IMAGES
of America

AROUND WINDHAM

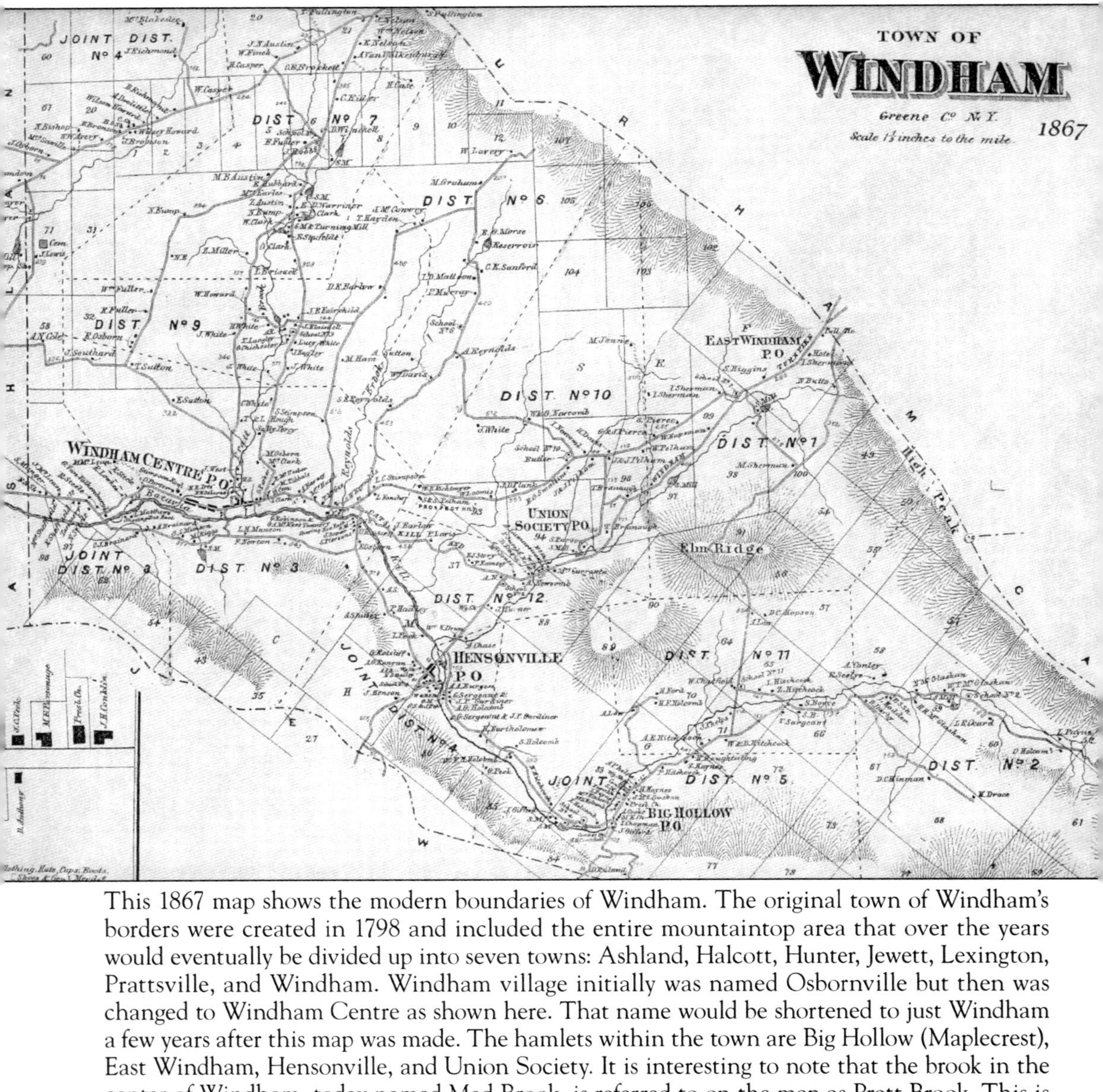

This 1867 map shows the modern boundaries of Windham. The original town of Windham's borders were created in 1798 and included the entire mountaintop area that over the years would eventually be divided up into seven towns: Ashland, Halcott, Hunter, Jewett, Lexington, Prattsville, and Windham. Windham village initially was named Osbornville but then was changed to Windham Centre as shown here. That name would be shortened to just Windham a few years after this map was made. The hamlets within the town are Big Hollow (Maplecrest), East Windham, Hensonville, and Union Society. It is interesting to note that the brook in the center of Windham, today named Mad Brook, is referred to on the map as Pratt Brook. This is obviously named after the most famous of the old tanners and businessmen of the mountaintop, Zadock Pratt. When and why the name was changed to Mad Brook is unknown. (Courtesy of Roy Davis.)

On the Cover: The guests who came to Windham from the New York City area every summer always brought their finest clothes with them. As casual, laid-back, and relaxed as the mountains were, these Victorian-era vacationers still loved to dress in their finest clothes for walks along the country lanes and especially for dining. The boardinghouses provided three formal meals a day, so people had plenty of opportunity to wear their best. In this c. 1905 photograph, the two summer guests were probably staying either at Crest Park or the Munson House on South Street. The house behind the ladies, which belonged to Silas and Phebe Munson, is at the corner of Church and South Streets. Built about 1893, it still stands today. (Courtesy of Roy Davis.)

IMAGES
of America

AROUND WINDHAM

Roy Davis

ARCADIA
PUBLISHING

ISBN 978-0-7385-7633-6

Published by Arcadia Publishing
Charleston, South Carolina

Printed in the United States of America

Library of Congress Control Number: 2011925287

For all general information, please contact Arcadia Publishing:
Telephone 843-853-2070
Fax 843-853-0044
E-mail sales@arcadiapublishing.com
For customer service and orders:
Toll-Free 1-888-313-2665

Visit us on the Internet at www.arcadiapublishing.com

This book is dedicated to those extraordinary pioneers who settled Windham and all who live in, visit, or read of its enchanting valley.

Contents

ACKNOWLEDGMENTS

Appreciation is extended to the following for their help in putting this book together: the Windham Historical Society; Charlotte Breeyear; Margy Davis; Harold and Evelyn Munson; Ruth and Richard Morse; Edwin, Charlotte and Janice Hitchcock; Barbara Tolley; Eleanor Lane; Mickey Goettsche; Roberta Christman; Christopher Garraghan; John and Carole Smith; Gary and Carolyn Wank; Ken Mabey; Peg Sokoll; Regina Kazman; and Pauline Lawrence.

Unless otherwise noted, all images appear courtesy of the Bill Davis/Roy Davis collection.

INTRODUCTION

The eastern facing slope of the northern Catskill Mountains was called the Wall of Manitou by the native Indians. Manitou was the spirit who lived in Onteora, which translates as "the land in the sky." From the Hudson River Valley floor, these peaks rise abruptly nearly 4,000 feet to their summit. It must have been an intimidating sight for the early settlers whose oxen had to pull their heavy loads up those steep slopes to Windham in the high valley.

The mountaintop area that would eventually become Windham was nothing but a wilderness with only a few brave and hardy families scattered far apart among the hollows. Batavia was the only name used on early maps and records to refer to that large area. By the 1790s, there was a cluster of houses and businesses located just east of the North Settlement Road (County Route 19) and State Route 23 intersection. This tiny settlement was given the name Batavia whenever someone wrote or spoke of it.

Old Windham is an important designation to remember when discussing the history of modern Windham and its boundaries. The town of Windham and its borders were officially established on March 27, 1798. At that time, there were no settled villages in these northern Catskill Mountains, so what could be called Old Windham then encompassed an area that, years later, would be divided into the seven mountaintop towns (with their years of establishment): Hunter (1813), Lexington (1813), Prattsville (1833), Ashland (1848), Jewett (1849), and Halcott (1851). Greene County was created on March 25, 1800, from parts of Albany and Ulster Counties two years after Windham was formed. The original four towns of the new Greene County were Freehold, Coxsackie, Catskill, and Windham. Today, the county has 14 townships.

The Town of Windham never changed its name, but the village did. First, it was called Osbornville, then Windham Centre, and finally, Windham. The Osborns were a prominent family in the early settlement, had many businesses, and were civic leaders as well. Bennet Osborn became Windham's first postmaster and, with that power, gave the village his name. Several years later, Zadock Pratt would be the postmaster, and he changed the village name to Windham Centre. It is speculated that Pratt did it because Osborn opposed him in an election for a public office. So, where did the name of Windham come from? One person who was most likely responsible for it was Stephen Simmons from Windham County, Connecticut. He came to the mountaintop area in the 1780s as a land agent for Robert Livingston and was a leader in the early development of Windham. He apparently liked the name of his former residence and felt that it would be a good name for his new home. Immersed in the local politics of the day, he was instrumental in the process that created the town with land taken from Freehold and Woodstock.

Going further back in time when the Dutch and British ruled here, kings and queens parceled out large plots of land called patents to individuals for military service or political connections. Maj. Johannes Hardenburgh purchased a huge tract of land from Nisinos, a Mohawk Indian chief, in 1707 for 60 pounds. The Hardenburgh Patent was issued from this acquisition of which Windham lies within.

Land ownership in the northern Catskill Mountains through the 1600s and 1700s was in a very unsettled state of affairs. There was a lot of fraud of ownership, and many unsuspecting buyers were swindled out of their money. To make matters worse, unscrupulous absentee landlords would renege on agreements with settlers who brought their families to these backwoods and worked hard for many years to clear the land as part of their rent contract. Agents for these landowners would be sent into the wilderness to appear one day at the door of the settler's log cabins and kick them off the land for trumped-up charges of not abiding by the rent contract. Eventually, the Anti-Rent Wars broke out when the pioneering families banded together to resist these landlords. The protests by the settlers led to enactment of laws that offered much-needed legal protection for these early pioneers, but all that took time, which was a contributing factor in the slow development of the area.

When property rights were guaranteed by law in the late 1700s, immigration from Connecticut and Massachusetts increased. It was a trickle at first, but by 1820, settlements were being established with a steady flow of hardy pioneers moving west from the New England states.

In the late 1700s, tough, strong, and resourceful Connecticut Yankees made up the bulk of immigrants to the Batavia Valley. They were well prepared for the hard work that lay ahead of them in their new home. Deeply religious, most were Presbyterian, Episcopalian, Baptist, Methodist, or Dutch Reformed. They must have felt greatly moved when they crested the summit of the Susquehanna Turnpike and found themselves viewing the thick forests and lush valley. From the notch they were in, they christened the mountains on each side with the biblical names of Mount Nebo and Mount Pisgah. These are names mentioned in the Bible relating to where Moses first saw the Promised Land. The settlers would find the local mountains practically uninhabited by Indians and found out very quickly that they should fear the wolves, panthers, and bears instead of Indians. Many stories are contained in the historical records of encounters with these wild animals that were the cause of many deaths until they were hunted practically to extinction locally.

Farming and tanning were a very good fit for Windham in the early years of settlement and were the economic incentives for most of the new settlers. There was a huge demand for tanned leather in this new and growing country at the beginning of the 1800s. The word *tanning* comes from tannic acid, which was essential for processing and preserving animal hides. Tannic acid is found in the bark of the hemlock tree, which the forests of the northern Catskill Mountains in Windham had an abundance of. Unfortunately, the Batavia Valley did not possess good fertile soil for crops; but when cleared of trees, it did have natural grasses that provided fine grazing pastures for cattle and sheep on the mountainsides. Today, new forest growth has reclaimed much of the open pastures. The stone fences, so carefully constructed by the farmers of long ago, can still be found standing in the quiet woods as monuments to those who toiled so hard to build them.

The Hudson River, 25 miles to the east of Windham, was the superhighway of commerce in the early years of the 1800s. Farms in upstate New York could ship their agricultural products to New York City via the river. The farmers west of Windham would pass through the town as they drove their livestock and products to the docks in Catskill. This activity created numerous drovers' taverns along the primitive roads where these herders could rest and securely pen their animals for a night on the long trip down the mountain. Such taverns were very profitable for those Windham residents who lived on the turnpikes of the day, but by 1830, two events would take place that caused the rapid disappearance of both the tanners and drovers.

First, the hemlock trees were harvested out. This left an unsightly mess on the barren mountainsides of fallen logs stripped of bark. By the 1850s, the tanners were leaving Windham behind and had moved on to new forests following the Appalachian Mountain chain south to Ulster and Sullivan Counties, taking their economy with them.

Second, the Erie Canal opened in 1825, bringing an end to the large volume of drovers passing through Windham. The farms west of Windham found it easier, faster, and less costly to take their products north via the Schoharie Creek to the Mohawk River, which was part of the new canal system. From the Mohawk River, goods traveled east on the Erie Canal by boat to Albany where it merges with the Hudson River. From Albany, the products continued by boat south to New York City, passing the much diminished docks in Catskill that had been handling the shipments before the canal opened.

From about 1830 to 1875, Windham's economy was farming coupled with manufacturing enterprises that prospered. Waterpower from the mountain streams supplied these companies with the energy source for their operations. Paper mills, foundries, gristmills, lumber mills, chair factories, and distilleries proliferated and are just a few examples of the manufacturing in Windham at the time.

Washington Irving's story "Rip Van Winkle," published in 1819, and the emergence of an American art movement from the prominent Hudson River School of painting later in the mid-19th century sparked the public's interest in the Catskill Mountains. Irving's mystical story and Frederic Church and Thomas Cole's beautiful paintings engaged people's imaginations, which put into motion a surge of summer vacationers to the area.

The new technology of the day would carry the crowds to the secluded valleys and mountaintops of the southern Catskills. Steam power on passenger boats plying the Hudson River and narrow gauge trains winding their way through the valleys brought millions of people to the peaceful hollows and challenging mountain peaks over the years, but Windham was in the northern Catskill Mountains and would never have a train connection. Tracks only came as close as Hunter, about 10 miles south. Windham was literally off the beaten path at the beginning of the resort business, and for this reason, the summer trade arrived later than what was taking place in the southern Catskill Mountains.

After the Civil War in 1865, this new tourism industry was discovering Windham and would create an economic boom that would be much larger and last longer than anything else the town had ever seen. The Industrial Revolution in America produced a middle class which would emulate the rich and famous by taking vacations in the summer to escape the stifling heat of the cities. In 1875, room and board in Windham was $6 per week for one adult compared to the $25 charged by the large, upscale hotels further south in the Catskills. These disparate rates reflected a distinct difference in clientele between the southern and northern Catskill Mountains.

Boardinghouses and resorts that catered to the crushing numbers of city dwellers flocking to the mountains would be the new economy for the town during the next 100 years. It all started with the farm families realizing a newfound cash source by offering room and board to these vacationers. Large farmhouses supplied the lodging and comfort, while the farms provided the food. It was a perfect match for Windham's new economy, and the residents at the many local farms and homes profited very well from the trade.

The vacationing crowds inundating Windham grew bigger every year. Anyone who had a spare room would take in boarders. There was such a high demand for rooms that it was typical in Windham for families to move out of their own houses entirely in the spring. The purpose was to make more rooms available to rent. These families would find other less glamorous accommodations, such as garages, cottages, or tents to sleep and live in during the tourist season before moving back into their homes in the fall. By the early 1900s, many boardinghouses expanded to become full-service hotels, and those owners would quit farming altogether, devoting their resources exclusively to catering to the summer visitors. Even so, these new, larger hotels were still referred to locally as boardinghouses.

One literary source in the mid-20th century noted that Windham was a metropolis in the wilderness. By 1960, it had three car dealerships, two jewelers, five grocery stores, one department store, several variety stores, gift shops and restaurants too numerous to count, two movie theaters, three hardware stores, and of course, so many hotels and boardinghouses that it defied the imagination.

Ringing a handbell to call the summer boarders to meals was a practical tradition at the boardinghouses. It originated in the farm days, when family members were in far-off fields or mountainsides, making a bell the most effective method to alert them that it was mealtime. As the late 1960s approached, more and more bells were falling silent at Windham's boardinghouses. There was change in the air blowing through the mountains, and not all of it was good.

By 1970, many developments had occurred that impacted tourism. The introduction of air-conditioning, inexpensive air travel, superhighways, and changes in vacationers' preferences all contributed to the decline and near total disappearance of the summer boarding trade in Windham. Transportation technology that brought people to Windham in the 19th century would now be replaced by 20th-century technology, which offered the vacationing public more choices that took them away from Windham.

But, at the same time, the skiing business was growing in the Catskill Mountains, and Windham was fortunate to have investors take a gamble on this new recreational business venture. Cave Mountain towers over Windham village, and this is where the first owners opened a ski slope in 1960.

It would take a few decades, several owners, and many doubts as to whether it could survive before the ski slope was able to become an economic force in Windham. Nothing could replace the scale of the prosperity the boardinghouse business had brought the local residents, but when the ski slope was finally able to establish itself as a public operation, it definitely helped the local economy.

In place of summer boarders, second homes were built for the winter skiers who came from the New York City area. Outdoor recreation in Windham's peaceful mountain valley would be the economic future for the town. Large events, festivals, and a growing art community draw crowds that make Windham a year-round destination.

For better or worse, Windham is located within the New York City watershed district. Because of that, many restrictive regulations have been enacted and enforced, which has had an economic effect on the town. The New York City Department of Environmental Protection (DEP), whose purpose ostensibly is to continue to provide high water quality for New York City residents, has the authority to purchase vast tracts of land in Windham. Unfortunately, when this land is purchased by DEP, it is lost forever to any economic or recreational use or development. The result of this policy is definitely a benefit for those living in New York City, but it is clearly at the expense of Windham's economy. The potential is greatly reduced for creating future employment opportunities that might otherwise become available to local residents.

Nevertheless, the natural beauty of Windham, nestled in the northern Catskill Mountains, has always endured and touched many lives through the years. It is an unforgettable, picturesque town with an intangible, mystical quality that affects each and every person who visits or lives there. And, if one is lucky enough to be in Windham during a summer rainstorm, he should listen for the thunder that echoes through the hills. Local residents will tell you it is just old Rip Van Winkle playing ninepin with Henry Hudson's crew in "the land in the sky" somewhere in the mountains around Windham . . . just as Washington Irving told the tale in 1819.

One

Early Settlement

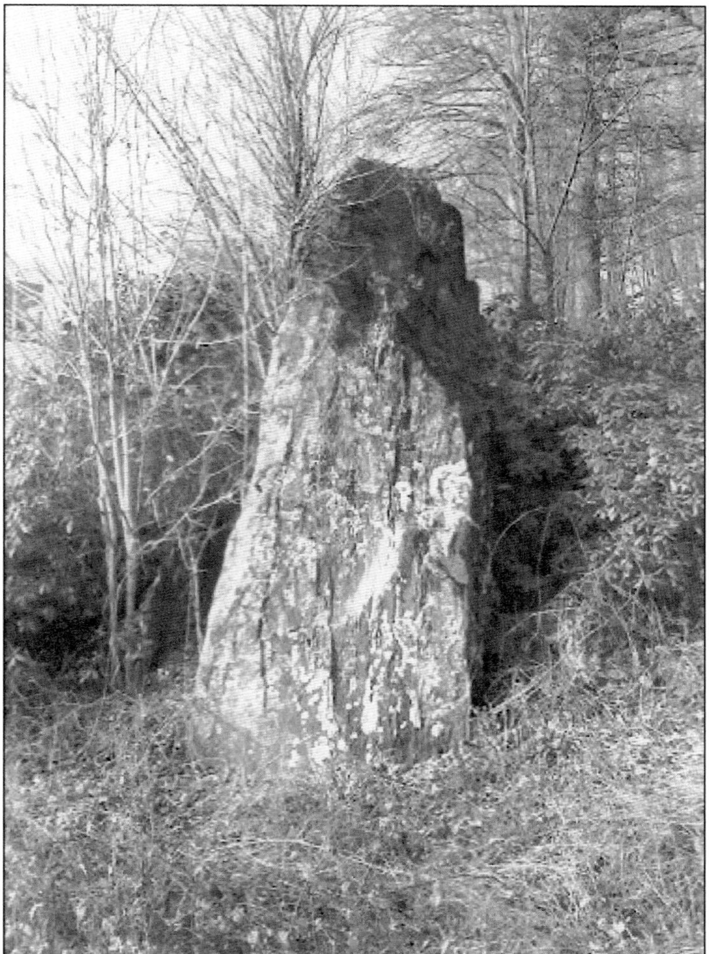

This is the iconic rock in the west end of Windham village where the first settler, George Stimpson, and his 13-year-old son Henry built a cabin in 1785. They came to the mountaintop area as cattle herders for Robert Livingston, the owner of a large tract of land that Windham was a part of.

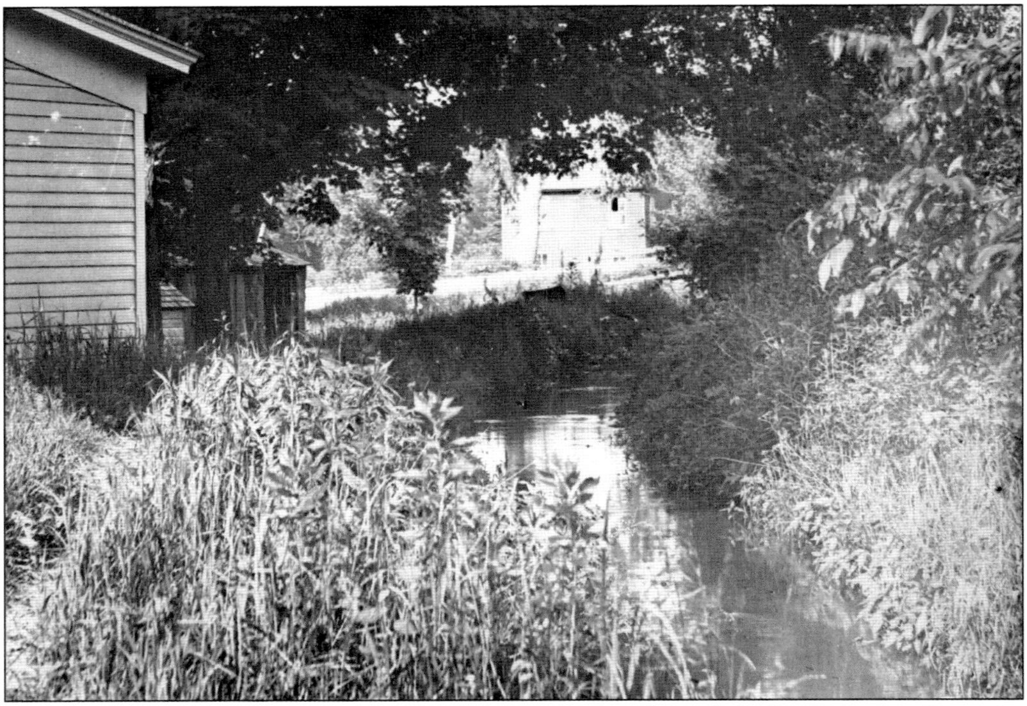

This is the east millrace that was dug from upstream of Mad Brook for homes and mills on the east side of the brook in Windham. The flow of water ran east behind houses and the Windham Methodist Church, under Route 23, and to the Creamery Pond. Remnants of the millrace can still be seen behind the church.

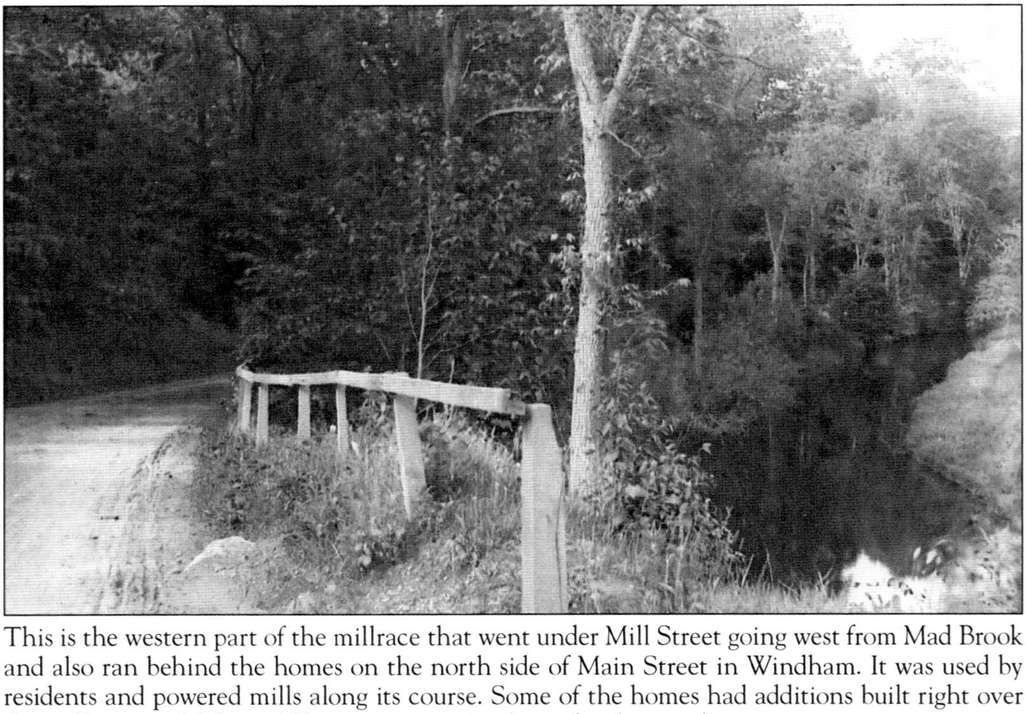

This is the western part of the millrace that went under Mill Street going west from Mad Brook and also ran behind the homes on the north side of Main Street in Windham. It was used by residents and powered mills along its course. Some of the homes had additions built right over the millrace, and fish could be seen swimming by under the trapdoor.

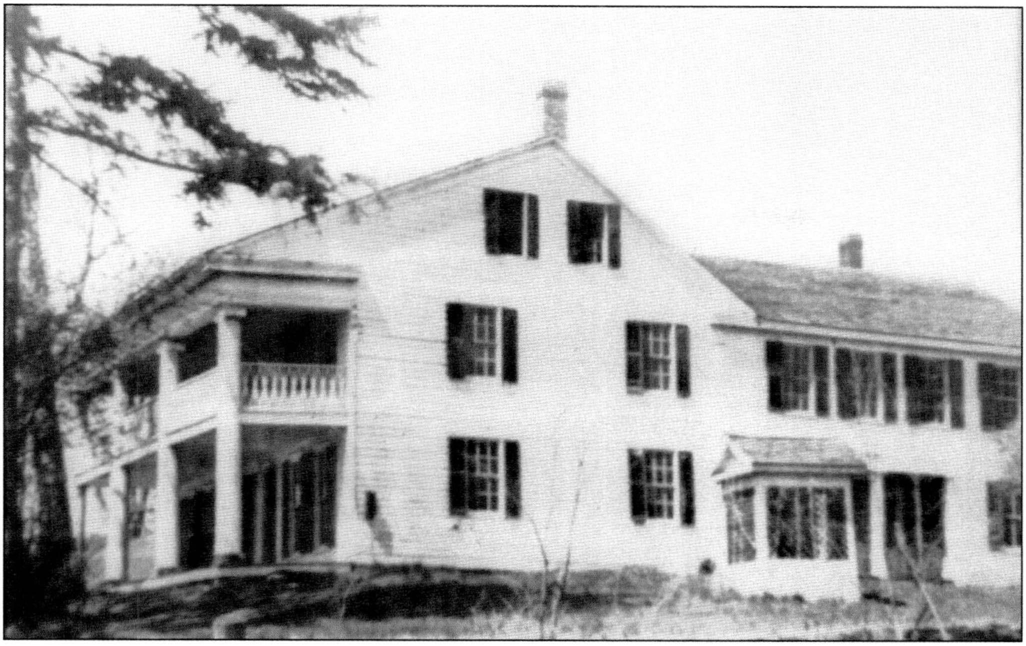

The Bump Tavern was built in the 1790s by Jehiel Tuttle, who operated it as a drovers' tavern until Ephraim Bump purchased it in 1842. It was located on the northeast corner of today's Route 23 and North Settlement Road intersection. In 1952, the building was dismantled into 16 pieces, transported to Cooperstown, New York, restored to its 1845 condition, and is now on public display at the Farmers' Museum.

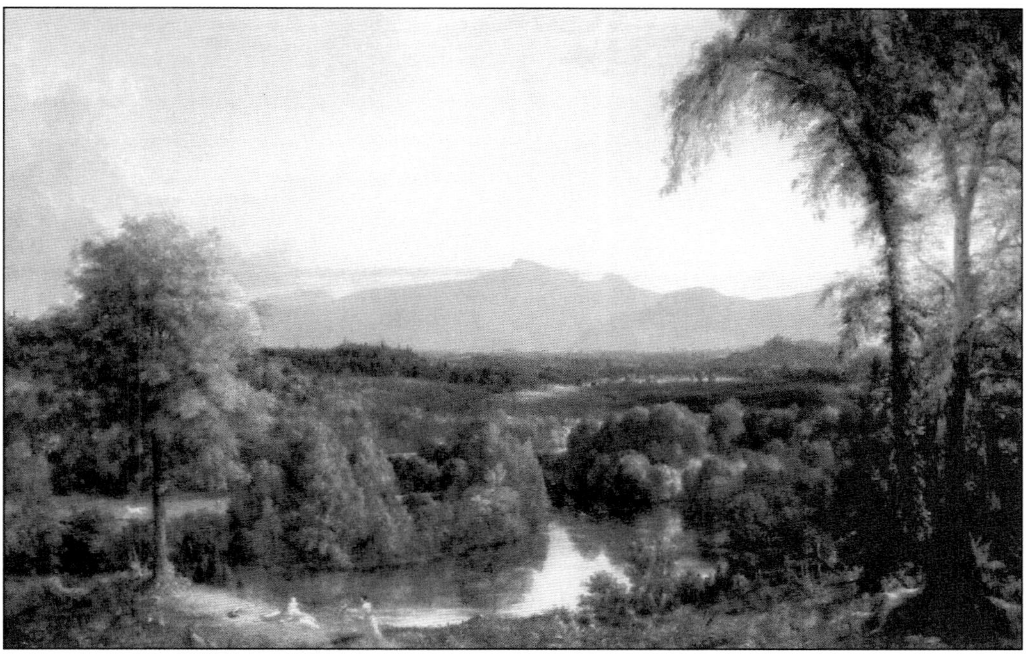

Thomas Cole's 1837 painting *View on the Catskill, Early Autumn* displays the grandeur of the east face of the Catskill Mountains' Wall of Manitou on the west side of the Hudson River. Manitou was the Indian spirit who dwelled in Onteora, translated as "the land in the sky." The summits of these mountains rise abruptly to nearly 4,000 feet above the Hudson River.

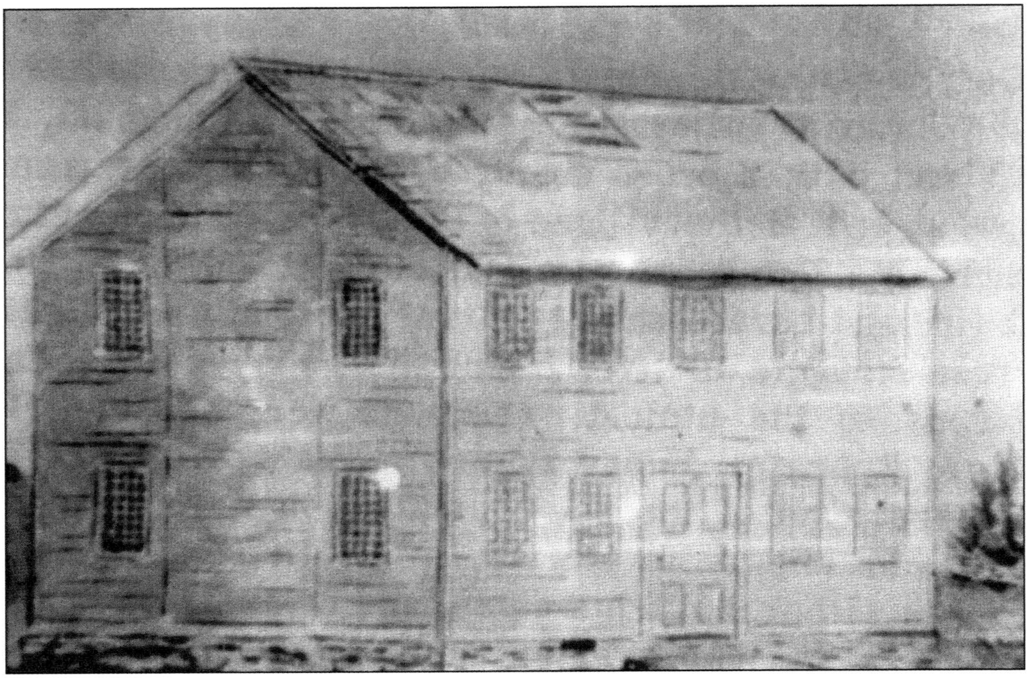

This is the Old Meeting House, built during 1799 to 1805, where the present Pleasant Valley Cemetery is. It was used for religious services and civic meetings. The small settlement here was called Batavia. When the building was abandoned in 1843, it reverted back to the original owners who used it for a barn and eventually dismantled it and reused the wood for other buildings. (Courtesy of Pauline Lawrence.)

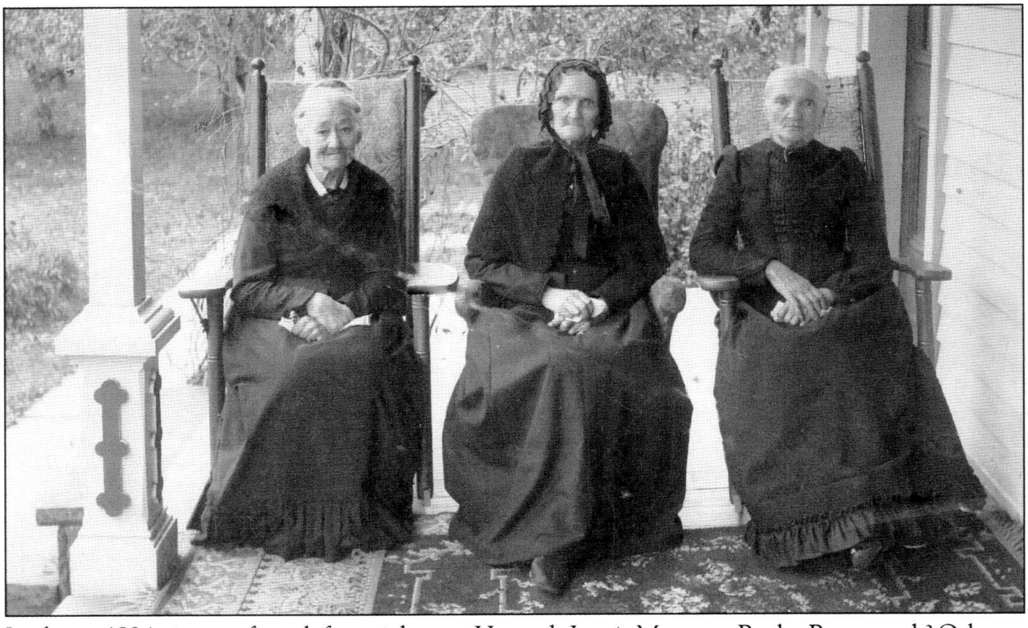

In this c. 1894 picture, from left to right, are Hannah Lewis Munson, Becky Bump and ? Osborn. All three are descendants of the original settlers of Windham. The Lewis, Munson, Bump, and Osborn names all appear in many historical records in the early settlement of the town. Hannah Munson was born in 1804 in Windham and died in 1895.

Two

BOARDINGHOUSES

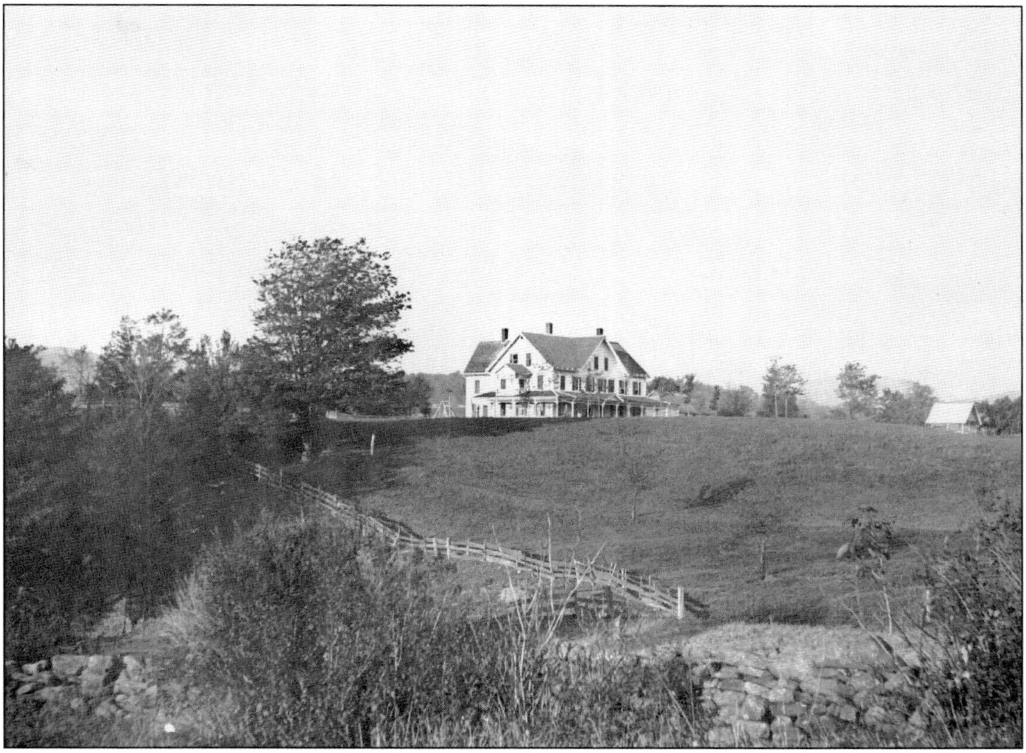

The Crest Park boardinghouse on South and Church Streets was built by Elmer Munson in 1900. This was the third Munson family hotel located on South Street. Like so many of the other boardinghouse owners, Elmer started as a farmer, ceased that occupation altogether, and made a very comfortable living serving tourists in summer. Crest Park was sold in 1960 and is now a private residence.

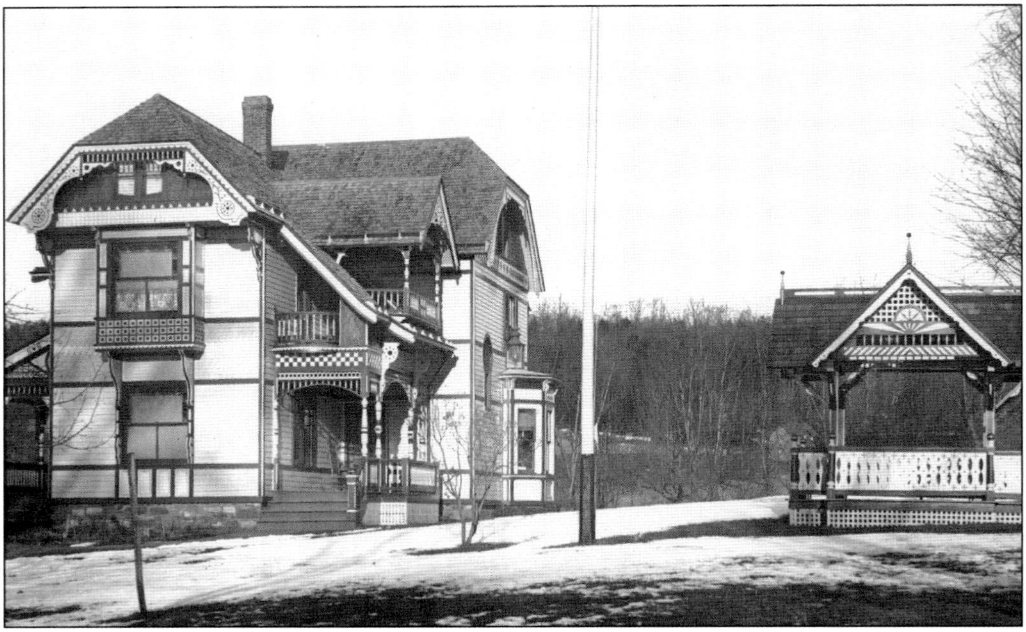

This 1900 picture is of the cottage at the Thompson House. In 1886, Ira and Christina Thompson purchased the farm of Elias Reynolds that included a house, barn, and acreage. This was the origin of the Thompson House, which is still operating today with the fifth generation at the helm. Victorian architecture was prevalent throughout Windham's boardinghouses and homes built in the late 1800s.

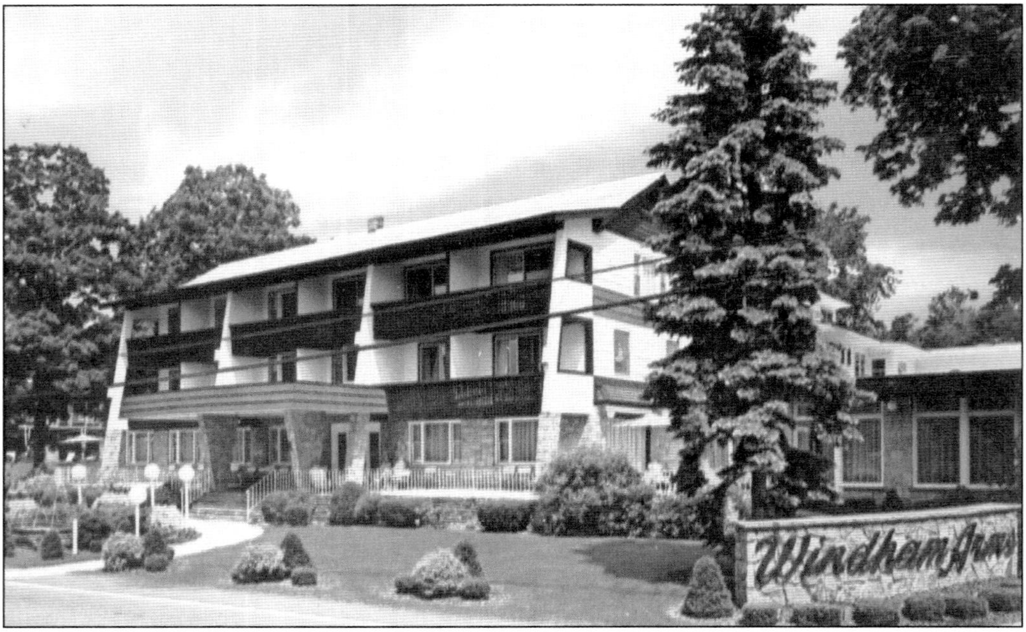

In this 1950s postcard, the Windham Arms sits at the top of Cemetery Hill (Route 23) a half-mile east of Windham village. In 1946, Larry and Eleanor Lane purchased the operation from Walter Soper. Larry was also a state assemblyman, and the Lanes kept expanding the hotel into a first-class operation well beyond a boardinghouse concept. In 1994, the entire hotel was sold to Ski Windham.

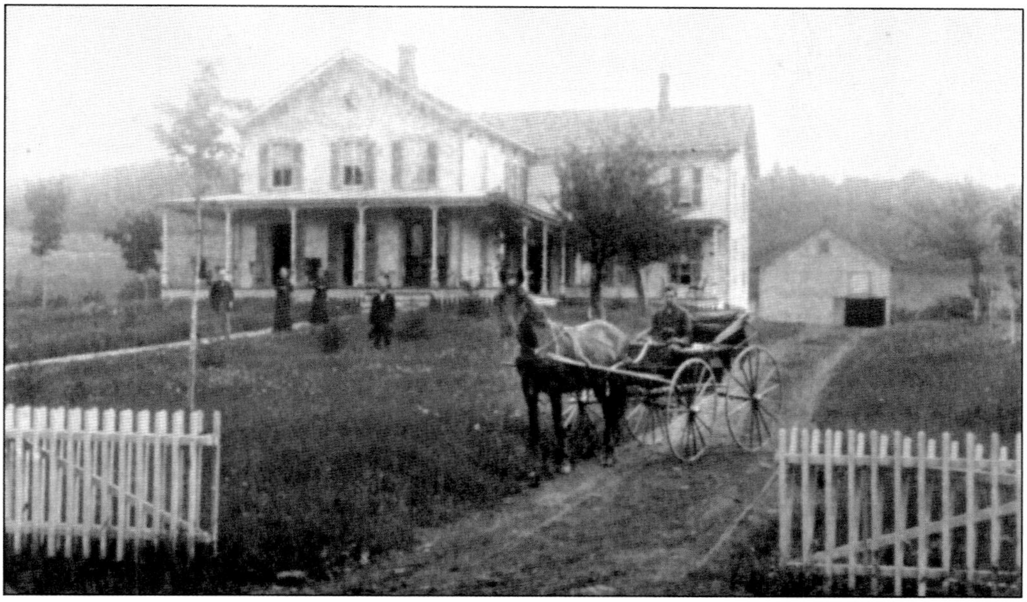

This photograph is of the Manor House, part of the Thompson House resort, in the 1880s. Ira and Christina Thompson are standing on the sidewalk in the background on the left with their son Herbert in the carriage. The two people in the middle are unidentified. Ira and Christina purchased the house and farm from the Elias Reynolds family in 1886. (Courtesy of Barbara Tolley and Mickey Goettsche.)

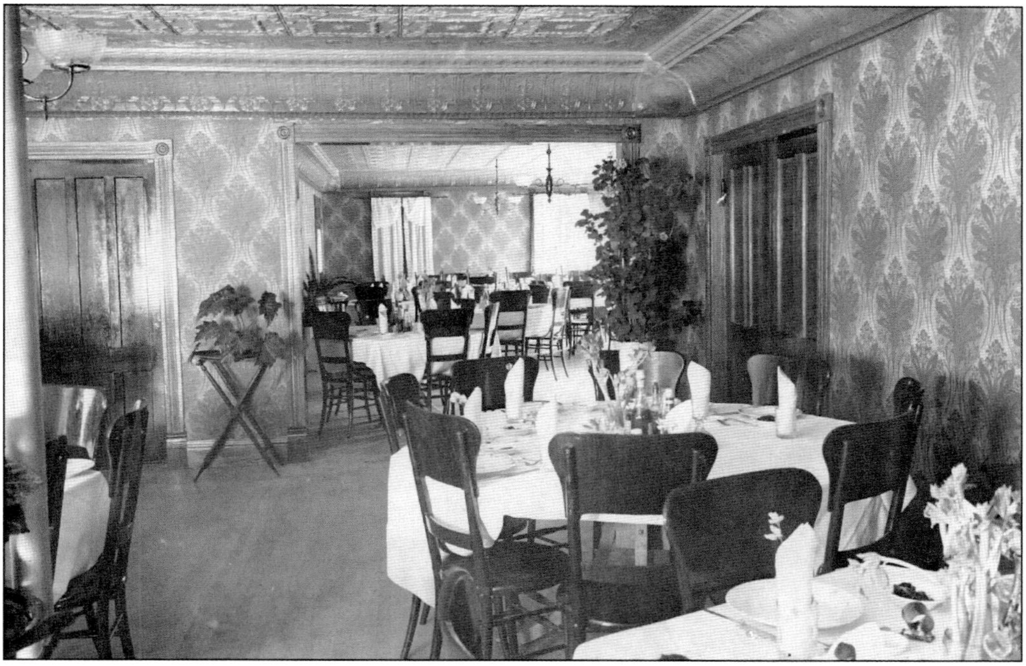

The dining room at the Thompson House in the 1880s is a very typical scene of the larger boardinghouses and how they served three formal meals every day during the summer. Waitresses lived right at the hotels and were assigned specific tables to attend to guests during their entire stay. They usually received a generous tip when the guests departed. (Courtesy of Barbara Tolley and Mickey Goettsche.)

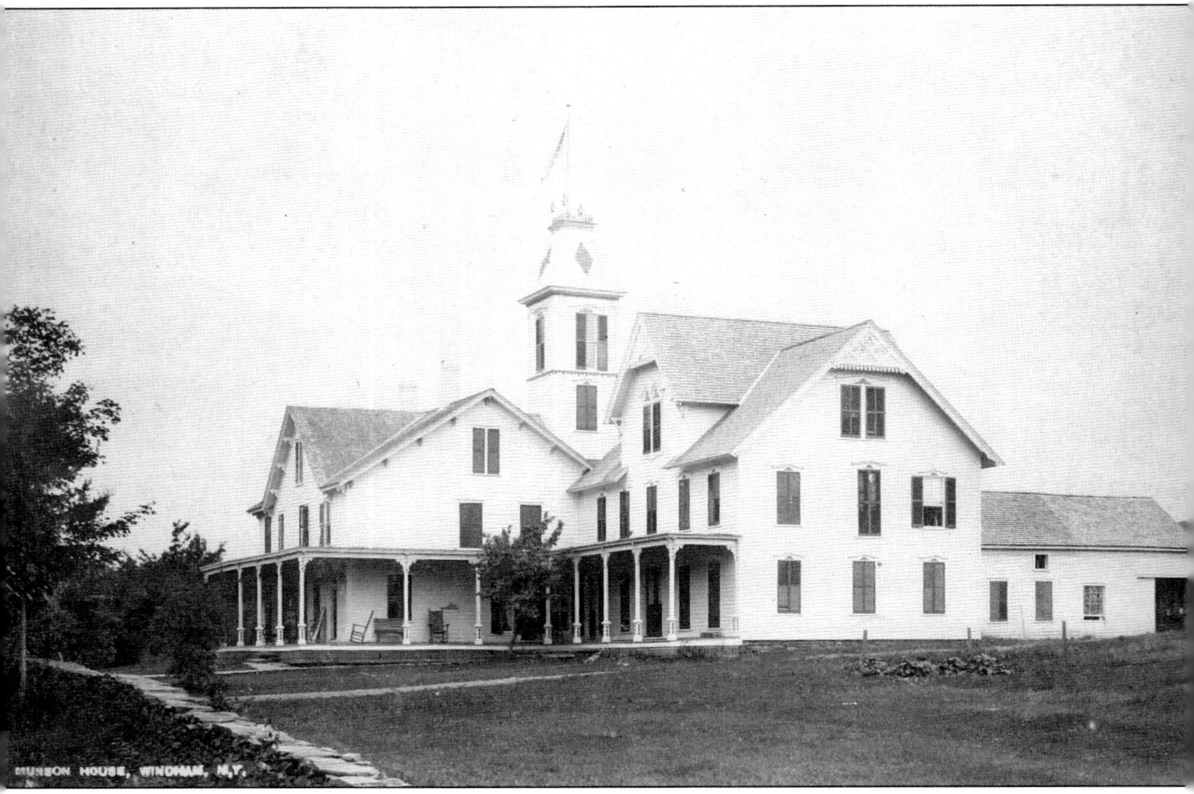

This picture of the Munson House on South Street, taken around 1900, shows how the simple concept of renting rooms in the farmhouse led to bigger buildings. Almost everyone who had a spare room rented to vacationers, whose numbers visiting Windham increased every year. At the beginning of the trade, there just were not enough rooms to rent. This led to the farmers moving out of their houses for the summer, sleeping wherever they could find a decent spot on the farm, and moving back into their homes in the fall when the paying guests went home. It was a yearly ritual that passed from one generation to another as the boarding trade expanded. Very quickly, many local farmers realized the potential for increasing business if they built larger structures with more rooms to rent. The result was that huge buildings like the Munson House covered the entire mountaintop and were always filled to capacity in summer. The concept evolved from traditional boardinghouses to hotel-like structures, but local residents still referred to them as boardinghouses.

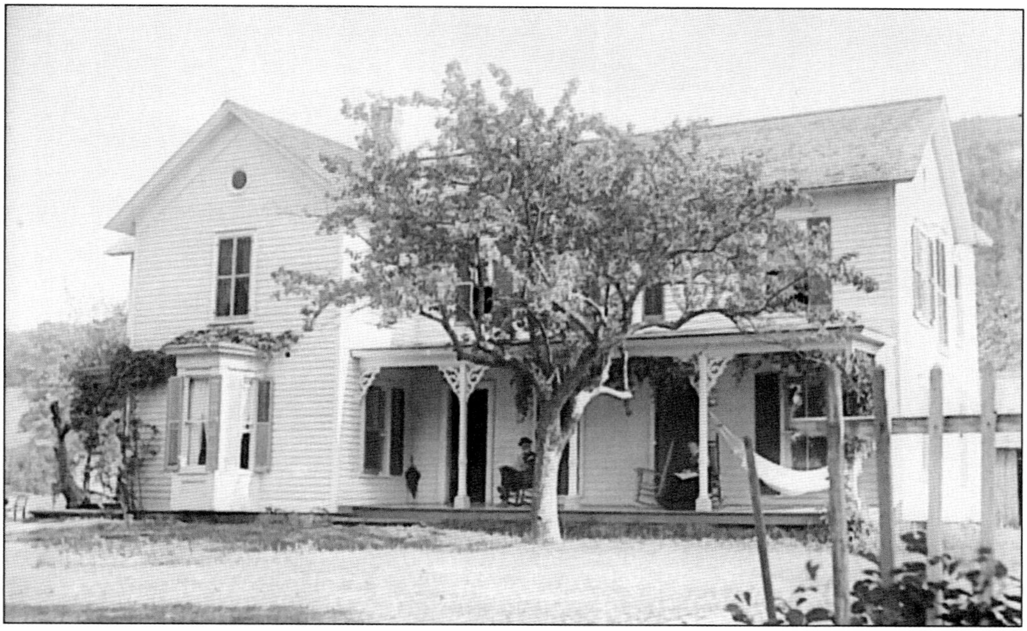

Named Elsie's Cottage by Alvah and Elsie Munson, the picture above was another of the three Munson boardinghouses built on South Street. Alvah died suddenly of appendicitis when only in his 20s in 1889, leaving Elsie with two small children. Elsie operated the cottage for many years but eventually sold it to Nicholas and Carrie West, who renamed it the Westmere. Their daughter Anita West would marry Ferris Thompson in this building in October 1916. Anita and Ferris would later become owners of the Thompson House. There are many instances where marriages and relationships between families in Windham also connected businesses. These buildings were sold a number of times after that, and an addition on the left side was constructed, as seen in the photograph below. It is currently operating as the Windham Mountain Inn.

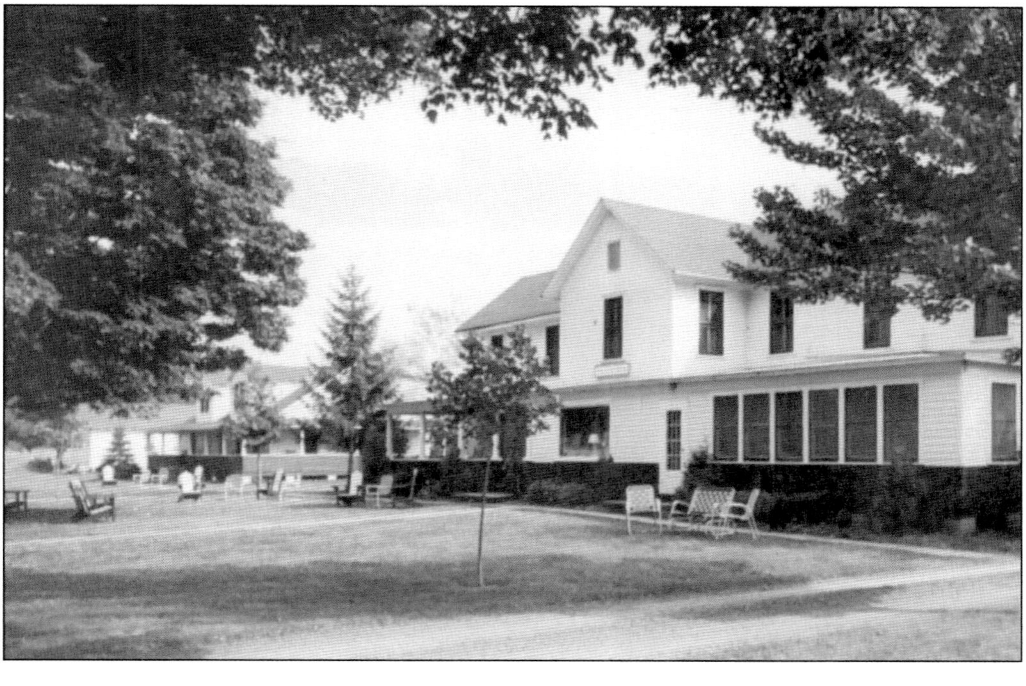

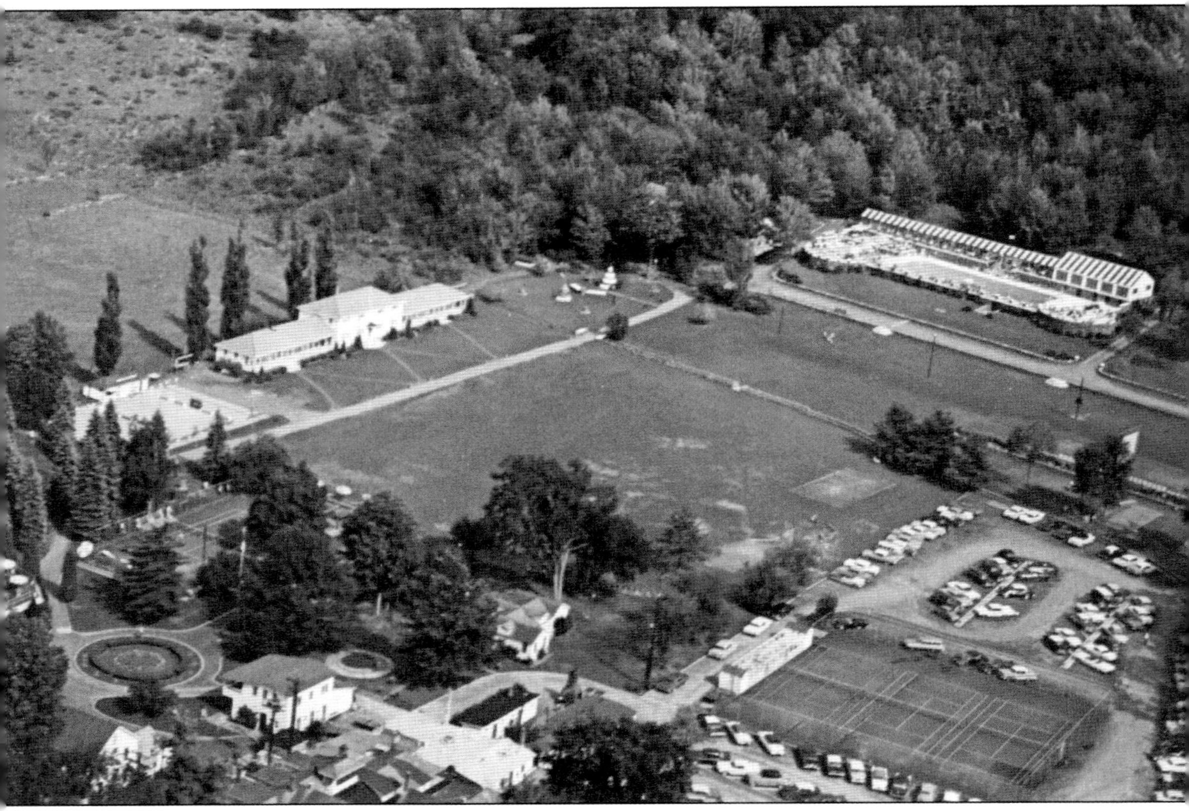

It is clear in this 1958 postcard photograph of the Sugar Maples resort in Maplecrest that it was by far the largest boardinghouse operation in Windham. Because its origin was not as a farmer's boardinghouse in the same way that most of the others were in Windham, Sugar Maples was clearly a hotel. Gus Moseman of Staten Island, New York, started it in 1925 and continued building on the 80 acres as the demand kept growing. Comfort and entertainment facilities for his summer guests included an Olympic-size heated swimming pool, roller-skating rink, library, orchestra, and a baseball field with roofed bleachers. The dining area seated 700 people and served, like the boardinghouses, three meals a day. But, after declining summer vacationers in the latter part of the 20th century, the resort closed in the early 1990s. In the beginning of the 21st century, several buildings of the original Sugar Maples were purchased for use by an art foundation and library.

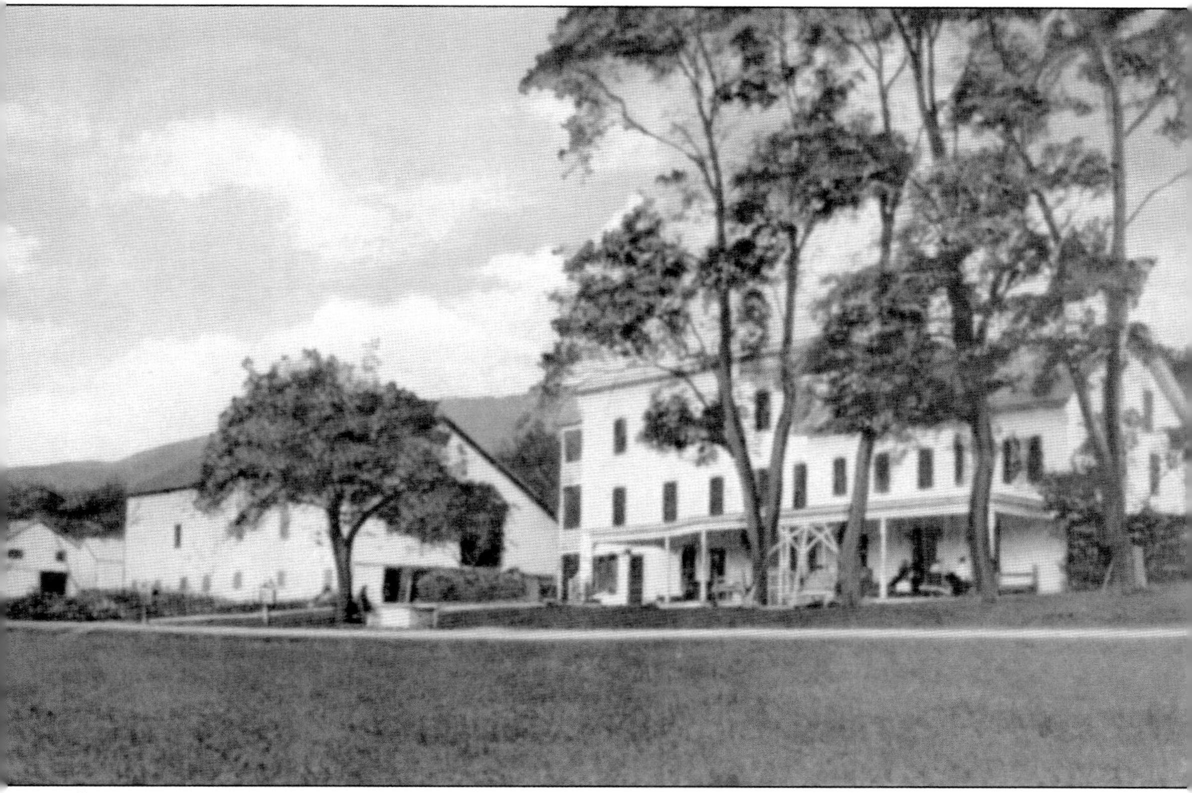

This 1944 postcard is of the Brainerd Farm boardinghouse on the west end of South Street. At its peak, it could accommodate over 80 guests. Like all the other boardinghouses, the Brainerd Farm slowly evolved to concentrate on the lucrative summer resort business. Josiah Brainerd purchased the 181-acre farm from George Stimpson in 1786. As the other boardinghouses evolved at the end of the 1800s, so did the Brainerd Farm. Locally, the farm operation was well known for its outstanding crops, horse breeding, and husbandry. But, by the arrival of the 20th century, efforts were devoted solely to the summer tourism trade, and farming ceased altogether. In 1960, as the development of a ski slope on Cave Mountain directly behind the Brainerd Farm was progressing, many residents who owned land there virtually donated acreage to facilitate the growth of the ski business and, hopefully, enhance the economic security of Windham. In 1964, the buildings were sold and became a private residence.

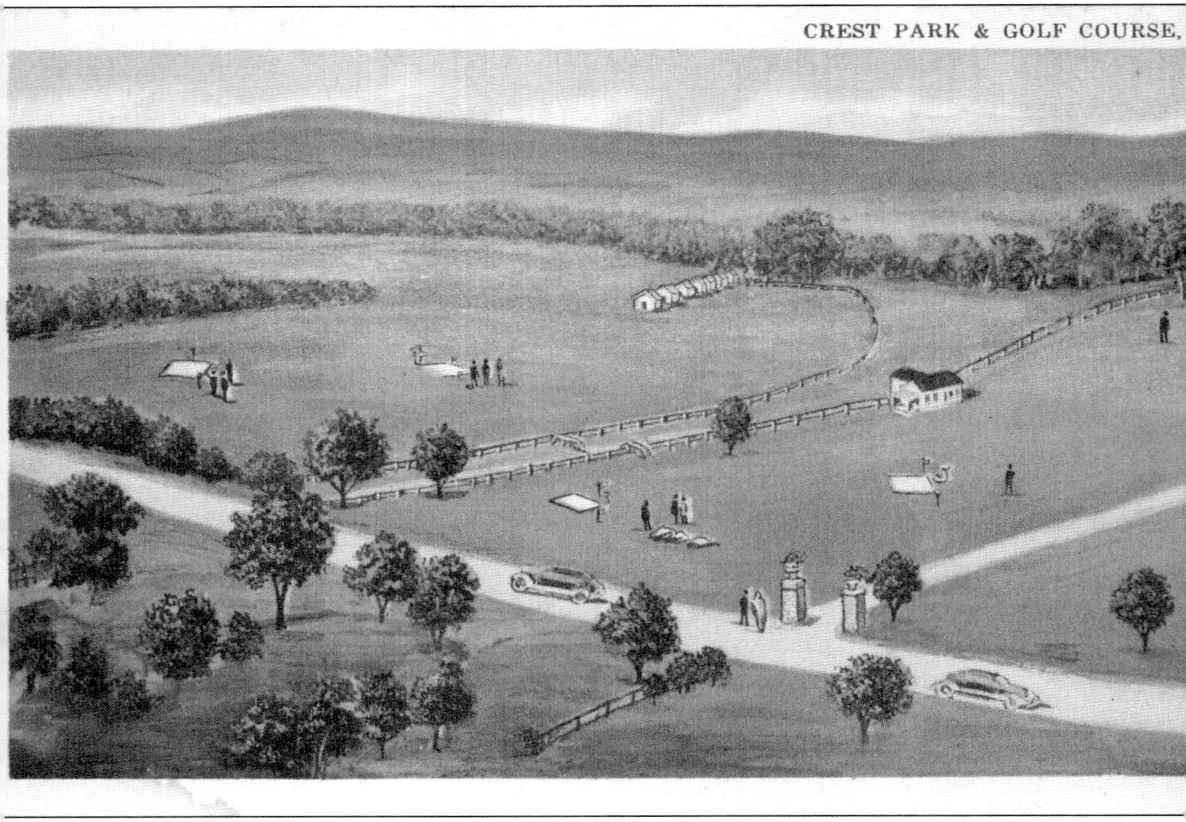

This type of postcard was very common, and practically all operating boardinghouses had one made for business advertising. This one of Crest Park on South Street is a good example of how these boardinghouses progressed to become full hotels. There was a main house, a smaller annex, and several outbuildings, which included cottages to rent, entertainment buildings, maintenance sheds, and beautifully maintained, expansive lawns. Most of the boardinghouses had regular

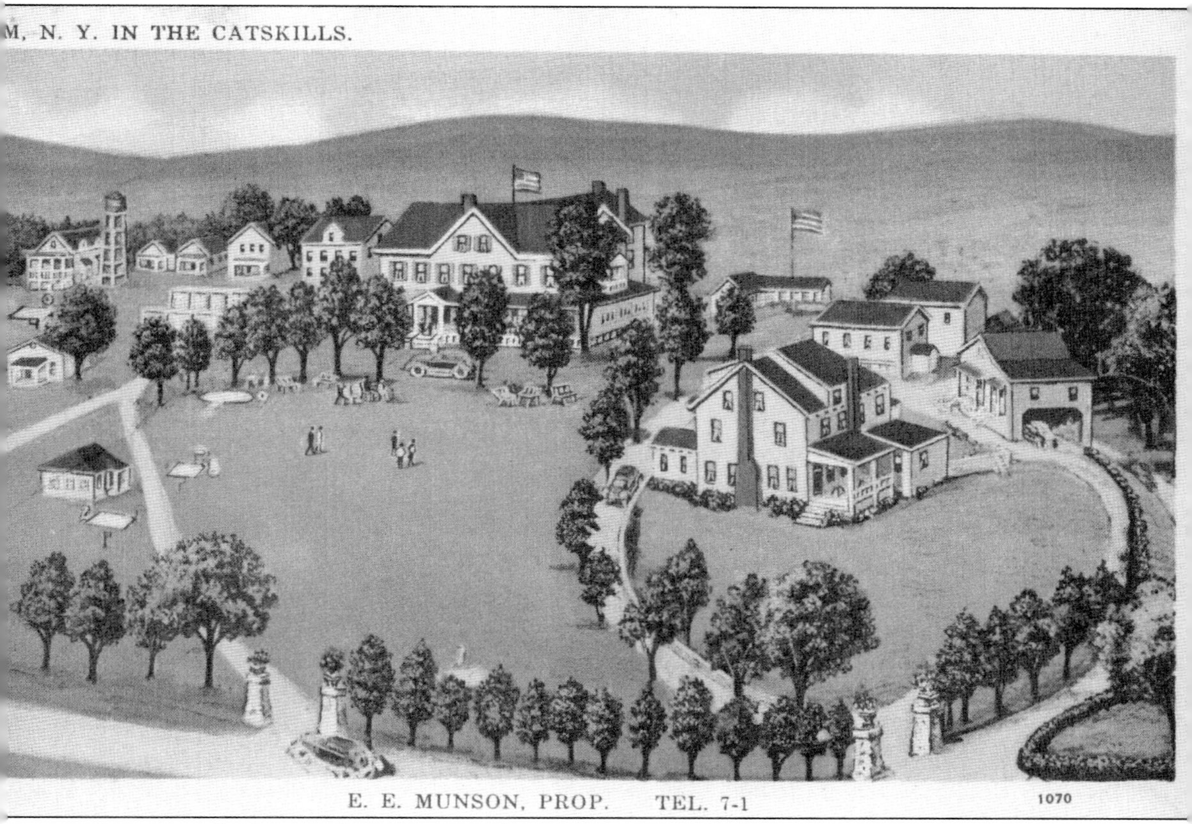

outdoor game facilities such as tennis and croquet. Crest Park also had a nine-hole golf course. The small buildings in the left background were for livestock. Boardinghouses started with farms, and farm products were needed to feed the guests. The larger hotels usually had working farms as part of their complex. Crest Park could accommodate up to 150 guests.

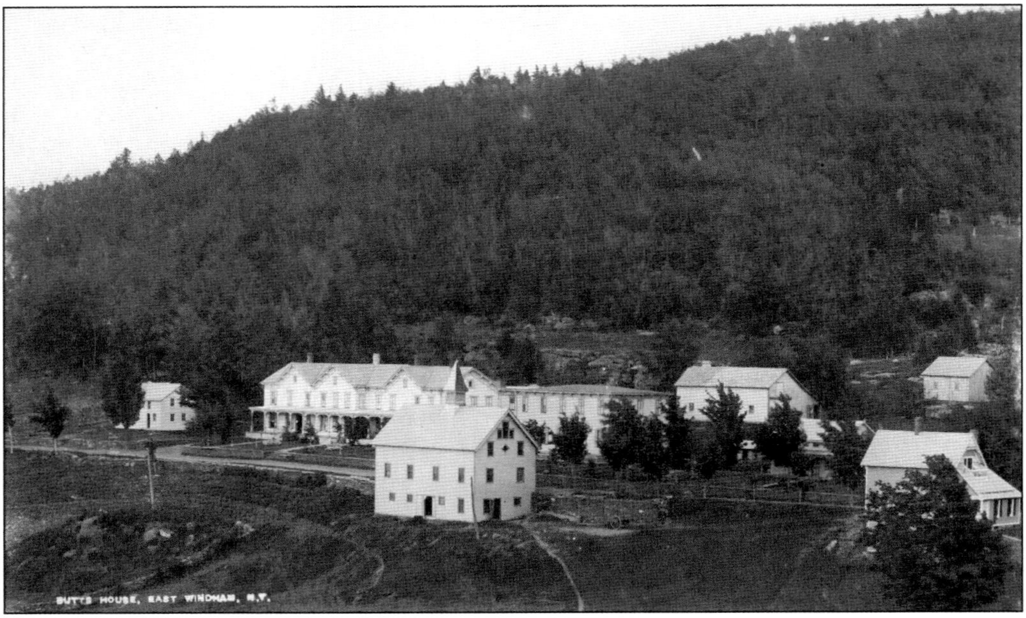

This c. 1900 image shows the Butts House in East Windham as seen from Mount Zoar. This is at the highest point the road reaches in East Windham, which offered the guests a stunning five-state view from the front porch. It was constructed in 1879 by Isaac Butts, whose brother Barney built the Summit House next door. Records mention that he kept 35 guests here, but the photograph below seems to show the building was large enough to accommodate more. All of these structures have burned down, and the stone walls are all that remain. (Above, courtesy of Christopher Garraghan.)

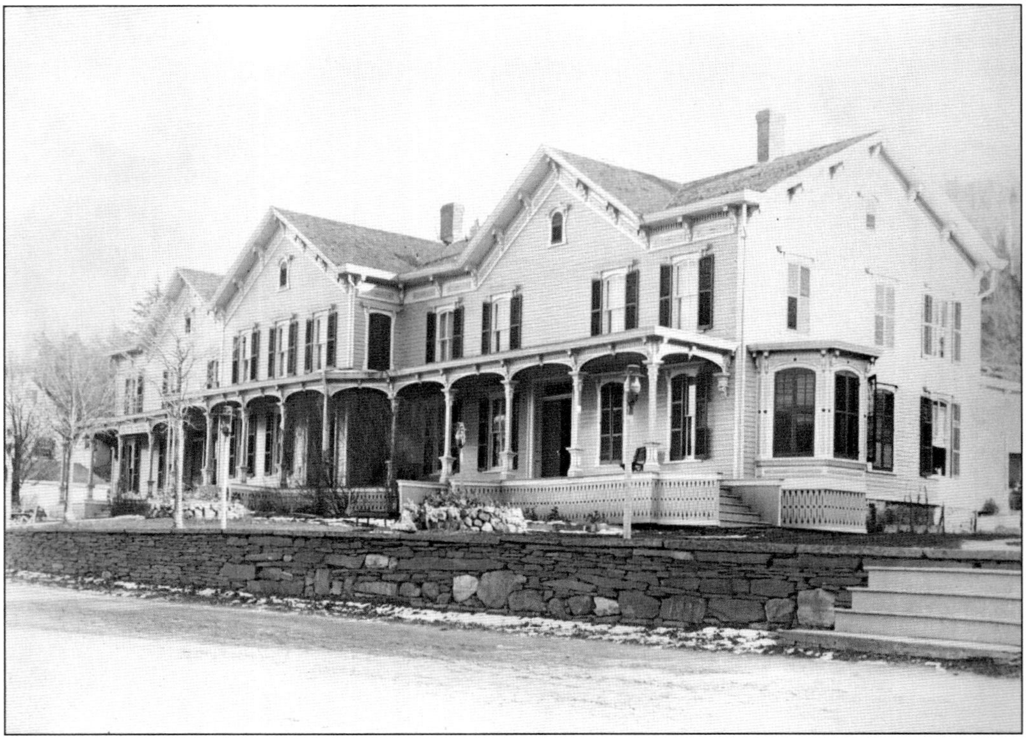

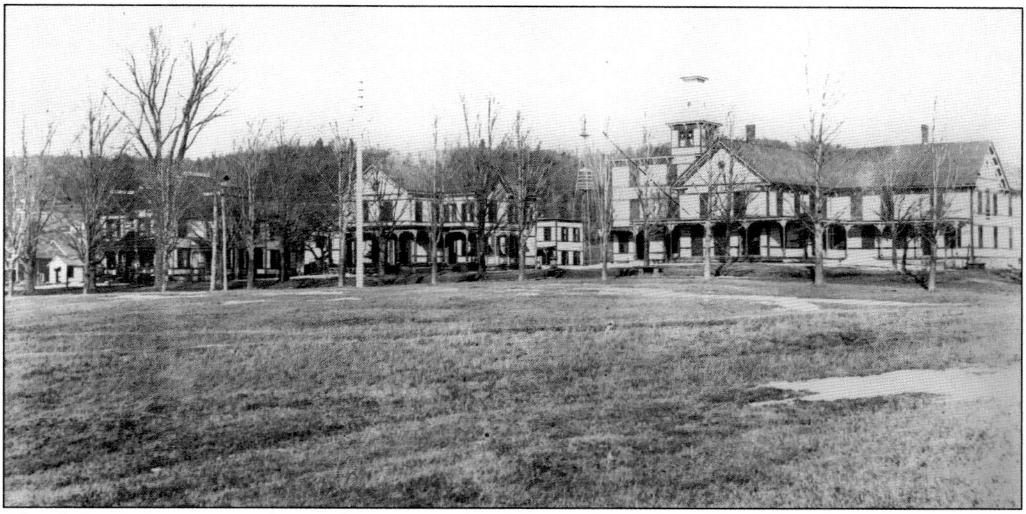

The Osborn House complex in the picture above also had a 300-acre farm in Brook Lynne, which was established in 1866 by Elbert Osborn. The Osborn name was prominent in the early settlement of Windham after Henry Osborn came to North Settlement in 1799. Subsequent generations in the 1800s had various businesses in Windham. Bennet, Merritt, Milo, and other Osborns had tanneries, a wine distillery, a gristmill, hotel, and more. Bennet was the first postmaster of Windham in 1830, and because of that, named the village Osbornville. Years later, the most successful tannery operator on the mountaintop, Zadock Pratt, renamed the village Windham when he was postmaster, reportedly because of a political feud he had with Bennet Osborn. The picture below is a close-up of the building on the left in the photograph above.

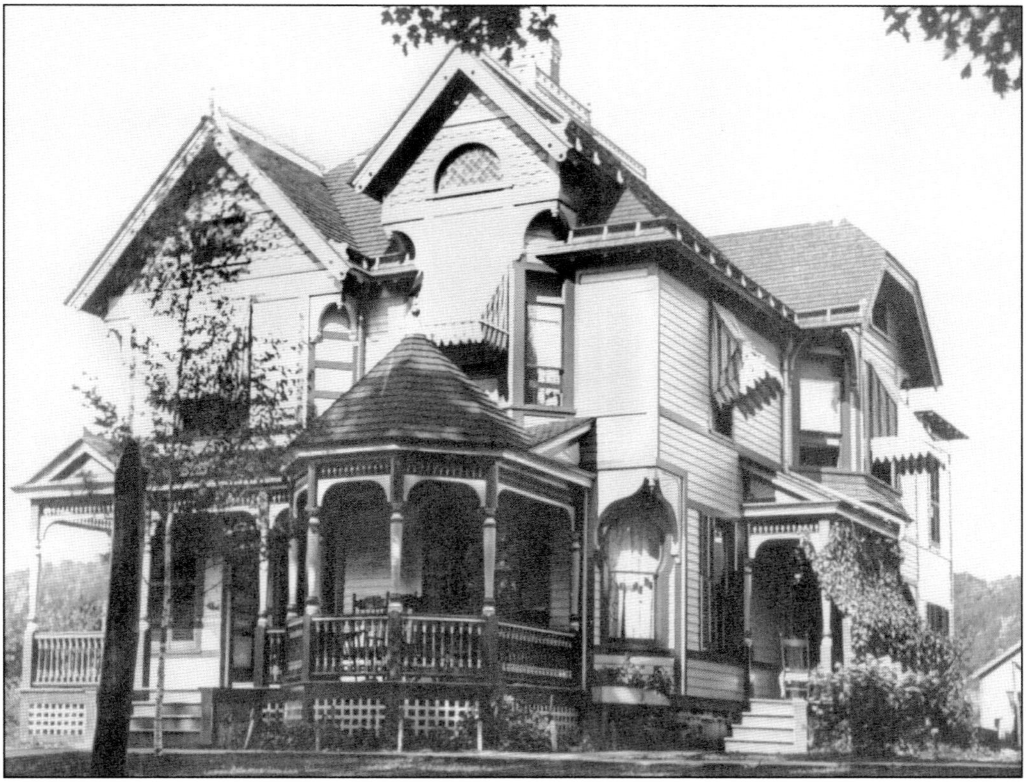

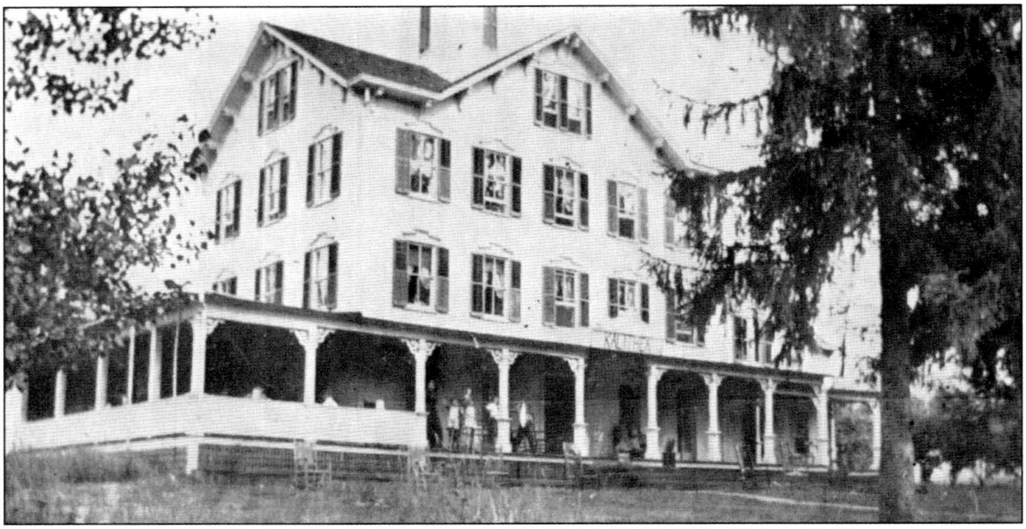

This 1960 postcard is of the Kallithea Farm boardinghouse in Hensonville on Seeley Road. Throughout the Catskill Mountains, various ethnic groups from the New York City area would vacation in particular towns. Hensonville became one such pocket in the mid-1900s for Greek Americans, and the Kallithea was one of the biggest in the area to accommodate them

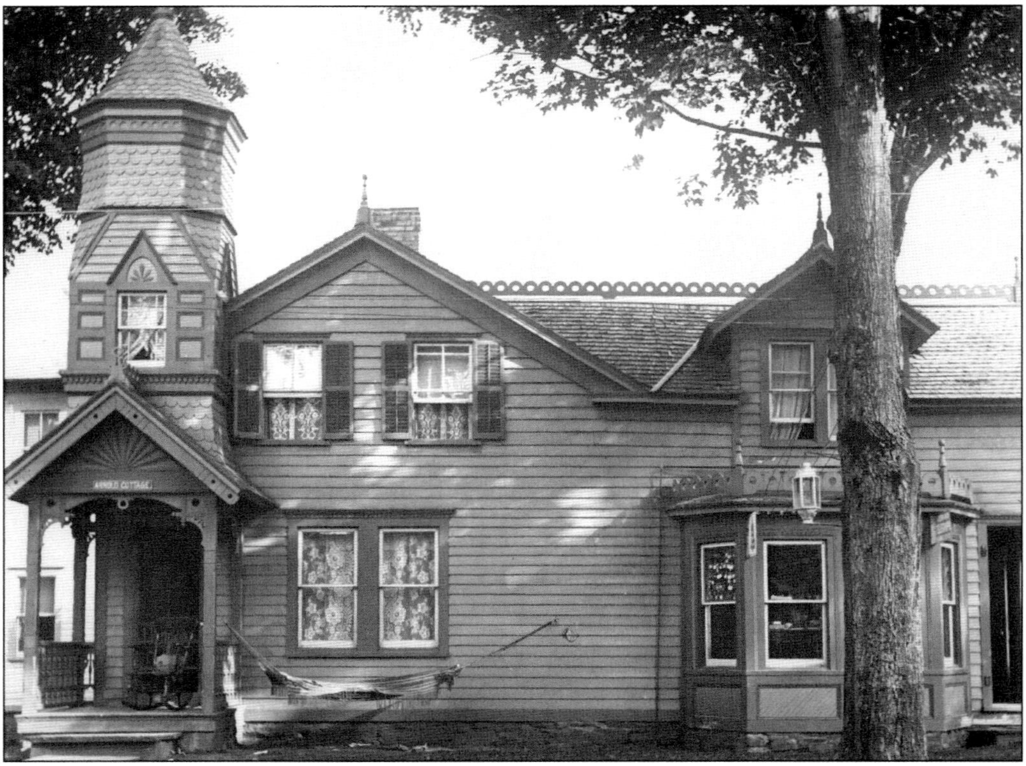

Many homes in Windham were given names by the owners to distinguish them for the summer boarders who came. This one, at the time this 1908 photograph was taken, was known as Arnold Cottage; it is located next to the Masonic Temple on Main Street in Windham. Windham has many homes and buildings with interesting Victorian architecture such as this. It is now Zerega's Restaurant.

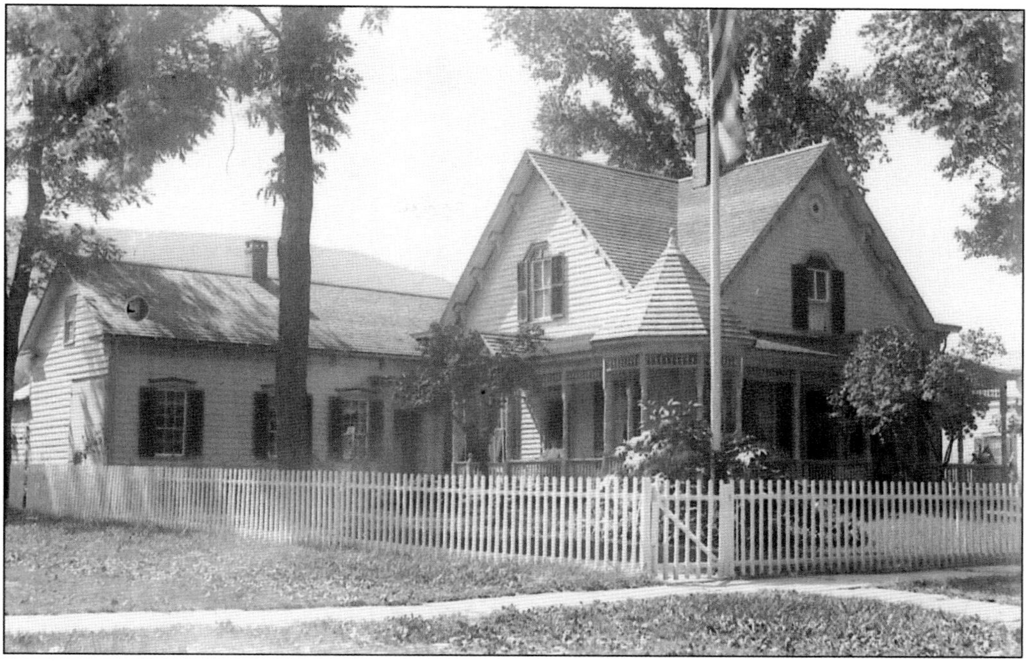

Washington Hunt was said to have been born in this house in 1811. He was the governor of New York from 1851 to 1853 and one of two state governors born in Windham. The other was Lucius Robinson, governor from 1877 until 1879. This boardinghouse had two names over the years—Windland Cottage and Briarwood Cottage. It is now owned by Graham and Kathy Merk/IA Financial Advisors.

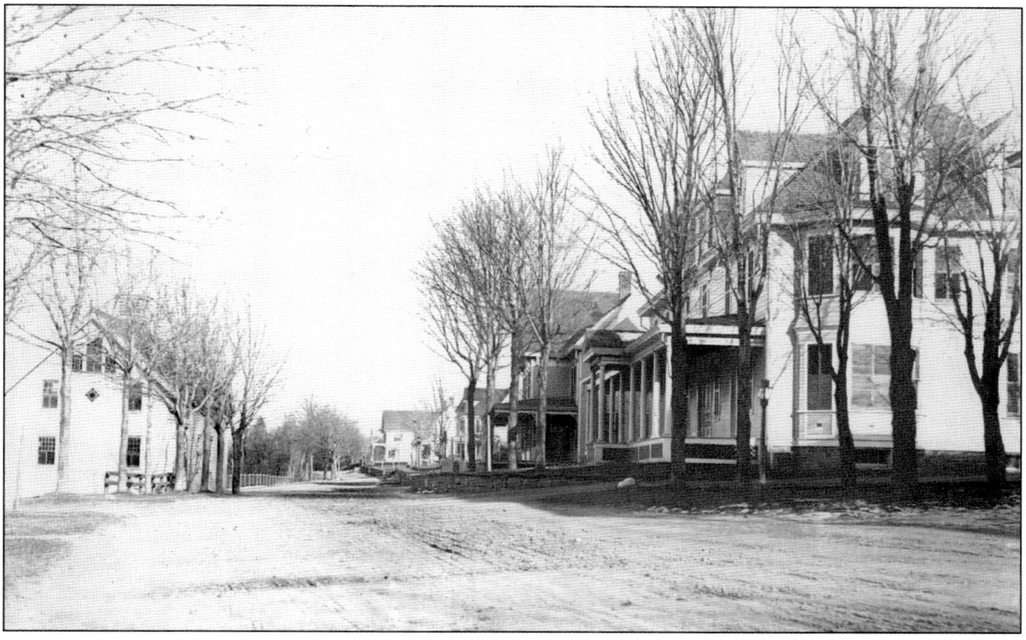

This 1905 view from East Windham looks south on the former Windham Turnpike, now State Route 23. Just west, about a mile from this point, is Silver Lake, where sawmills were operating in the 1800s. Silver Lake is now home to a summer camp for girls, Camp Oh-Neh-Tah. All that is left here is the stone wall, which can be seen when driving by on the road today.

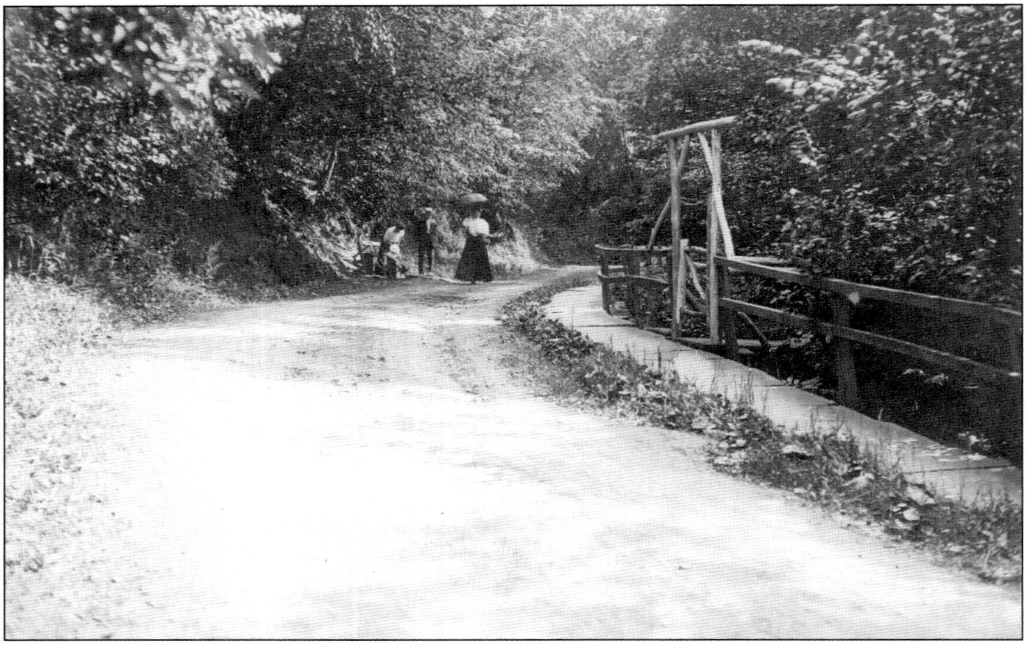

Summer guests enjoy a leisurely stroll down Church Street on a warm summer day in 1900. Country lanes and fresh air beckoned city residents to Windham for generations. By the mid-20th century, it often seemed as if everyone in the crowds that gathered in Windham all knew each other, and in fact, most did.

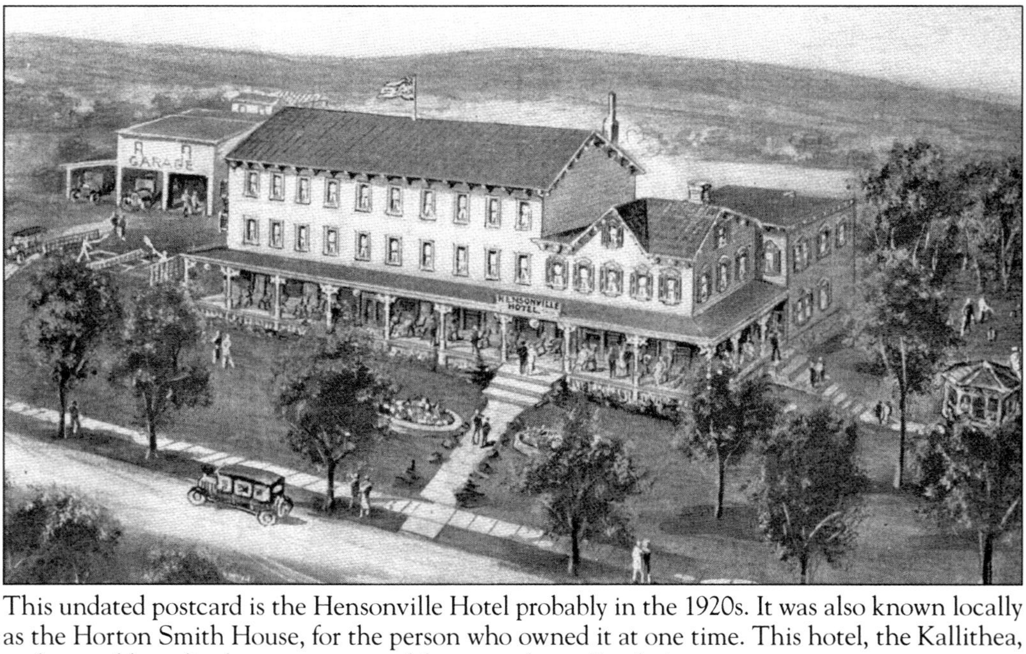

This undated postcard is the Hensonville Hotel probably in the 1920s. It was also known locally as the Horton Smith House, for the person who owned it at one time. This hotel, the Kallithea, and several boardinghouses accounted for a very large Greek American vacation community in Hensonville in the mid-1900s.

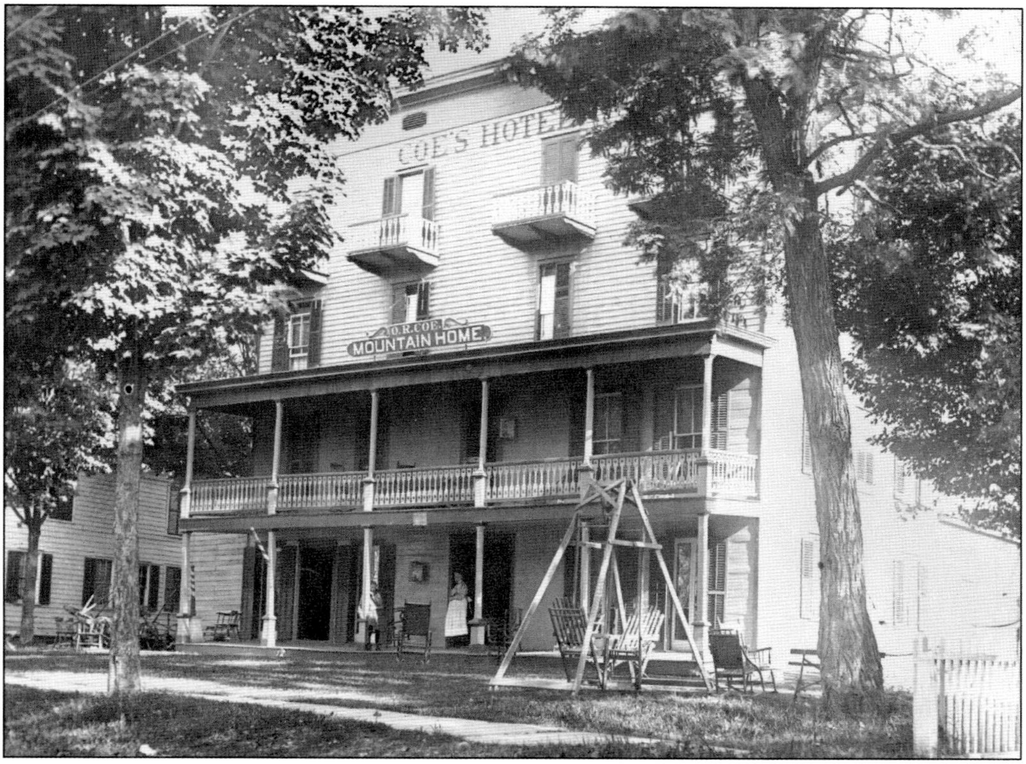

Coe's Hotel, or the Windham Hotel, was greatly expanded over many years. In this 1910 picture, the hotel had reached its final four-story size. Located at the bend on Main Street and with an imposing presence from either direction, it was by far the largest building in Windham. Unfortunately, the old wooden structure burned completely to the ground in 1966. Key Bank is now at the site at the Vets Road intersection.

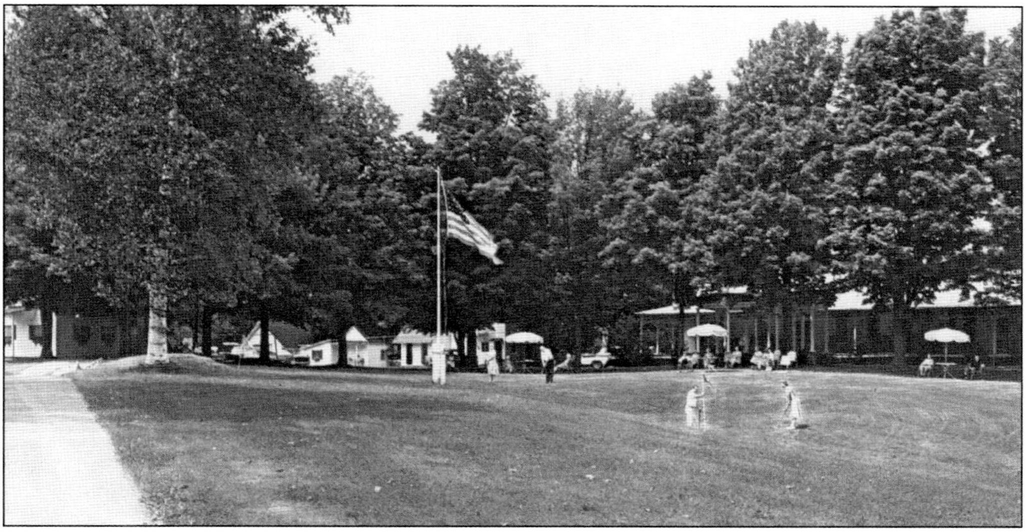

The leisure lifestyle of summer vacationers to Windham is captured in this 1950s postcard. The small nine-hole golf course seen here was at the Crest Park boardinghouse on South Street. Note the beautiful large porch on their main house in the background, a common feature of homes in the day. A waitress would stand there and ring a handbell when meals were to be served.

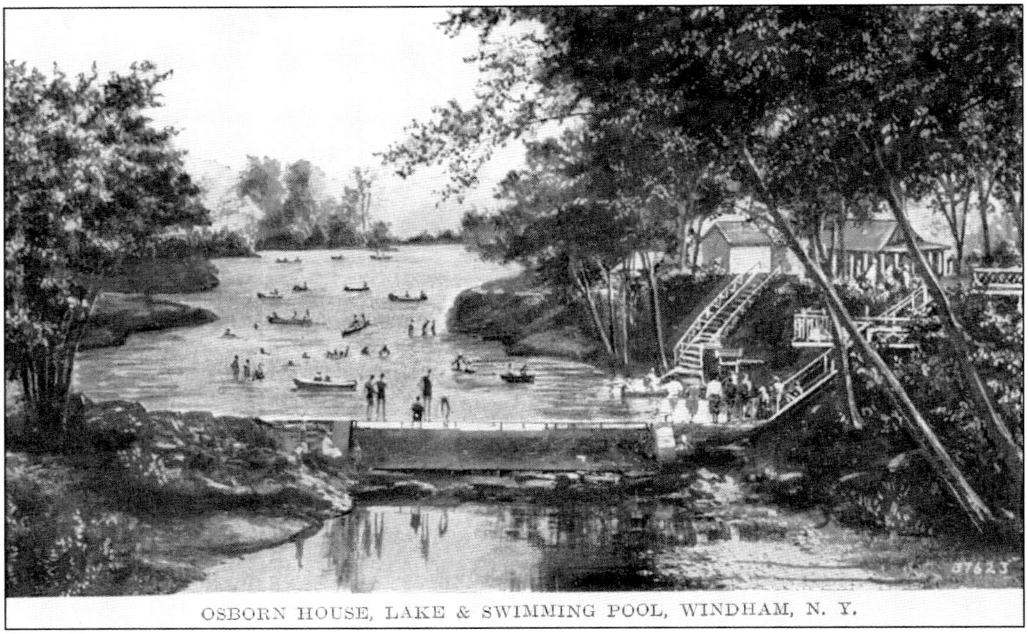

This 1946 postcard shows the dam built as a joint effort between the Thompson House and Osborn House in 1932 on Batavia Kill (creek) at Brook Lynne. When completed, guests staying at either boardinghouse could use the lake, which was created for swimming, boating, and other watersports. By the 1950s, the proliferation of swimming pools caused these natural or man-made swimming holes to fall out of use.

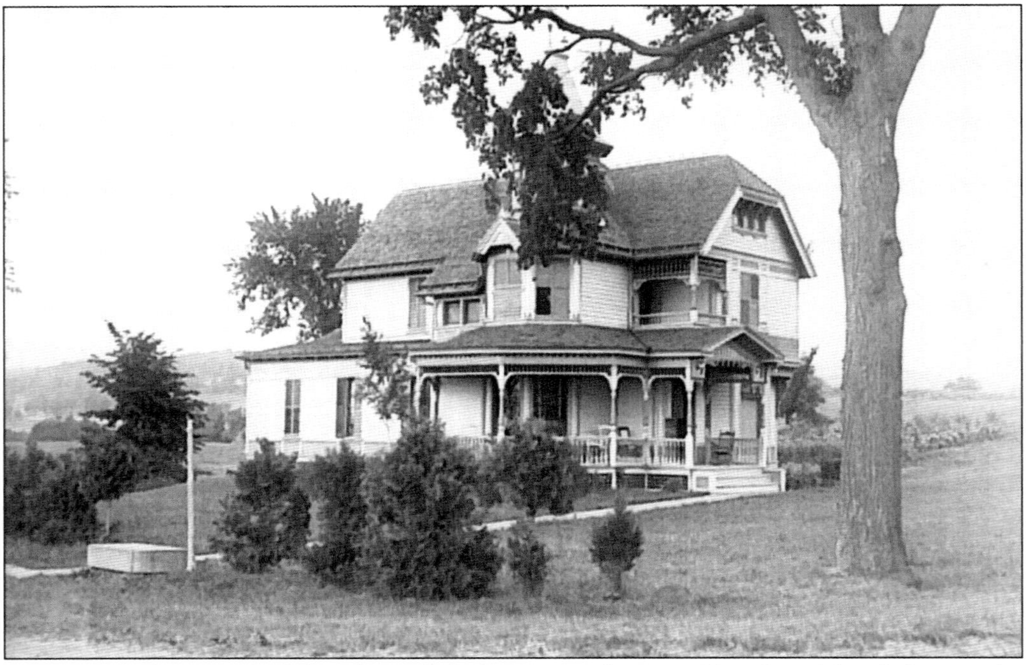

In this 1900 photograph of the Silas and Phebe Munson home at Church and South Streets, the unique Victorian architecture that was so popular at the time is evident. It was built around 1893 as a retirement home for Silas and Phebe. The Munsons were prolific builders, and their expert craftsmanship is evident here. As a boardinghouse, it was later known as the Elmcrest Inn.

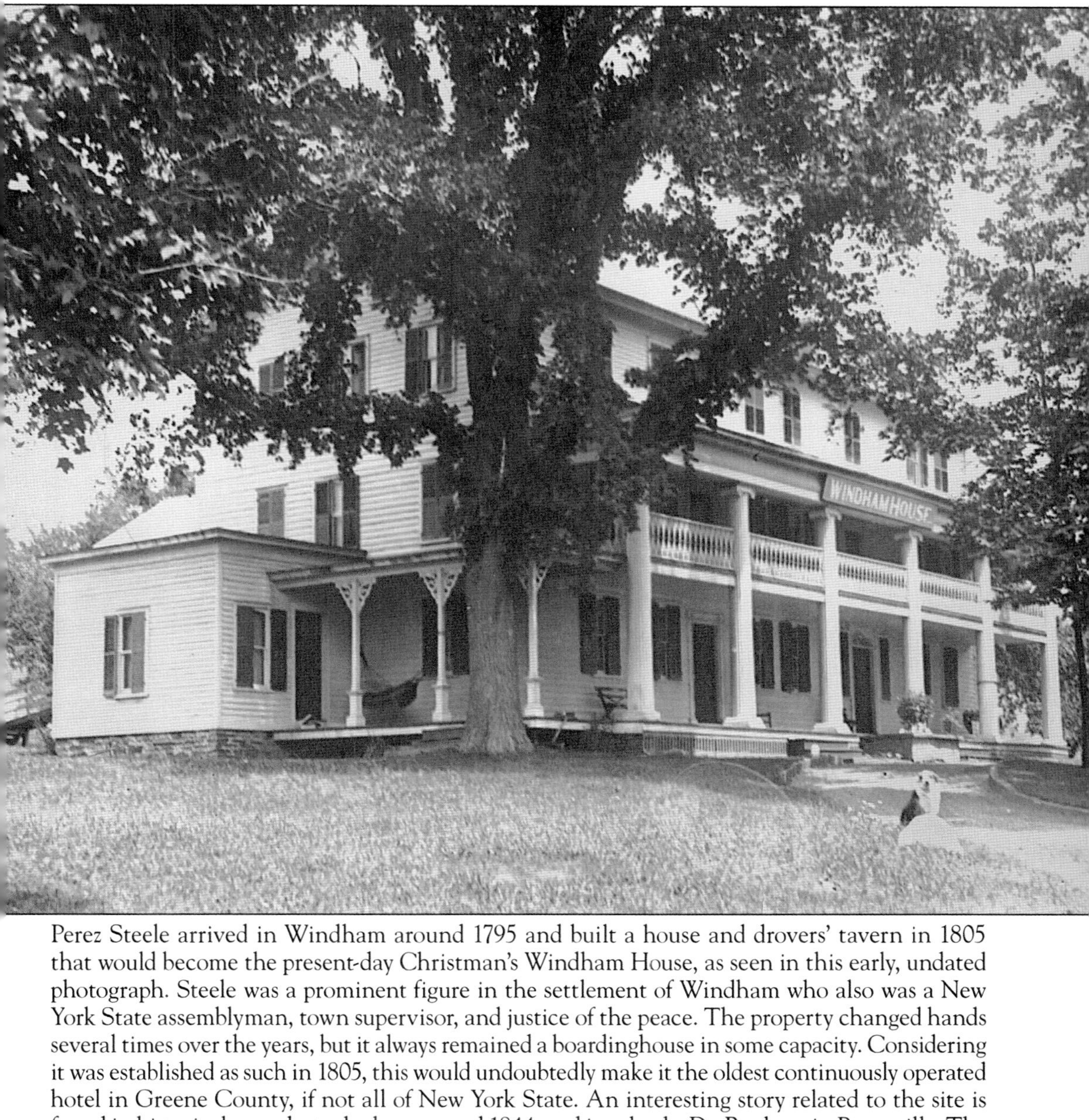

Perez Steele arrived in Windham around 1795 and built a house and drovers' tavern in 1805 that would become the present-day Christman's Windham House, as seen in this early, undated photograph. Steele was a prominent figure in the settlement of Windham who also was a New York State assemblyman, town supervisor, and justice of the peace. The property changed hands several times over the years, but it always remained a boardinghouse in some capacity. Considering it was established as such in 1805, this would undoubtedly make it the oldest continuously operated hotel in Greene County, if not all of New York State. An interesting story related to the site is found in historical records, took place around 1844, and involved a Dr. Benham in Prattsville. The doctor was called to a sick woman's house, but when he arrived, he found the woman strangled to death. Dr. Benham had met a man earlier on the road, so he told the authorities investigating the case about him. According to the 1884 J.B. Beers *History of Greene County*, the search found the man "asleep in Colonel Steeles' wagon house at Windham." He was taken to Catskill, tried, convicted, and hanged.

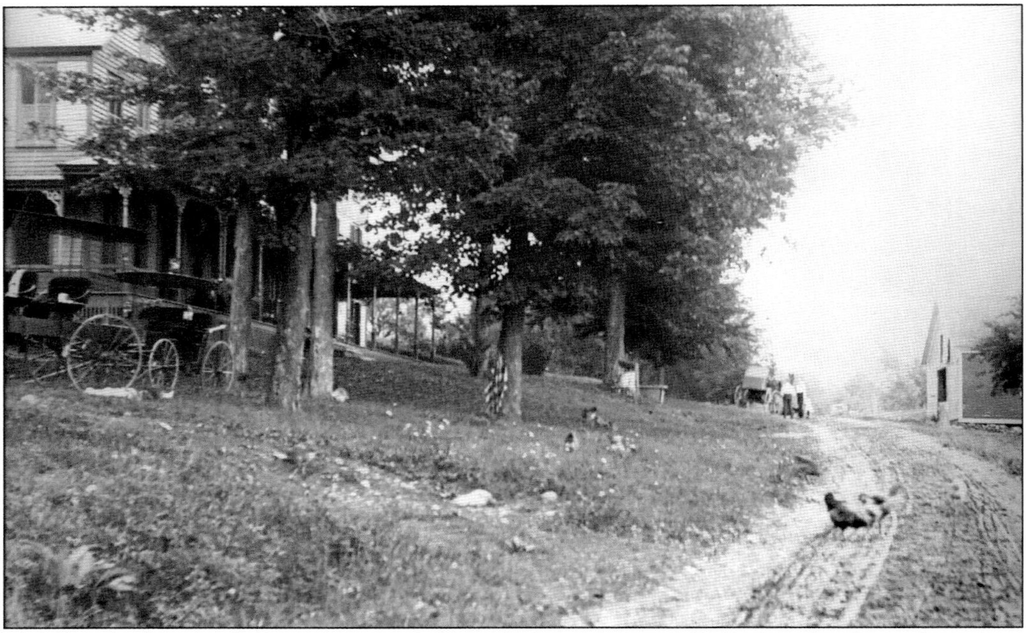

Mary Dewell operated the Howell Holiday Home and farm in this c. 1900 photograph. It later became a children's orphanage for a time. Eventually, it was purchased by the Westchester Police of Westchester County, New York, near New York City. They operated it as the Westchester Police Anchor Camp, a summer camp for children, until the 1980s. Many camps such as the Boy Scouts were in the mountaintop area. The barn seen at right stood for over 100 years, but in a February 2010 snowstorm that dumped over six feet of snow on Windham, the barn could take no more and collapsed.

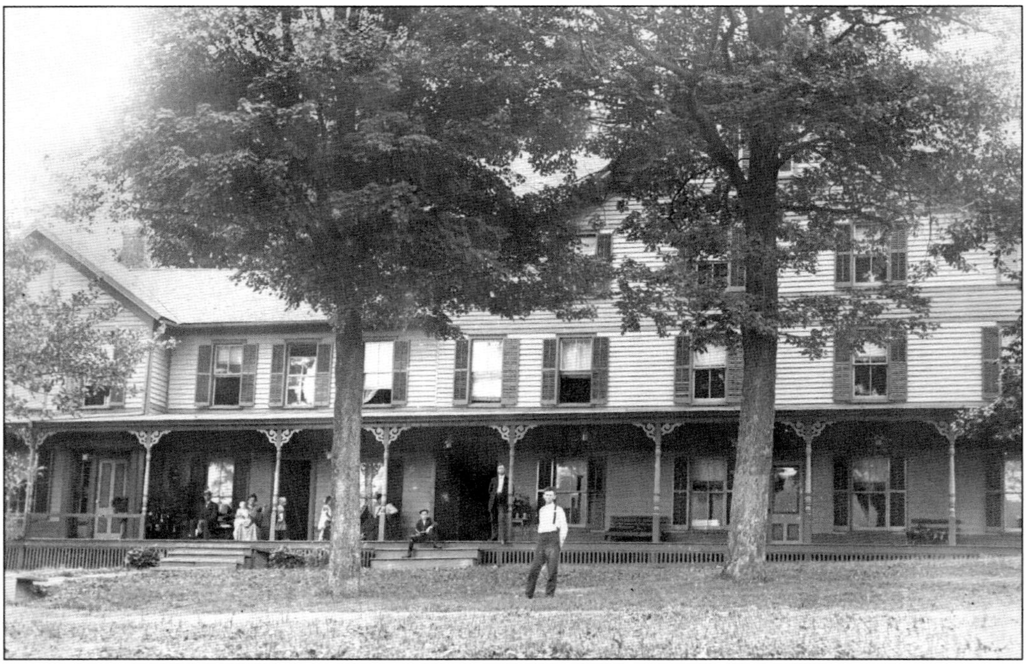

Pictured here around 1900 is Mary Dewell's Howell Holiday Home, seen from the road that is now Route 23. This boardinghouse was located about three miles east of Windham village.

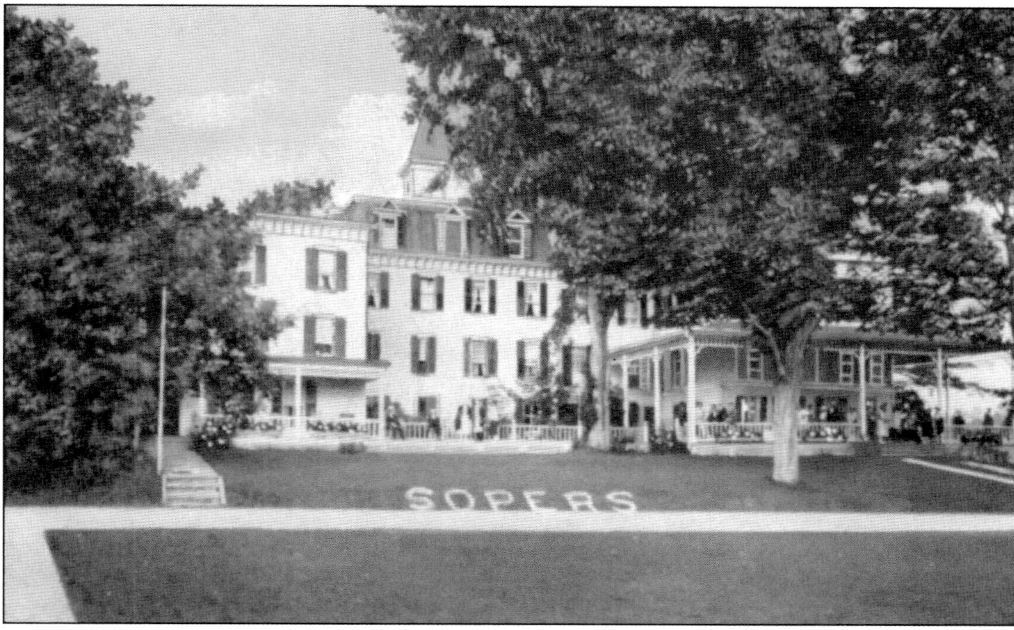

In the above 1920 postcard, the front of Soper's hotel stands on the west side of Route 296, adjacent to the Brook Lynne Bridge. In 1825, John Soper manufactured shaving boxes at his mill on Batavia Kill near this spot. He opened his hotel, formerly the Evergreen Park House, in 1870 and christened it Soper Place. It is now owned by the Thompson House. The 1906 photograph below is from the south side of the old Brook Lynne Bridge; the approach to Soper's was much lower than it is in 2011. Over the years, the road has been built up to where today it is level with the front of the building on the right. Upon reaching the crest of the hill in this picture, the 1906 Thompson House is on the left, and past that, the Osborn House.

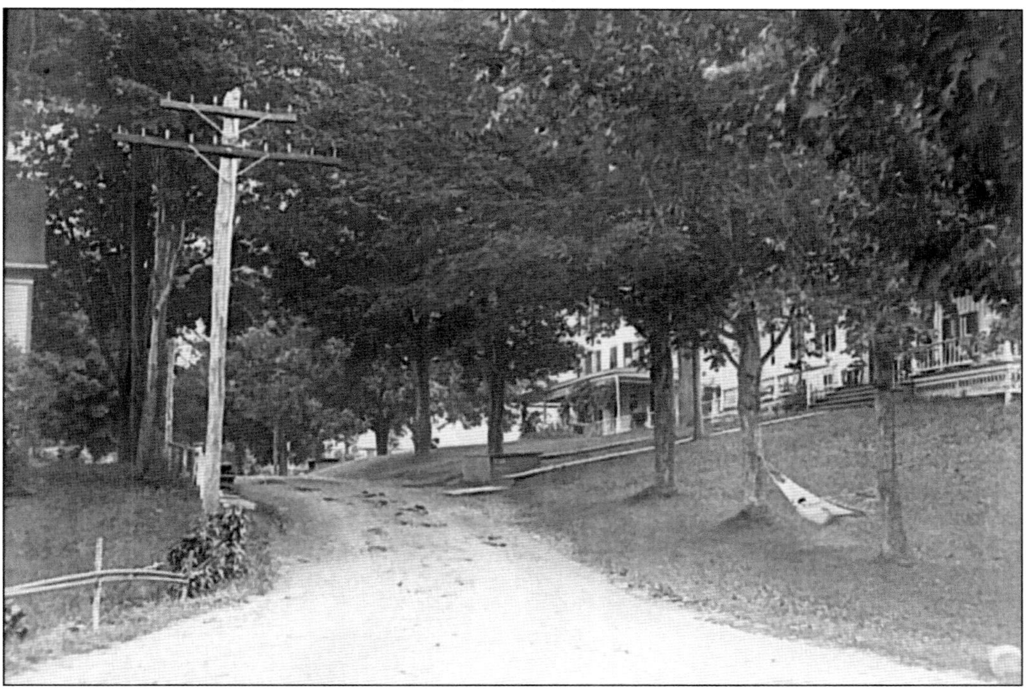

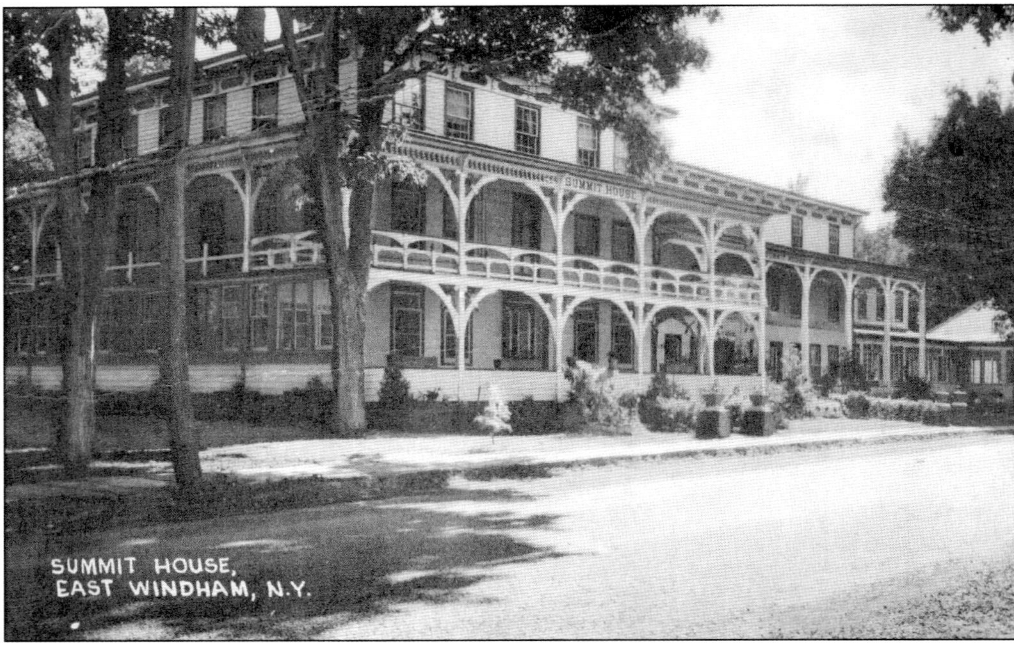

The Summit House was built by Barney Butts in 1848 on the Windham Turnpike in East Windham. Barney's brother Isaac later built the Butts House next door. It was said that Barney was a superb bear hunter, with a reputation for having captured or killed over 100. He kept three live bears chained behind the hotel for guests' entertainment.

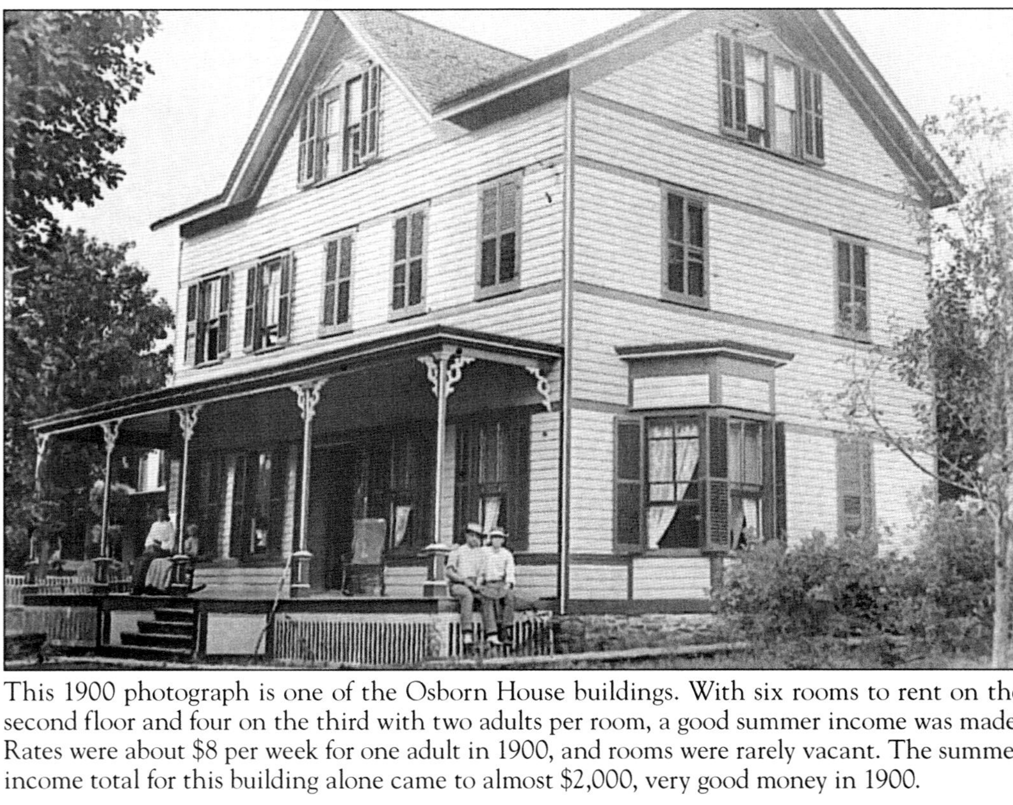

This 1900 photograph is one of the Osborn House buildings. With six rooms to rent on the second floor and four on the third with two adults per room, a good summer income was made. Rates were about $8 per week for one adult in 1900, and rooms were rarely vacant. The summer income total for this building alone came to almost $2,000, very good money in 1900.

Three

The Floods

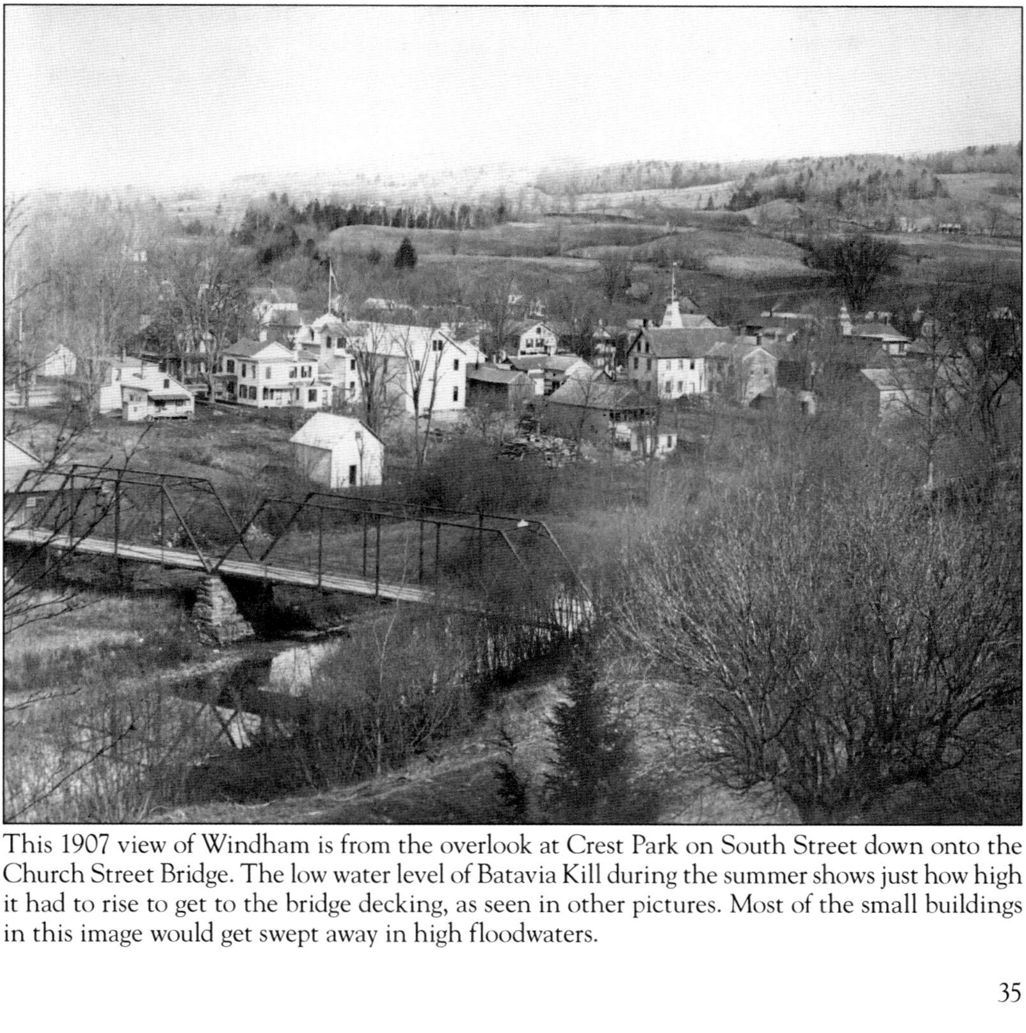

This 1907 view of Windham is from the overlook at Crest Park on South Street down onto the Church Street Bridge. The low water level of Batavia Kill during the summer shows just how high it had to rise to get to the bridge decking, as seen in other pictures. Most of the small buildings in this image would get swept away in high floodwaters.

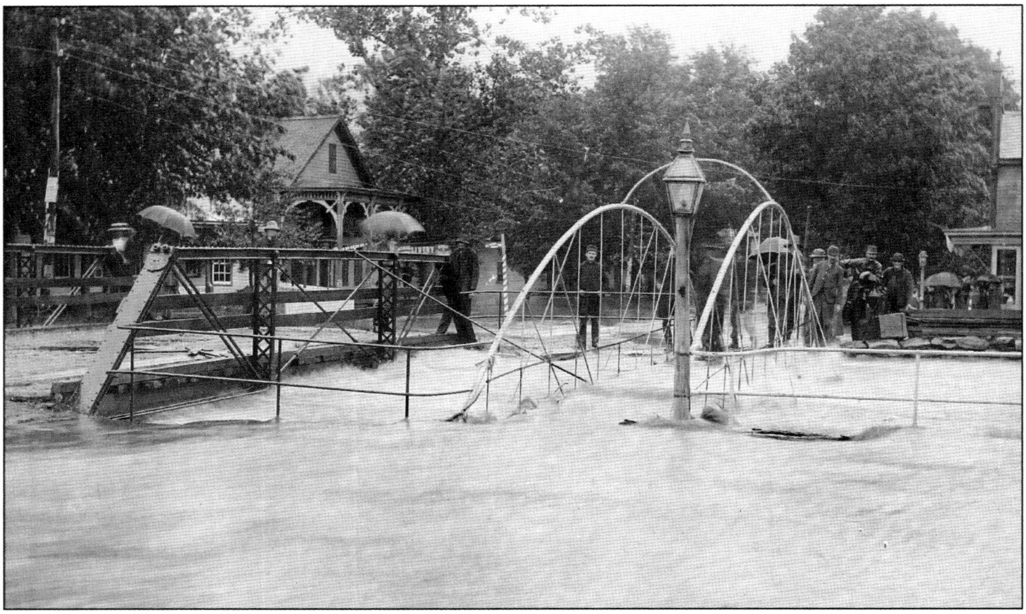

This photograph, taken during the 1893 flood, looks west on Main Street Windham at Mad Brook. Dams built further upstream often burst during downpours similar to this. On the night of April 18, 1870, after a violent storm with an enormous amount of rain, Sherman's Dam, located at Jennie's Notch, broke, sending a wall of water down that caused even more damage. (Courtesy of Richard and Ruth Morse.)

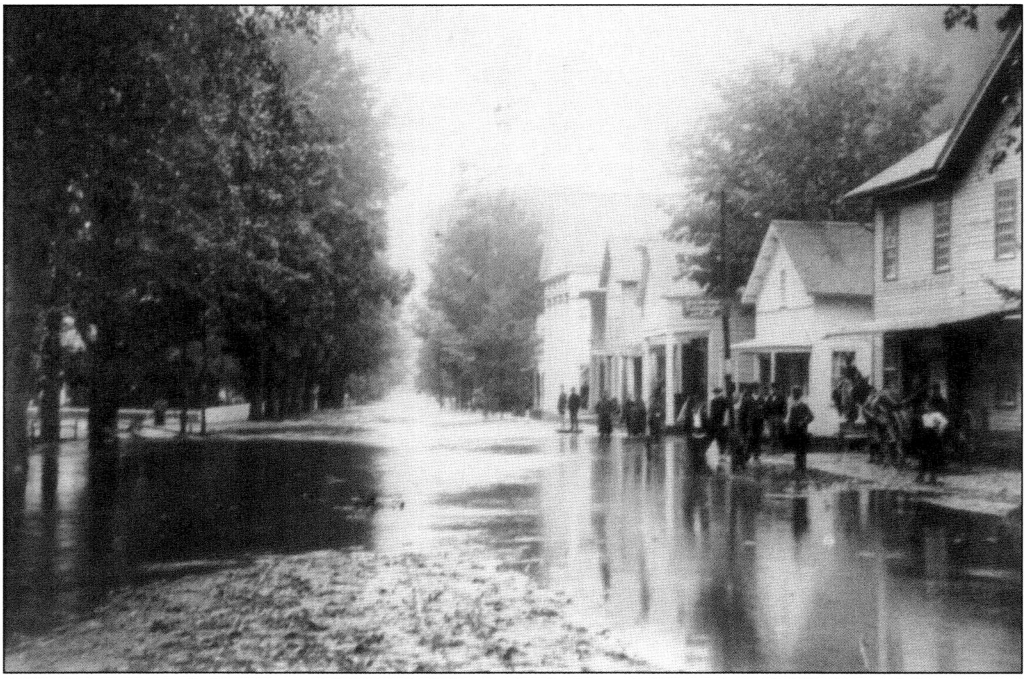

This 1892 view of Main Street faces west, but only the second house on the right is still standing in 2011. This location is across the street from today's school. All of the large buildings are manufacturers or mills that used waterpower supplied by the millrace, which ran from Mad Brook just east from here. The millrace ran behind these buildings to the west end of town.

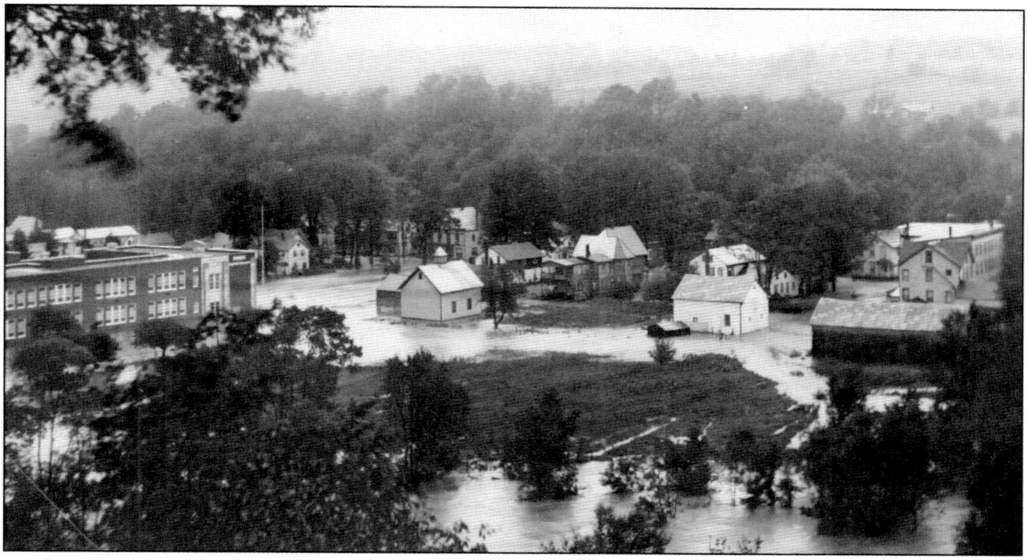

In this photograph of a late-1930s flood in Windham, water surrounds any obstacle on its flow westward. The Windham-Ashland-Jewett Central School, built in 1934, is on the left. Flooding occurred in Windham every time there was snow melt or heavy rain. Until catch basins were built higher up on the mountainsides in the 1960s, annual flooding was a problem. (Courtesy of Harold and Evelyn Munson.)

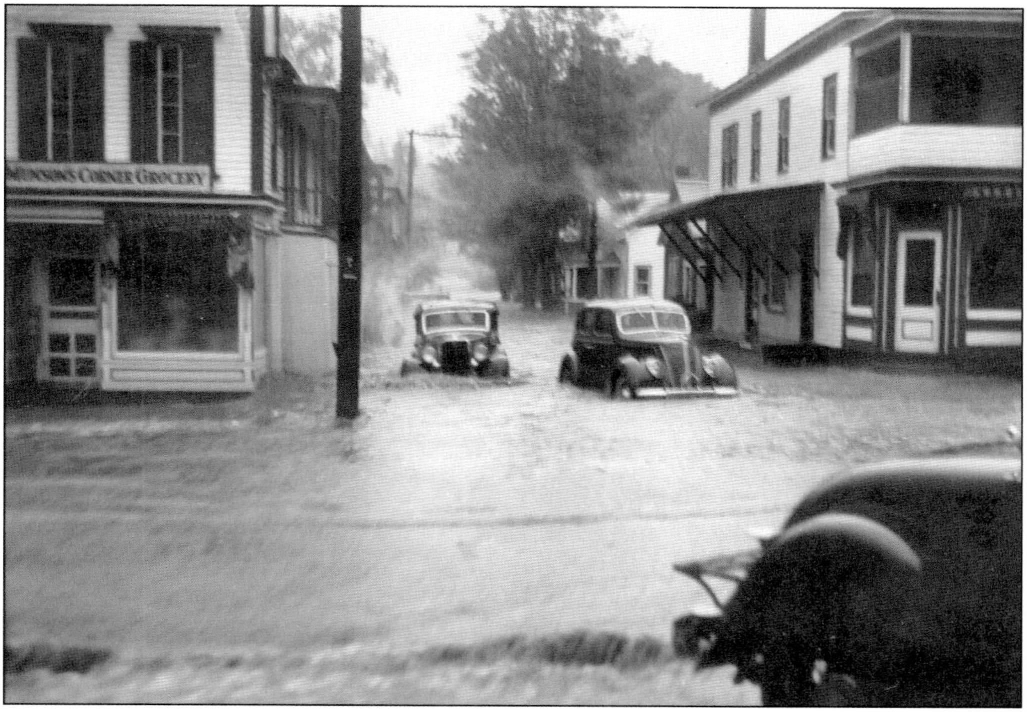

This is the corner of Main and Mill Streets in Windham during the 1930 flood. The Munson Grocery building later became the Blue Moon gift shop and restaurant, which burned down in 1967 and was later replaced by Todaro's Salumeria. The structure on the right in the image was originally a feed store, then a post office, and is now Roshkowska Galleries. (Courtesy of Harold and Evelyn Munson.)

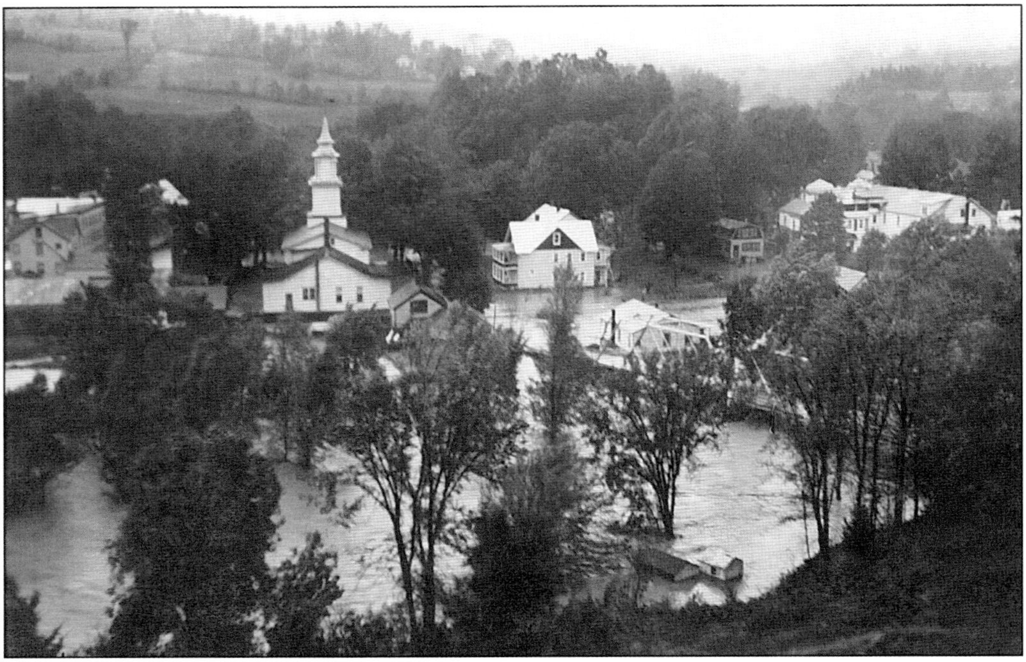

In this image from the 1930 flood is the Windham Centre Presbyterian Church, now the Windham Civic Centre and Library, at the corner of Main and Church Streets, completely surrounded by floodwaters. Elmer Munson built the two structures in the bottom of the image to house a pump for his water supply at Crest Park boardinghouse. (Courtesy of Harold and Evelyn Munson.)

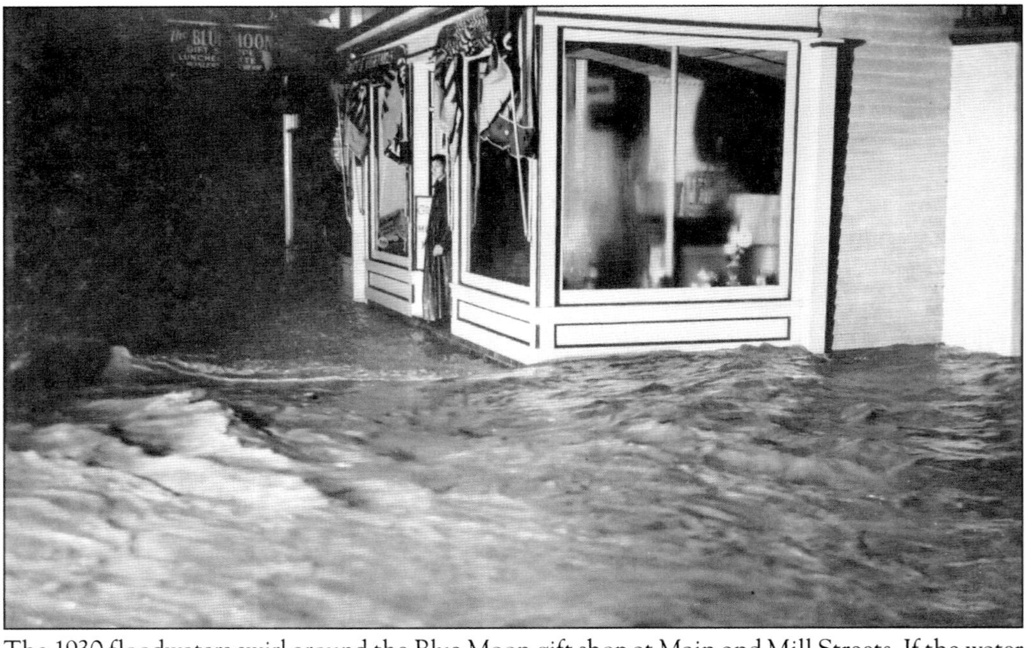

The 1930 floodwaters swirl around the Blue Moon gift shop at Main and Mill Streets. If the water rushing down Batavia Kill rose rapidly to a dangerous level in Windham during the night, someone in the town firehouse would sound the siren, warning sleeping residents. Flooded basements and floors were a regular occurrence that the population had to contend with. (Courtesy of Harold and Evelyn Munson.)

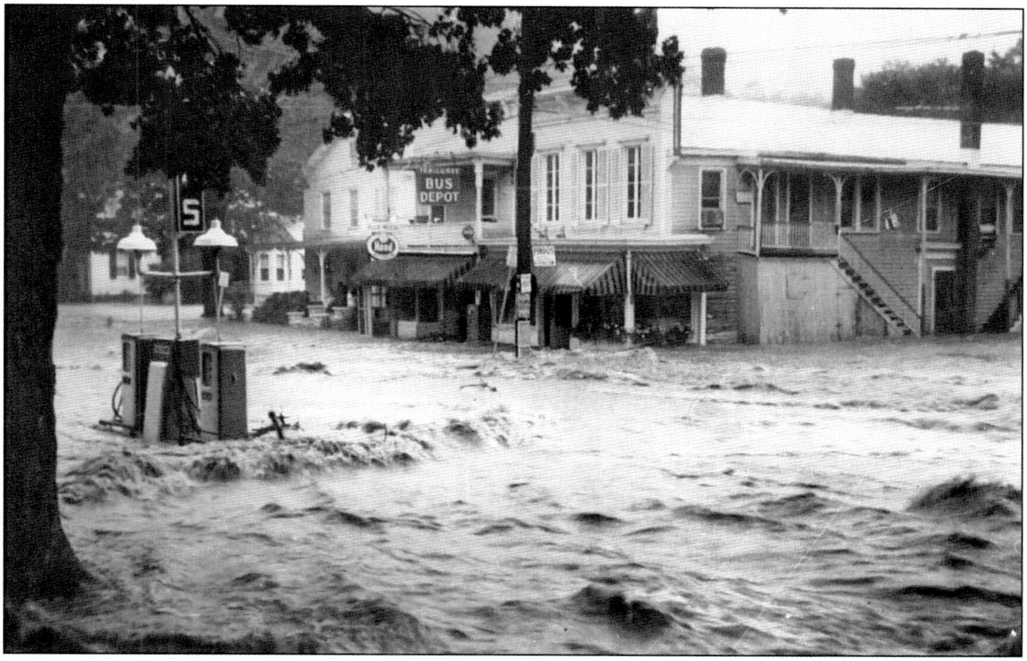

This view is looking west toward the corner of Main and Mill Streets during the 1960 flood. The gas pumps on the left are in the front of Sokoll's Ford dealership, which is now Michael's Diner. The early settlers certainly faced a dilemma: they needed to be close to the streams, but in Windham's mountain valley, that came with a price of yearly flooding.

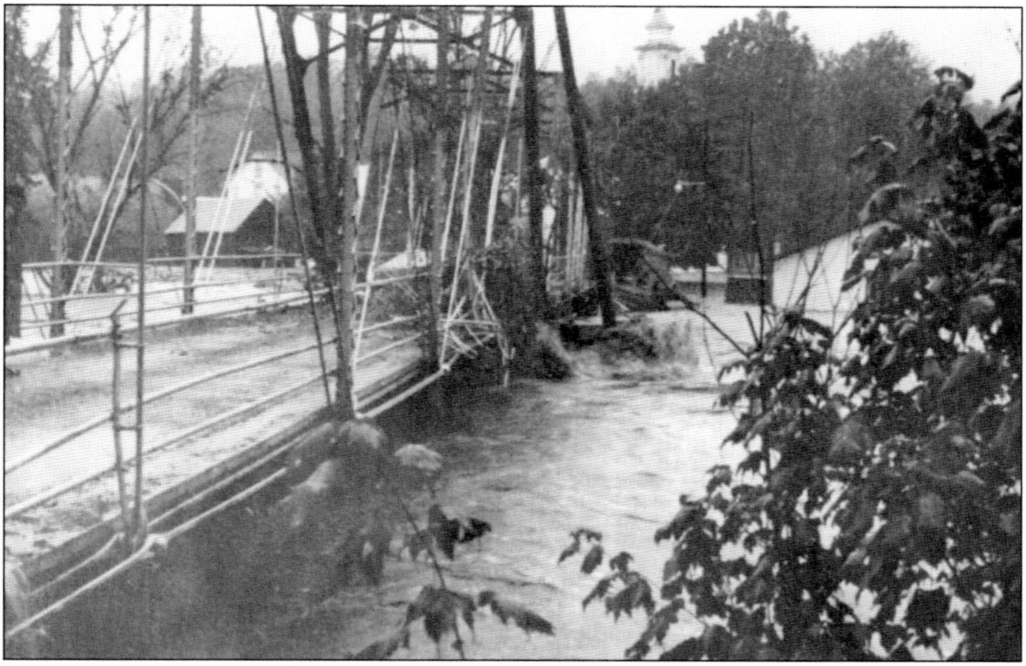

Debris being washed downstream can be seen piling up on the Church Street Bridge in this September 1960 photograph. The pipe rails have been twisted beyond repair from previous impacts. What appears to be an electric pole has struck the middle abutment and is jammed against it by the water pressure.

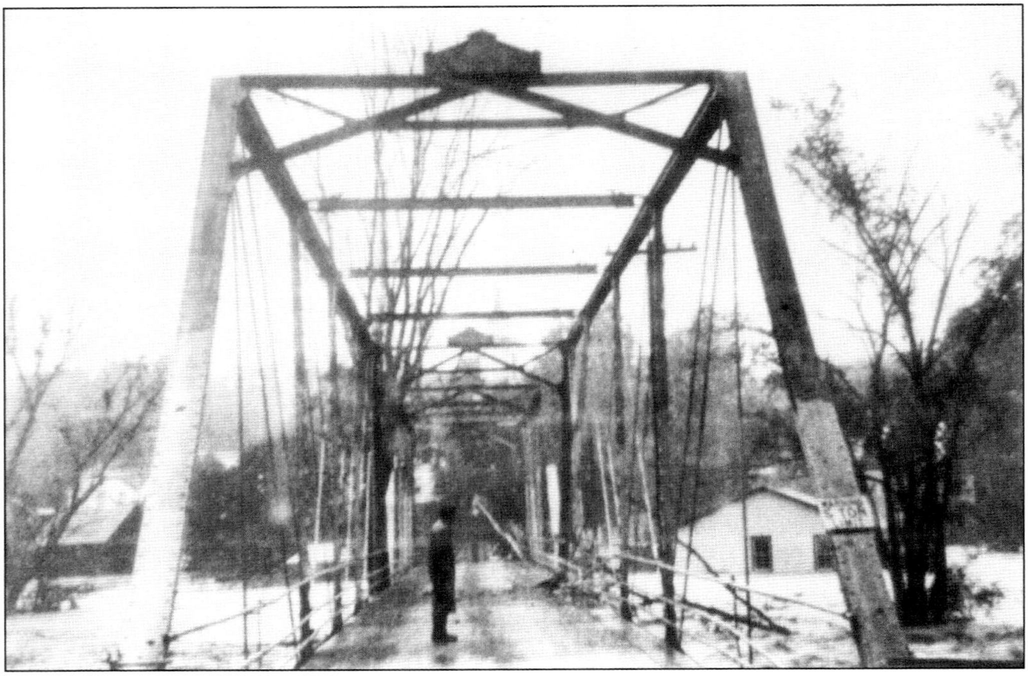

One might question the intelligence of the man in this photograph. During a different flood on August 24, 1893, another summer boarder had done the same thing, only to be swept away with the bridge. The group of trees in the water to the right of the bridge is not part of the landscape—they were ripped from wherever they stood further upstream and had floated down. It appears that they are about to impact the bridge.

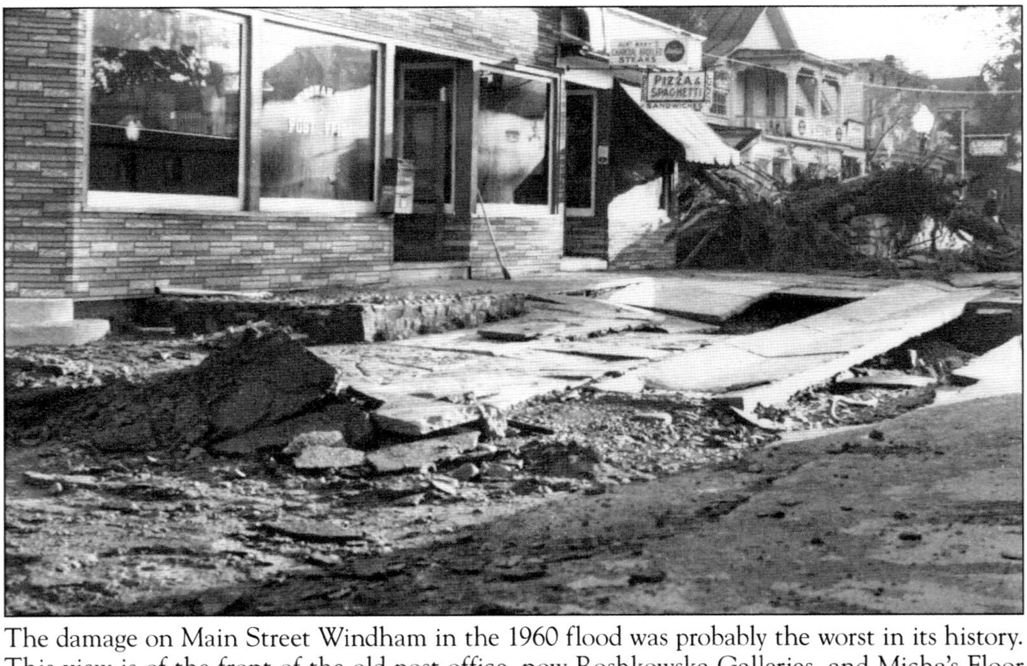

The damage on Main Street Windham in the 1960 flood was probably the worst in its history. This view is of the front of the old post office, now Roshkowska Galleries, and Micha's Floor Covering, adjacent to Mad Brook. Debris washed down by the flood is piled high on the bridge that spans Mad Brook.

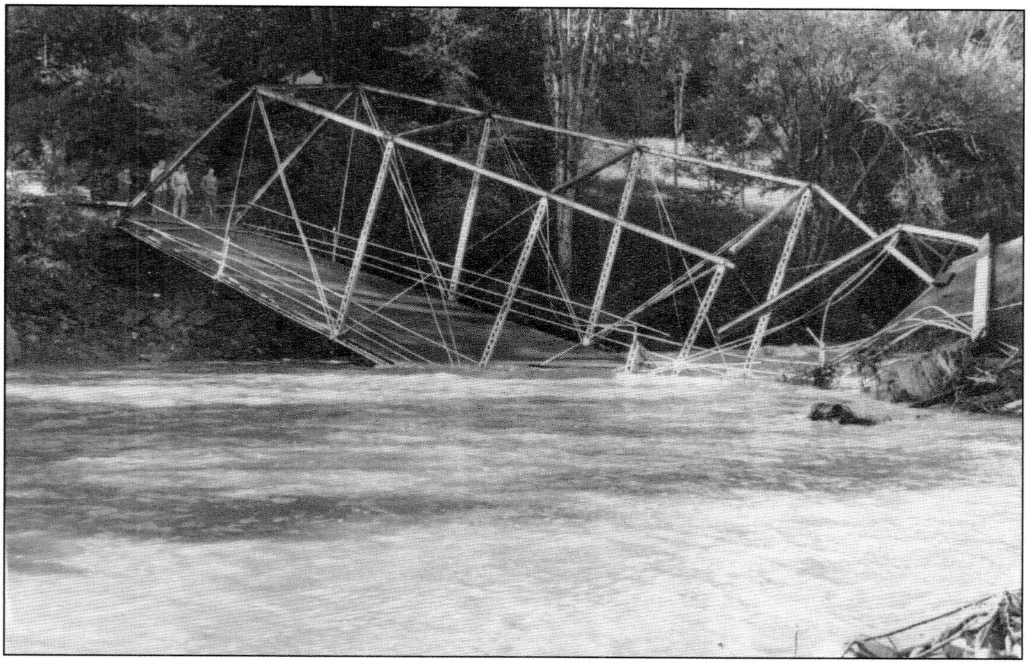

Residents view the destruction of the Church Street Bridge that was caused by the 1960 flood. Built in 1903, the bridge endured years of constant water pressure and, particularly, the impact of debris swept downstream during floods that finally took its toll. For the residents of South Street, this created a three-mile detour until the following year when the bridge was replaced.

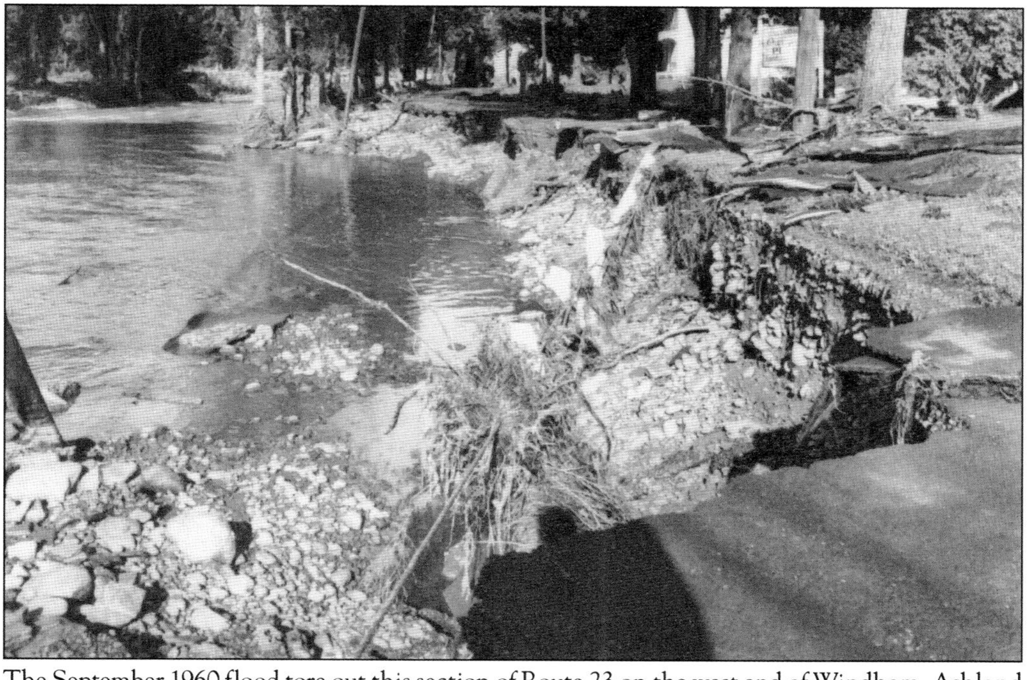

The September 1960 flood tore out this section of Route 23 on the west end of Windham. Ashland fire chief Paul Alle was wading in water carrying a lamp in front of a rescue truck to guide it when he was swept away at this washout. The Church Street Bridge displays a plaque dedicated to his memory and service to the town.

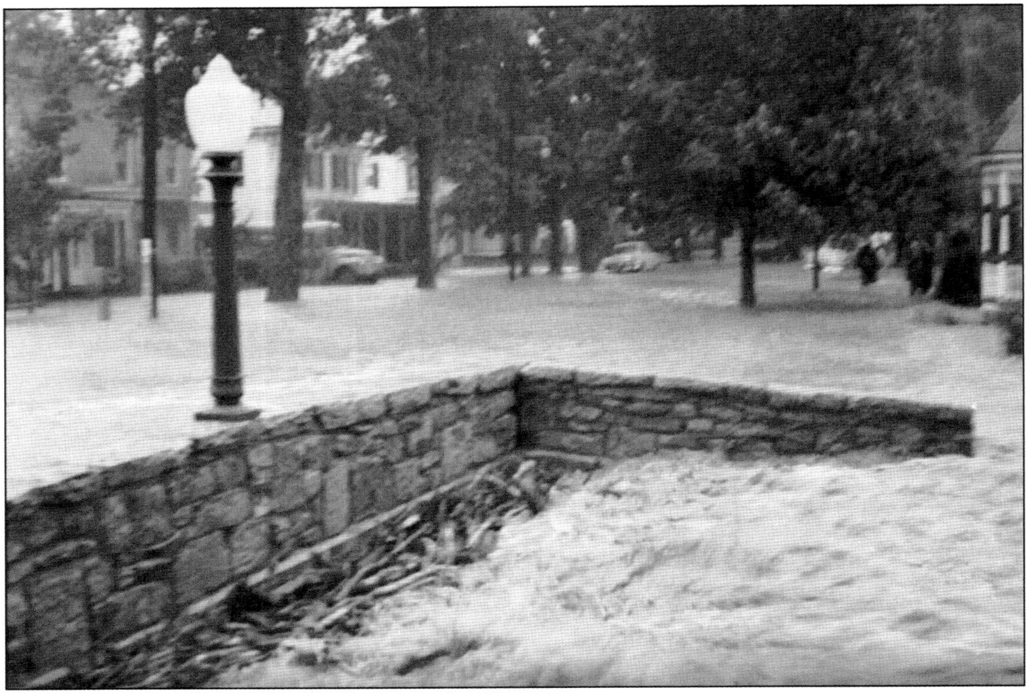

These pictures of the 1960 flood damage on Mad Brook show the force of the water as it came downstream onto Windham's Main Street. The debris would pile up on the upstream wall of the bridge in the picture below and be held there by water pressure as it overflowed the top of the wall. The tremendous force from the floodwaters caused incredible damage to the street and buildings. Everything inside the Victory Store adjacent to the bridge was destroyed. The floodwaters in the background of the photograph above are from the Batavia Kill overflow on the east end of town.

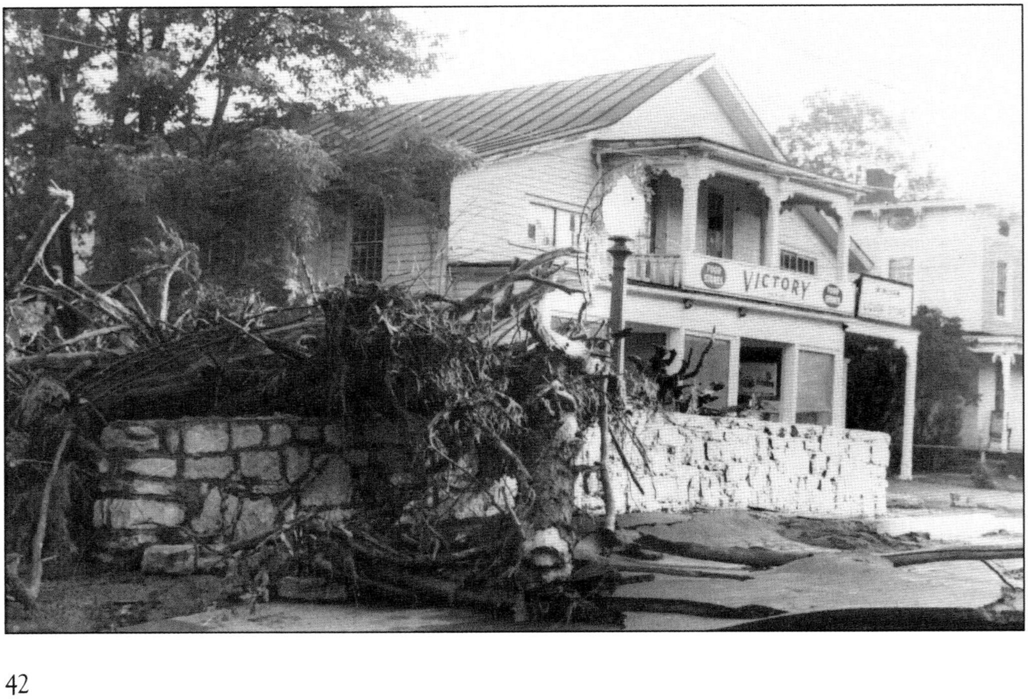

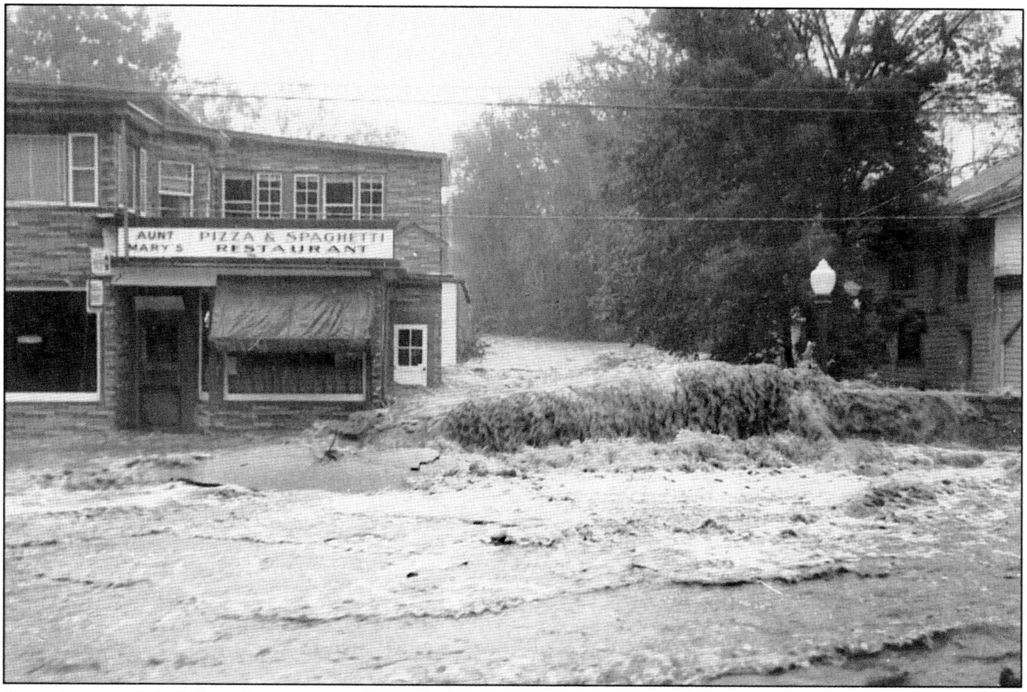

Seen here is Mad Brook as it overflowed the north side of the bridge on Main Street in the 1960 flood. The pizza restaurant on the left now houses Micha's Floor Covering. As debris piled higher on the bridge, so did the water as it spilled over onto Main Street.

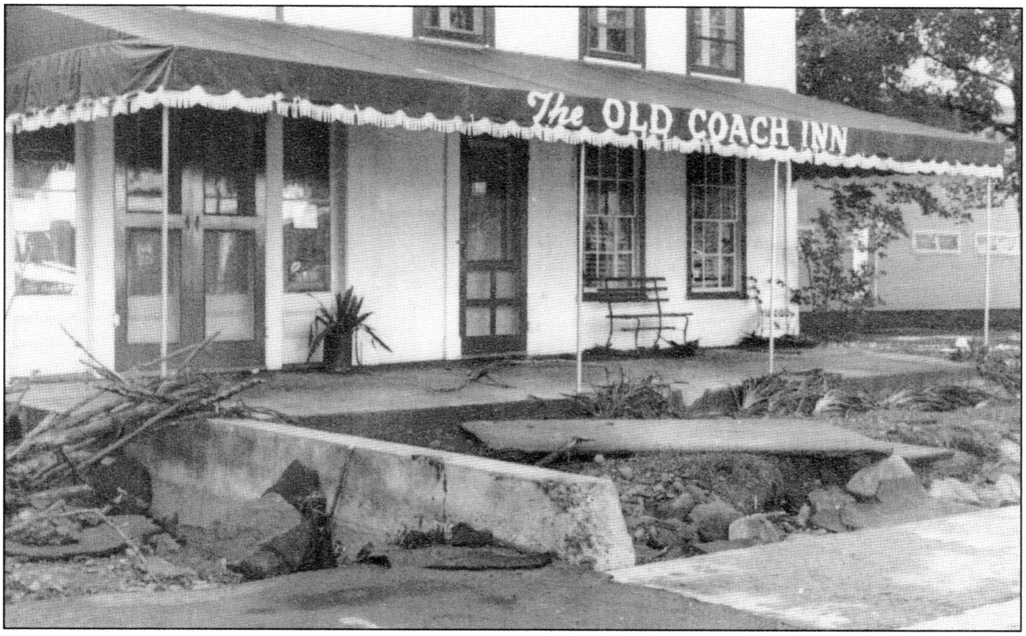

The Old Coach Inn had many lives in its 100-year existence. It was located between Sokoll's Ford dealership (now Michael's Diner) and the Masonic Temple before it was torn down, and the site is now a parking lot. Taverns in the old villages were important in the day. They were places where people could go for news from the outside world as well as to attend civic meetings and entertainment events. (Courtesy of Peg and Lyle Sokoll.)

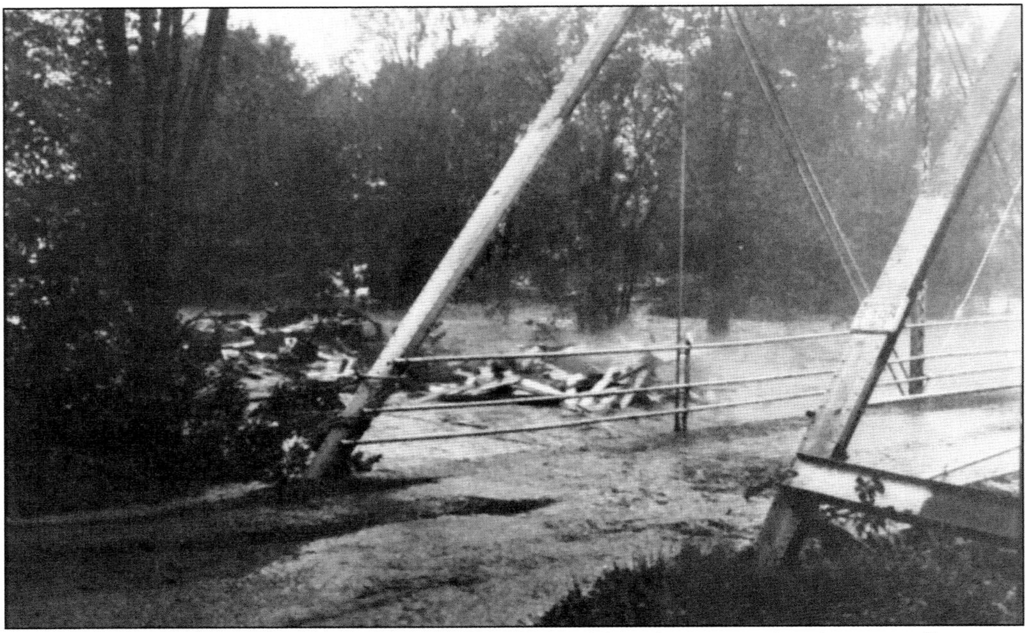

The shattered remains of a storage building from the Welsh and Grey Lumber Company float away after impact underneath the Church Street Bridge. This terrible flood was caused by Hurricane Donna in September 1960. That storm holds the record for the longest major hurricane affecting the largest land mass in history. It is ranked fourth highest of all time on the Accumulated Cyclone Energy (ACE) scale.

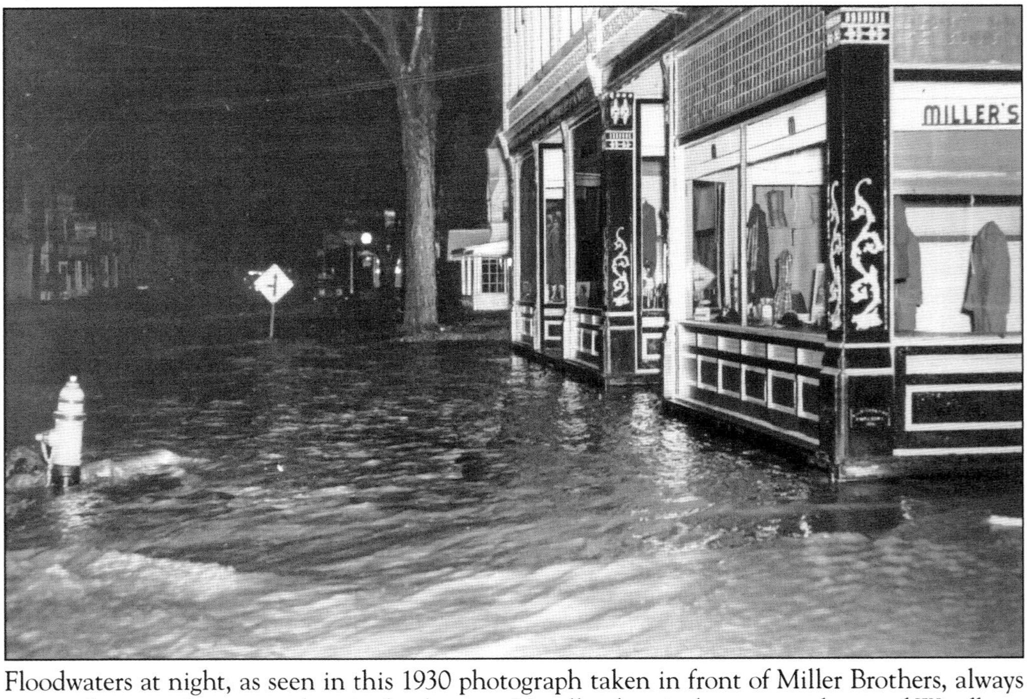

Floodwaters at night, as seen in this 1930 photograph taken in front of Miller Brothers, always seem to be more dangerous than in the daytime. Usually, electrical power was lost, and Windham residents were forced to move to higher ground until the floodwaters subsided. The water is about one foot deep, but the strong current caused most of the damage.

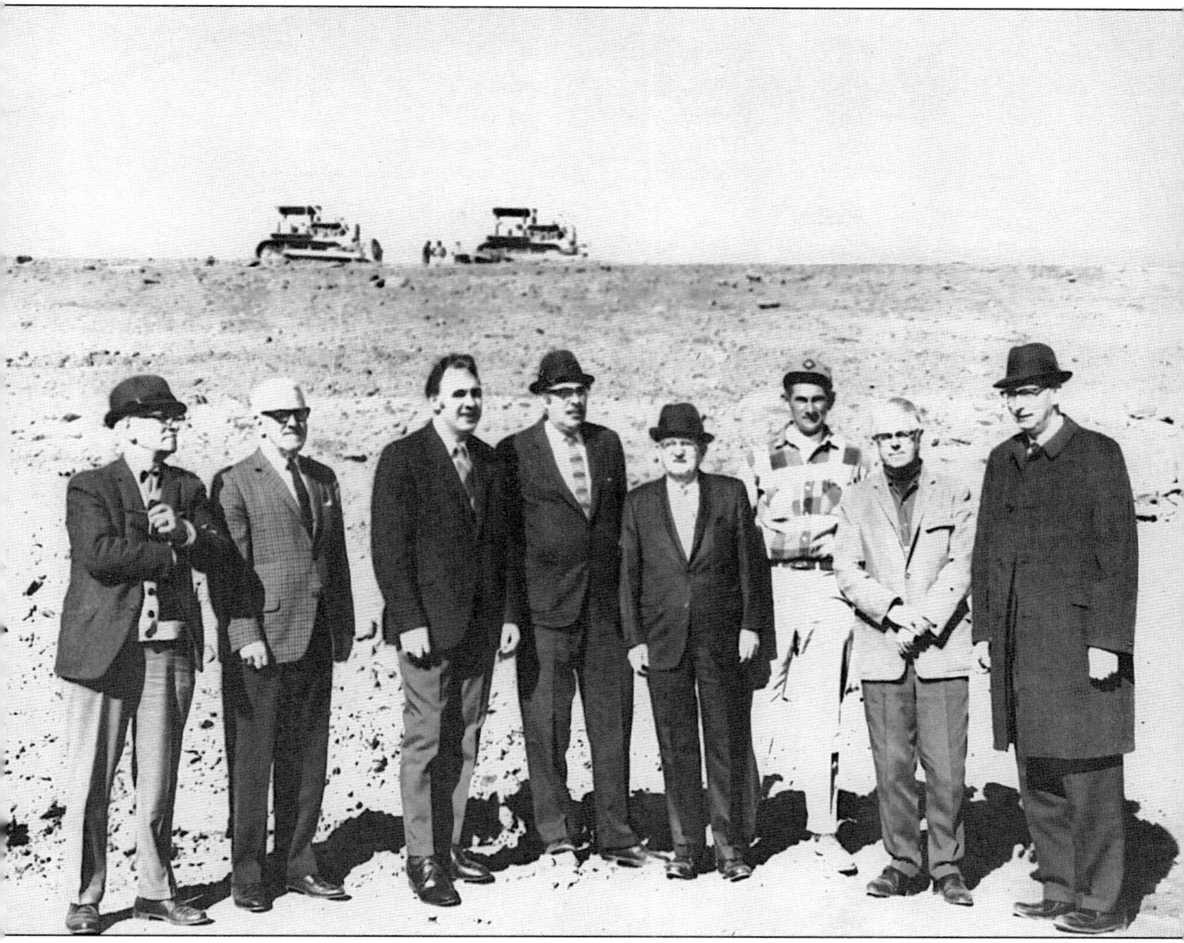

Relief from the endless cycle of flooding in Windham village finally arrived when Windham resident and state assemblyman Larry Lane was able to acquire government funds to build a flood-prevention system in the early 1960s. Seen here are dignitaries who were involved with the project as they stand at the base of one of the government-funded barrier dams. They are, from left to right, William Koonan, George Osborn, Larry Lane, Lee Decker, V.W. Morrow, two unidentified men, and John Smith. The purpose of these catch basins was to retain the excessive water runoff from the mountainsides, hold it behind the dams, and release it slowly over many days. The whole project works perfectly, and the constant destruction and anguish from floods has ceased completely. In addition to constructing the catch basins, Batavia Kill was cleared by bulldozers of all obstructions that caused water to back up. (Courtesy of Windham Historical Society.)

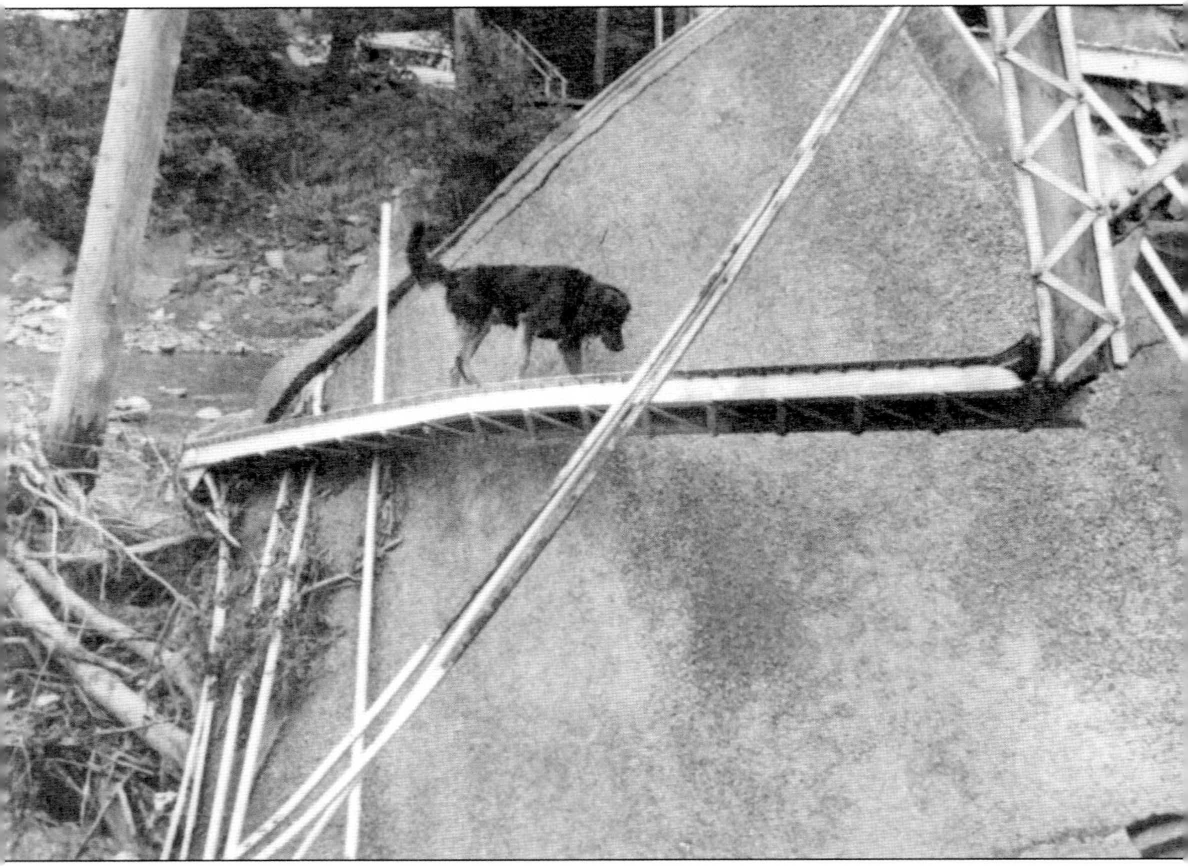

After the 1960 flood caused the Church Street Bridge to collapse, along with all the other destruction it inflicted upon the town, not only did the people of Windham have to cope with the aftermath, but so did the animals. To the amazement of onlookers, Nipper traversed up and down the twisted wreckage of the bridge until he was able to cross over the creek without getting wet.

Four

HOMES AND BUILDINGS

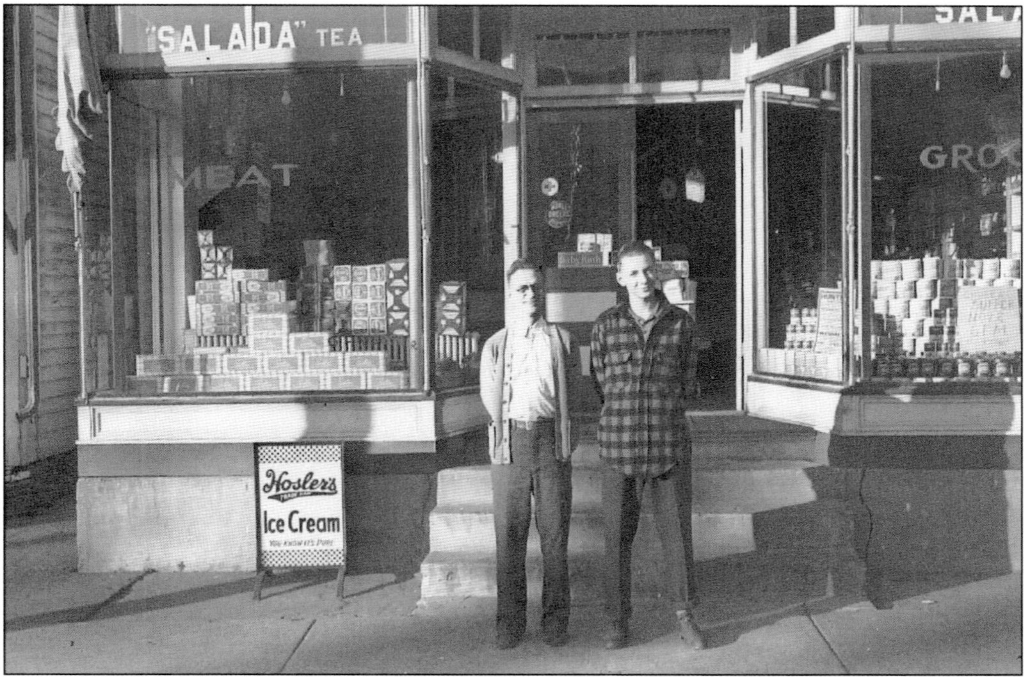

Standing in front of his store in this early-1940s photograph are Grant Morse (left) and his son Richard. Morse's Grocery was located across Route 23 from the Windham-Ashland-Jewett Central School. There were several large buildings erected very close together, and in 1972, a fire started in a structure adjacent to Morse's and burned all three buildings to the ground. (Courtesy of Richard and Ruth Morse.)

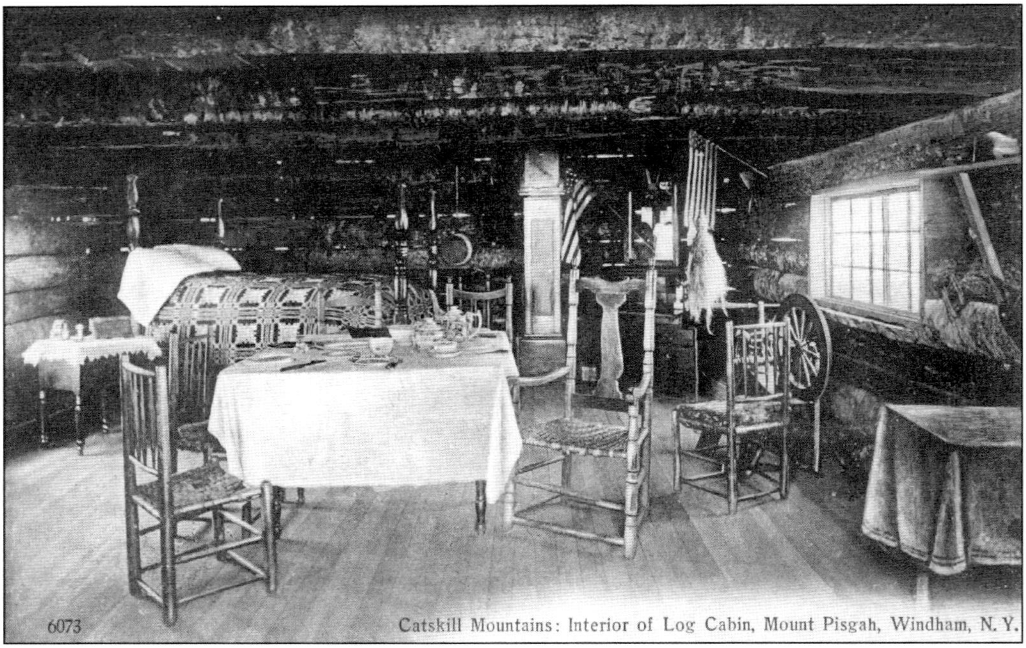

The image above is a 1908 postcard showing the interior of the log cabin on the summit of Mount Pisgah, seen in the photograph below. The Doolittle family owned the summit of the mountain and turned it into a profitable observation deck and dance hall business. These accommodations may seem very rugged, but when the settlers first arrived in Windham, living conditions were even worse. Hard work and determination produced these log cabins, which, to them, must have seemed like palaces compared to what they first lived in. It was unusual for anyone to build such a structure on top of a mountain, considering that water would not be nearby. After lumber mills began operating, the houses would be constructed with wood planks.

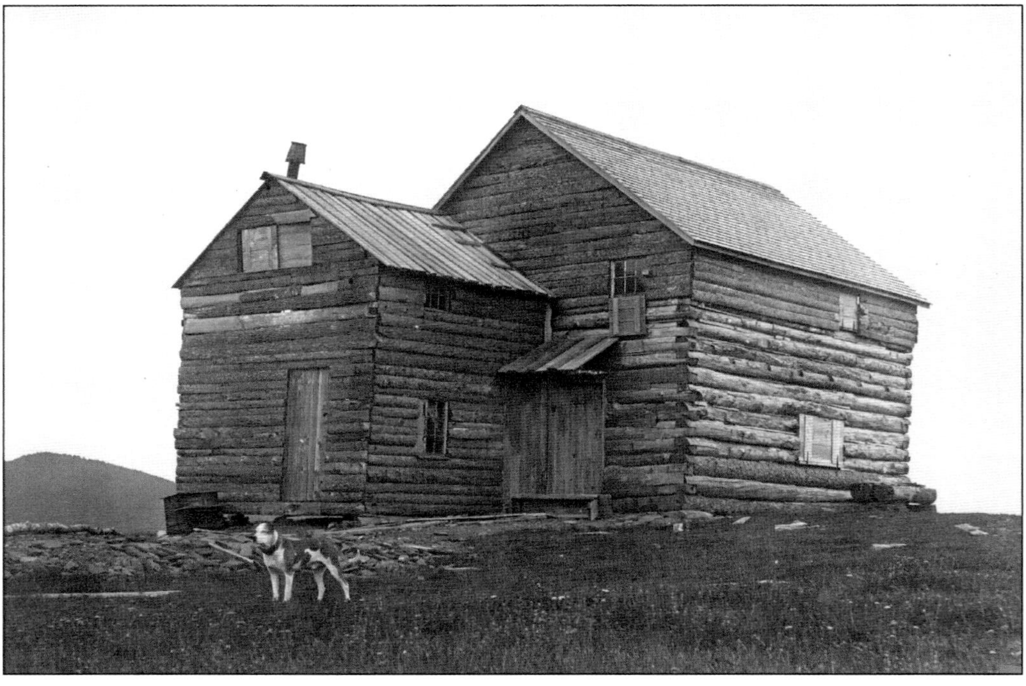

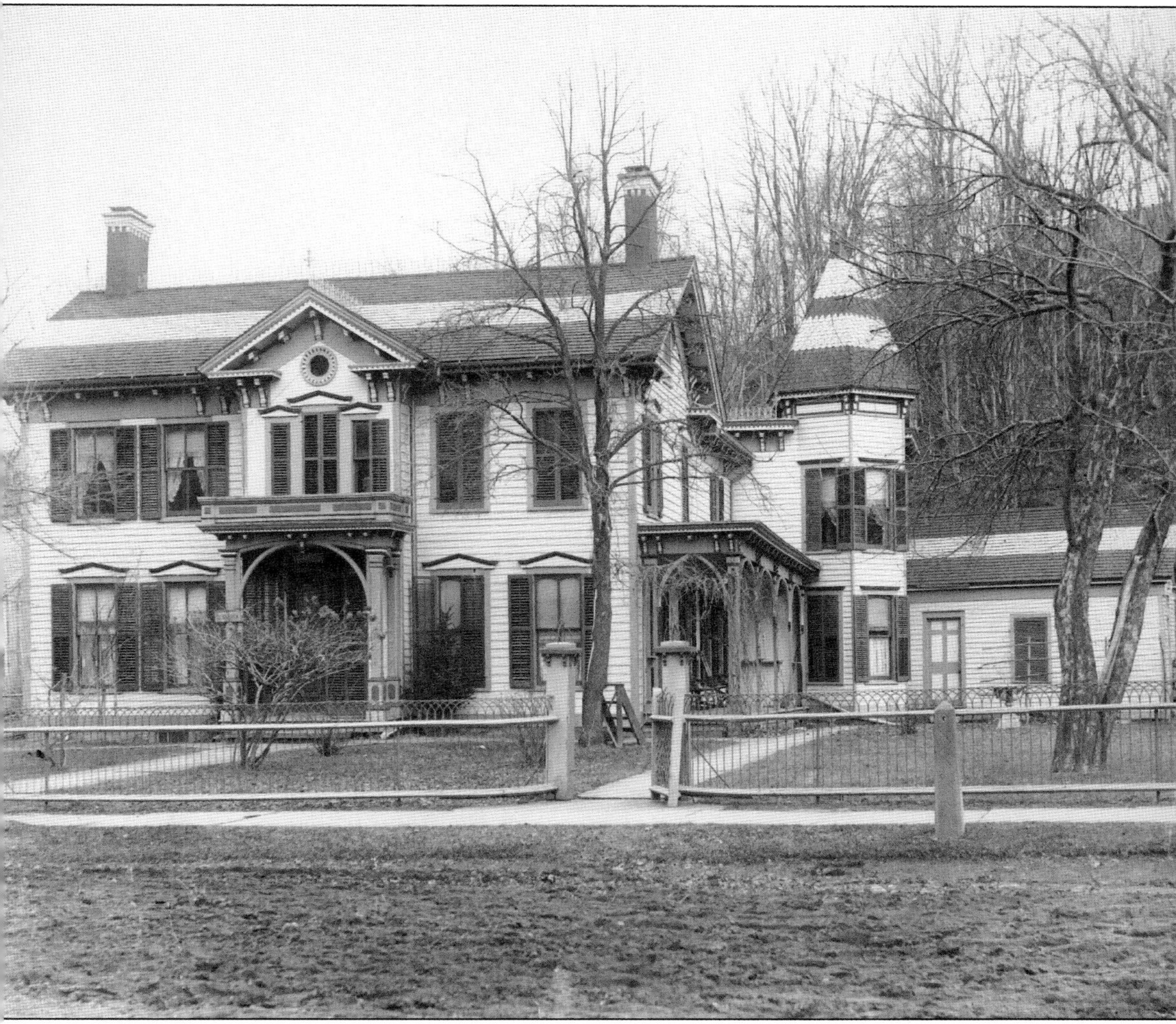

Built by Dr. Hervey Camp in 1814, the house in this 1900 photograph was continuously occupied by doctors until 2004. The most recent resident was Dr. Edwin Mulbury, who passed away in 2004 at the age of 98. Located right in the center of Windham, it has been the single most recognizable home in the town. In addition to being a good old-fashioned country doctor, Mulbury was very involved in community organizations. He was the school physician, belonged to the Masonic lodge, and was a lifelong member of the Windham Fire Company. In his profession, he was affiliated with many medical organizations and was a Federal Aviation Administration medical examiner. He, along with the younger Dr. Blakeslee, provided Windham residents and nonresidents alike with excellent medical care through most of the 20th century.

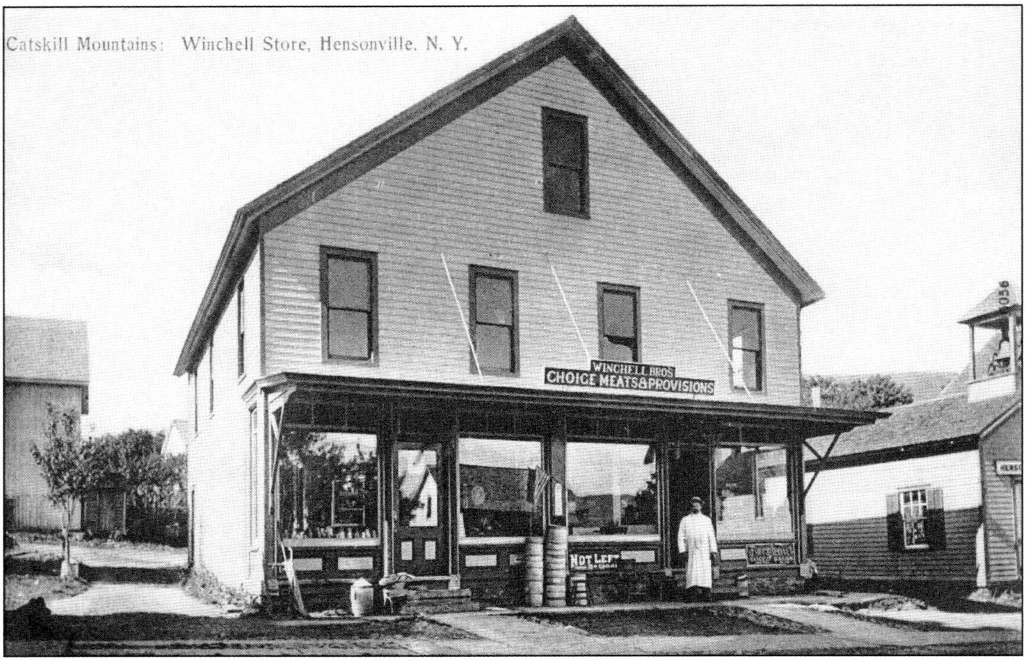

The Winchell Store in Hensonville, as seen in this 1898 postcard, sold meats and provisions. This building has housed a variety of businesses over the years, including a Laundromat, and has now been converted to apartments. For such a small hamlet, Hensonville had many commercial buildings at the four corners and was a hub of local activity in 1900.

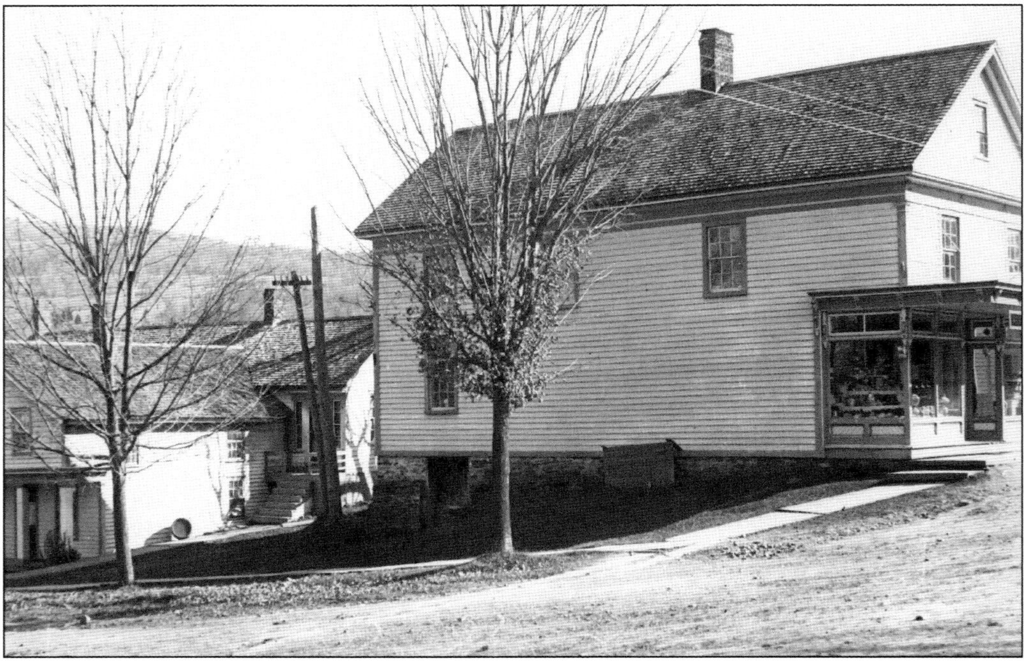

Slater's Store stands at the corner of Route 296 and Brooksburg Road in Hensonville in 1905. John Henson was the first settler in this hamlet (which was named after him), and this is near the site where his log cabin, built in 1818, once stood. In the mid-1900s, an addition was built to the left side of the structure, which became the Frog's House restaurant and bar for many years.

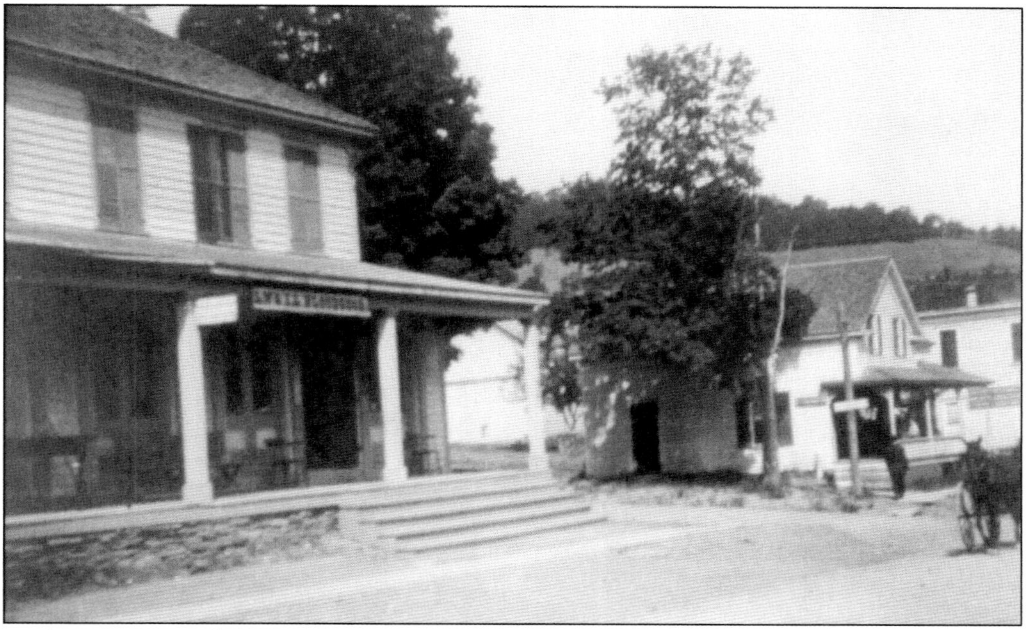

In this 1900 view facing west is Bloodgood's store in Hensonville, located at the corner of Brooksburg Road and Route 296. In the mid-1900s, this building was joined by an addition to the house next to it, which provided a large store interior. Owned by Walter and Ellie Jacobs, it operated as the Hensonville Supermarket for many decades.

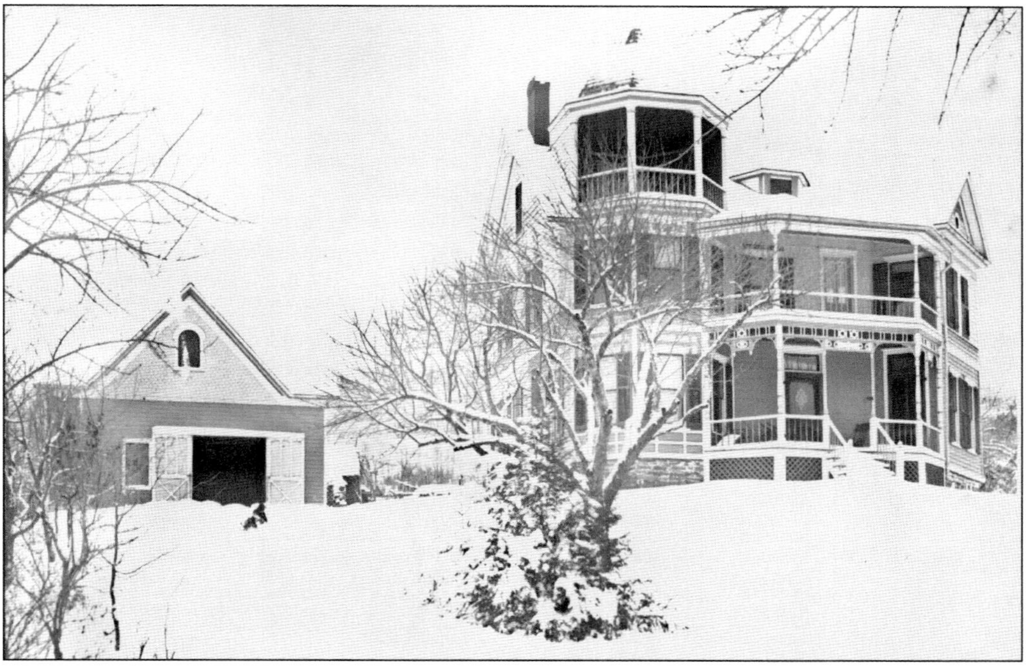

This 1900 photograph is the former residence of Dr. Ford in Hensonville, later owned by Walter and Ellie Jacobs, owners of the Hensonville Supermarket. It is currently the Catskill Lodge, a bed-and-breakfast. Many of the beautiful old homes have been brought back to life by people moving to the town with the resources and passion to preserve the unique architecture of the buildings in Windham.

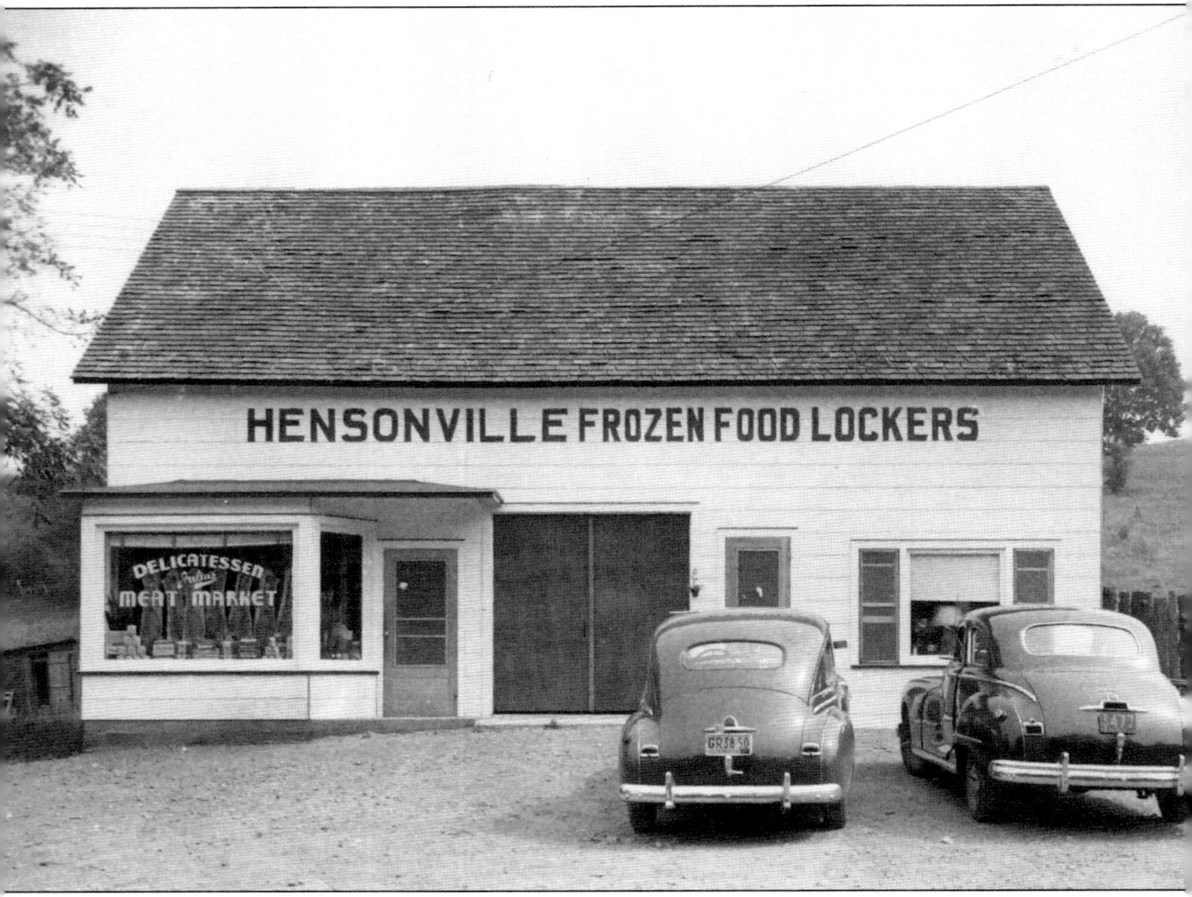

Julius and Lena Gooss came from Germany and purchased the barn belonging to Willis Dunham on Maplecrest Road. They renovated the side facing the road for the storefront of the Hensonville Frozen Food Lockers, seen here in 1952. Meat-cutting was Julius's specialty, and he would butcher and piece animals such as cows and pigs for local farmers as well as deer that were brought in by hunters. In the back of the store, Julius had freezer lockers of various sizes where people could rent and store their own meat that was cut and packaged at the store. Few people in the early days of refrigeration and freezers could afford their own appliance, so this was a convenient way to store meat and other products for the long term. The Goosses' son Ernest took over the business before handing it down to his son Ted and his wife, Janet. Their son Brett is operating the store in 2011 and is the fourth generation of the family to do so. (Courtesy of Gary and Carolyn Wank.)

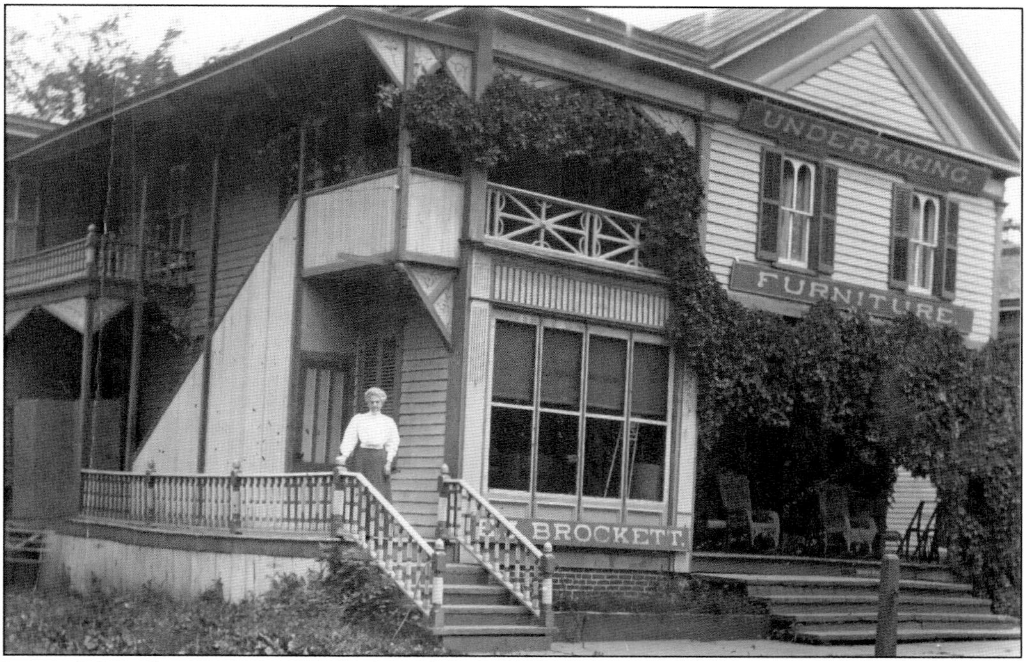

Located directly across Main Street from the Windham Civic Centre, this 100-plus-year-old building has been home to many enterprises. In addition to the undertaking and furniture business seen in this 1900 photograph, it has also housed the *Windham Journal*, established in 1857. It is now the Bistro Brie & Bordeaux restaurant.

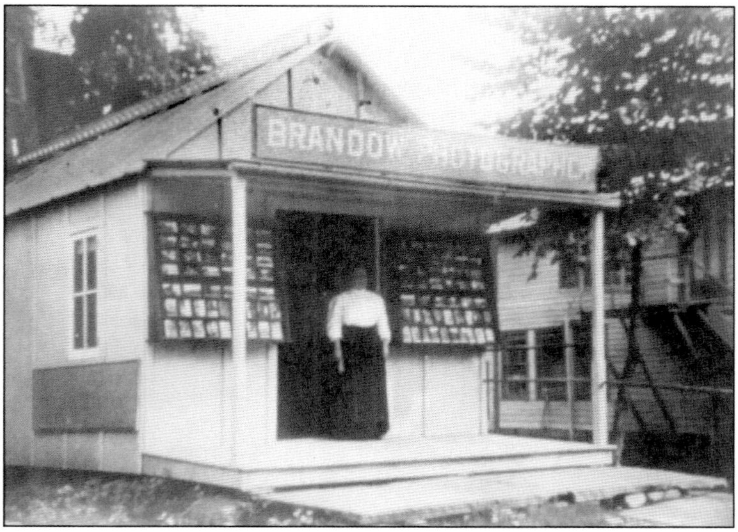

This 1895 picture is of the Brandow Photography shop located on the west side of Mad Brook in Windham. Fieldstones such as those used for the steps to the store were plentiful in the mountains and were cut and shipped by local quarries to New York City for its sidewalks. The widespread use of cement would later end these quarry businesses.

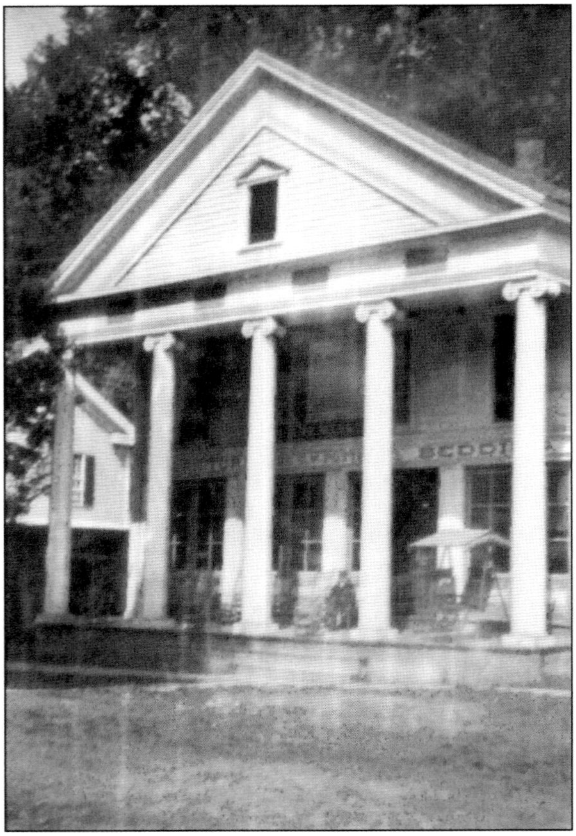

This is the Potter & Newell Furniture and Bedding store building as it looked in the 1890s. It once stood across Main Street in front of the present-day Windham School but is now gone. The house seen next to it is one of the oldest in town and still stands today. The west millrace ran behind these homes between the buildings and a steep hill.

Built in 1882 by A.E. West, the Glen House could accommodate 40 guests. It was set back east of Mill Street in a cozy hollow hugging Mad Brook, north of Windham village. This building is still standing today as a private residence. Because it was constructed to accommodate so many, it can be assumed that it was built solely for boarding summer guests. The photograph was taken around 1900.

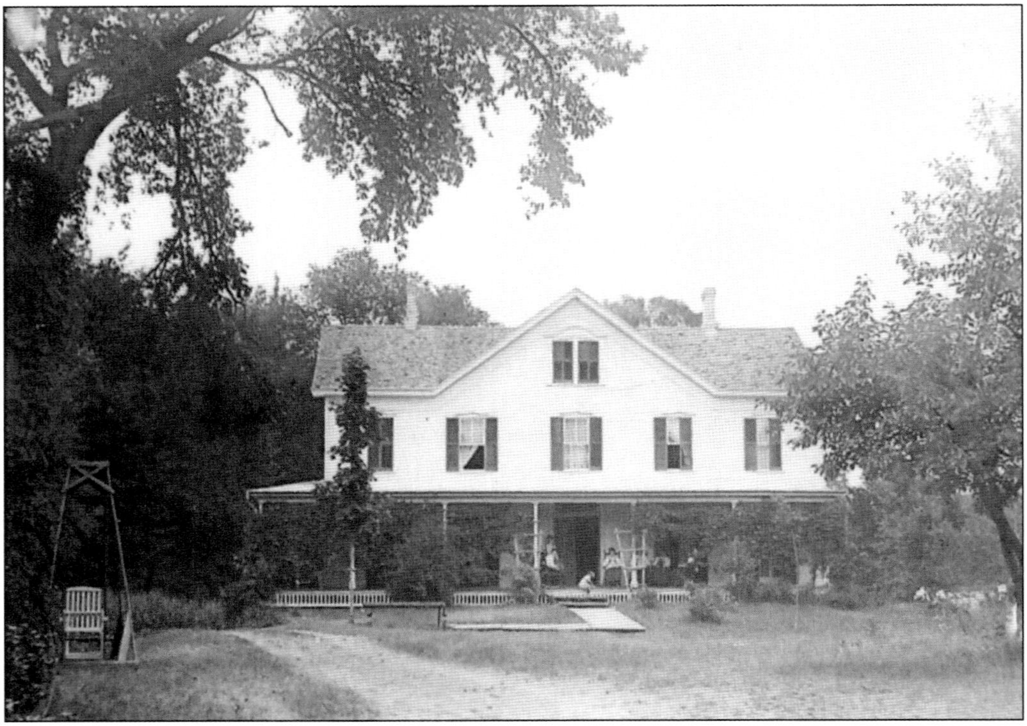

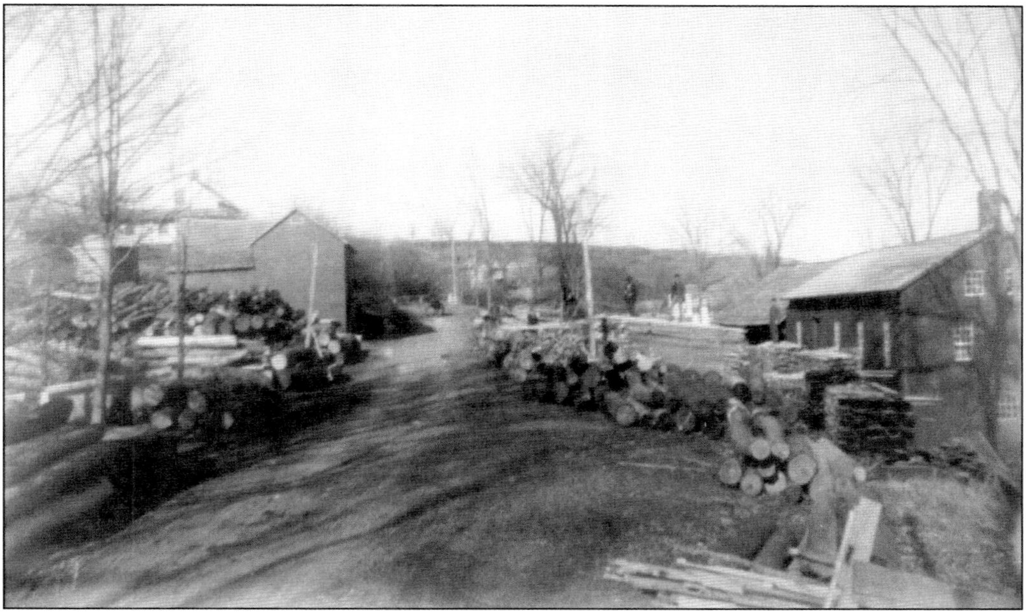

Seen here is Kelly's Saw Mill, as it stood in 1900, on Route 23 on the west end of Windham where the current Veterans of Foreign Wars (VFW) Hall is. Windham had countless numbers of streams that would drive waterwheels for making a variety of products to sell. Milled lumber was in high demand, as was mill grinding for food processing and driving various types of mechanisms for manufacturing. In the later 1800s, steam power spelled the demise of local manufacturing and waterpower. Previous to steam power, waterpower was the mechanical force used to drive the wheels of industry. With steam power, manufacturing facilities could be built closer to the markets in the cities and shipping centers. Consequently, manufacturing declined in Windham.

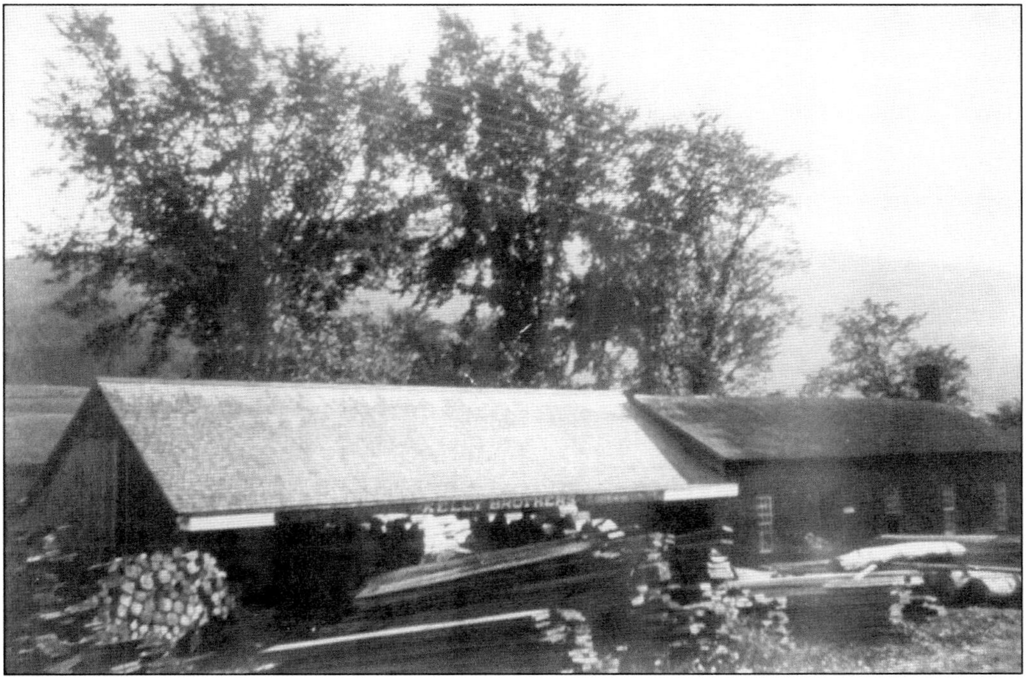

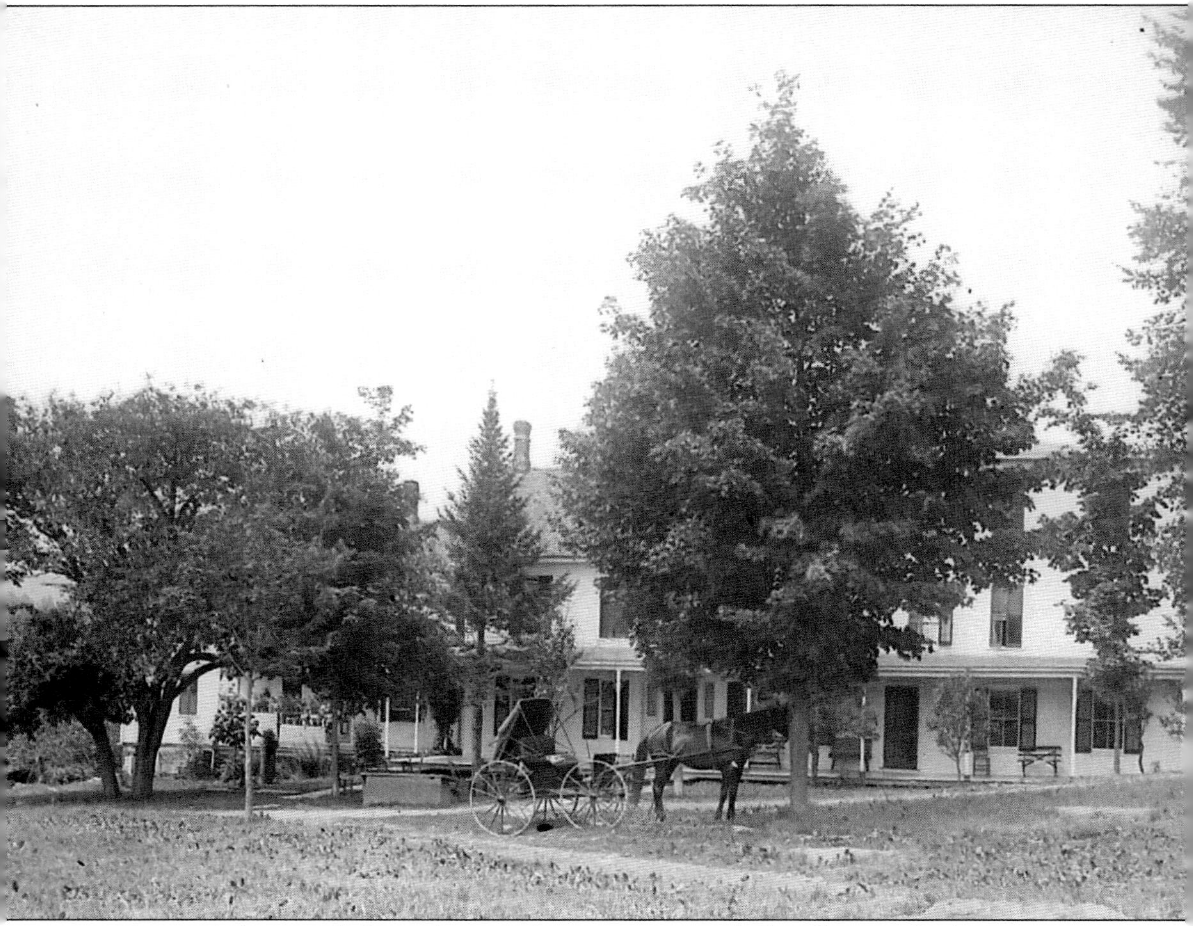

This 1905 photograph shows the Hidecker House on Mitchell Hollow Road, which, many years later, would become the Wagon Wheel Resort, operated by the Anderson family. So many homes in Windham were built initially as simple farmhouses or residential homes in town. When the summer resort business was in full swing by 1900, these buildings were enlarged to truly magnificent proportions to accommodate more paying guests. The trees partially obscure it, but three different sections are visible. No doubt, each was added as the years went by, and when done, they provided the owners with a comfortable income from summer tourists. Many residents in Windham constructed even bigger complexes of various buildings and facilities that accommodated hundreds of guests. Some are still operating today as hotels since the term "boardinghouse" has passed from the local lexicon.

Another farmhouse that expanded to accommodate more summer guests was the Bronson House, seen here in 1900 at North Settlement. The smaller, left part of the house was probably the original farmhouse, and the larger, right section was added to take in summer boarders. Farmers would simply seal off the larger part of a home during the winter when it was unused.

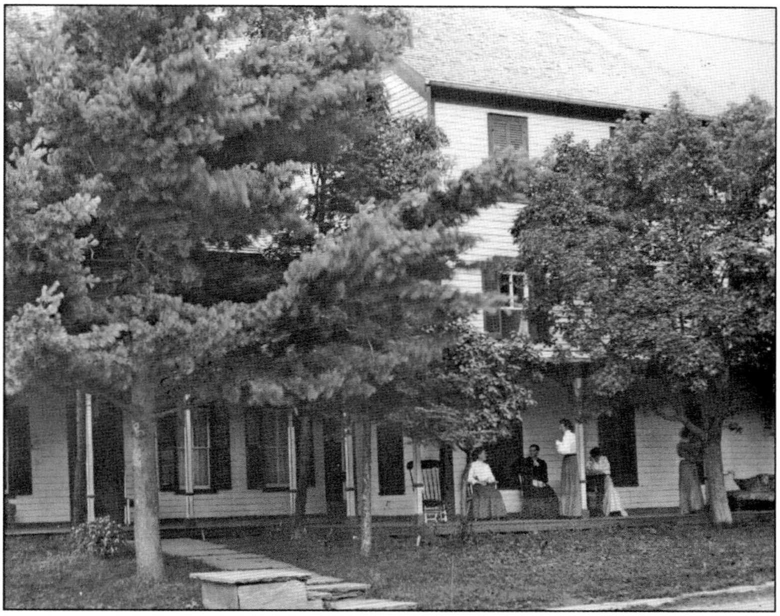

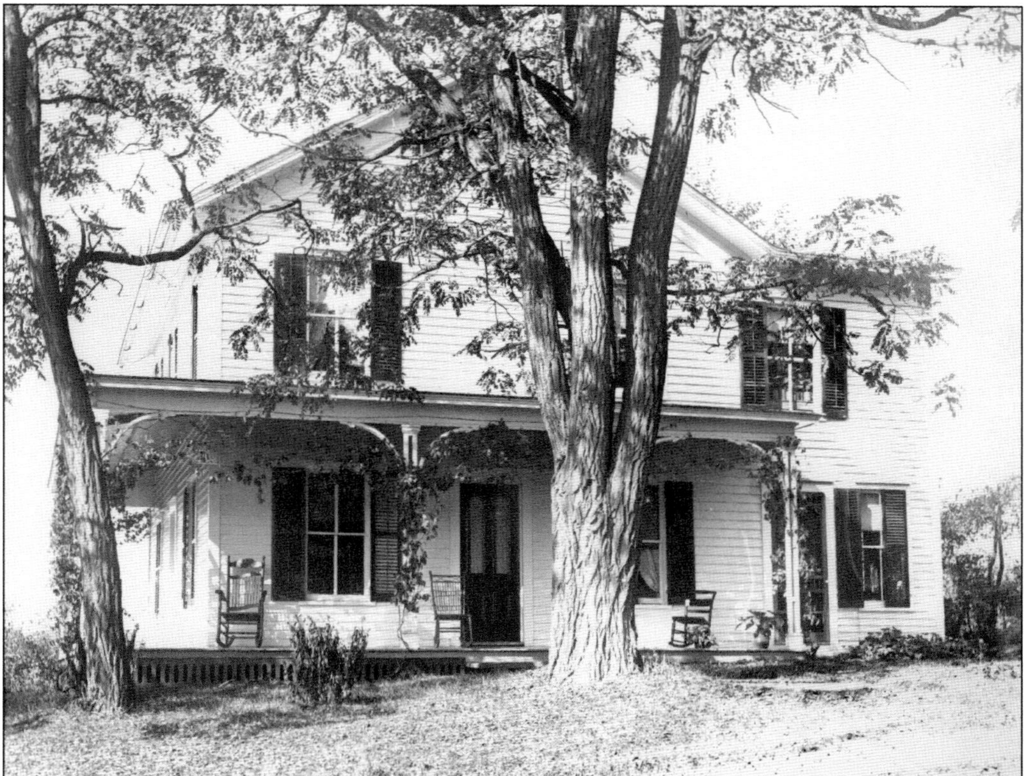

This is Cyrus Tibball's house at Route 23 and Mitchell Hollow Road in 1900. Behind this house was a hill with a small shack used for spotting possible Russian aircraft. After 1945, the Cold War with the Soviet Union created a fear that Soviet aircraft would penetrate American borders. Civilian spotters like Margaret Munson compared airplanes overhead to silhouette charts of Russian aircraft and were ready to sound an alarm if necessary.

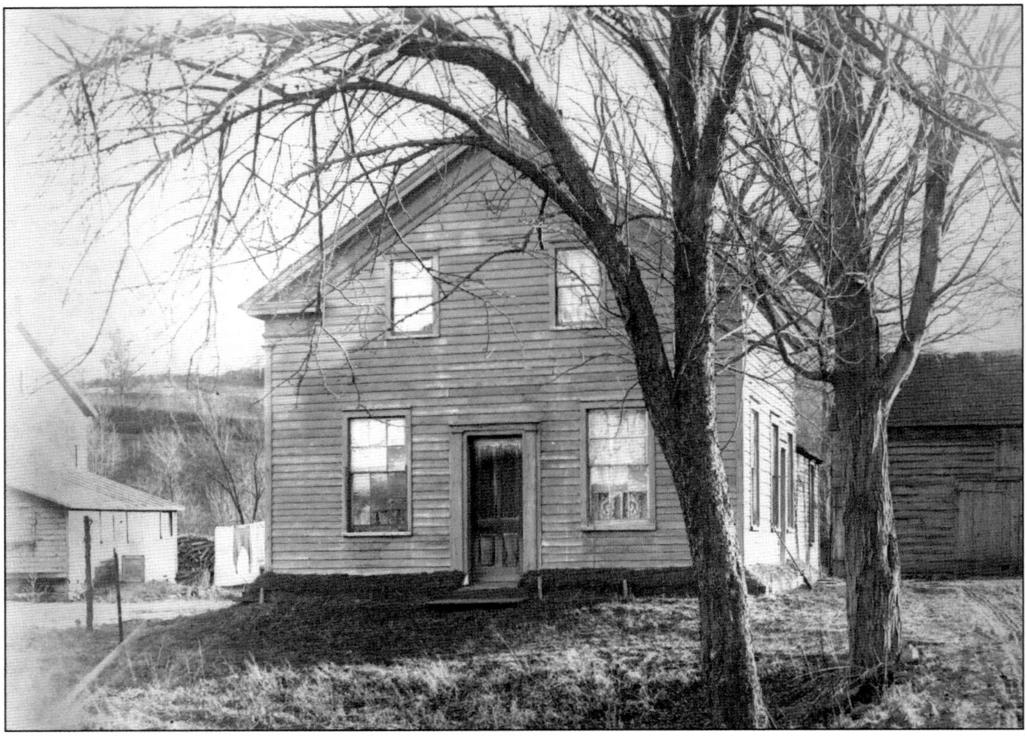

In this 1900 photograph is the former John Osmon house at the Creamery Pond on the east end of Windham village. The Windham Creamery building can be seen to the left. It was a very busy place, as the numerous farmers in the area would bring their milk here to sell. The creamery closed in 1936.

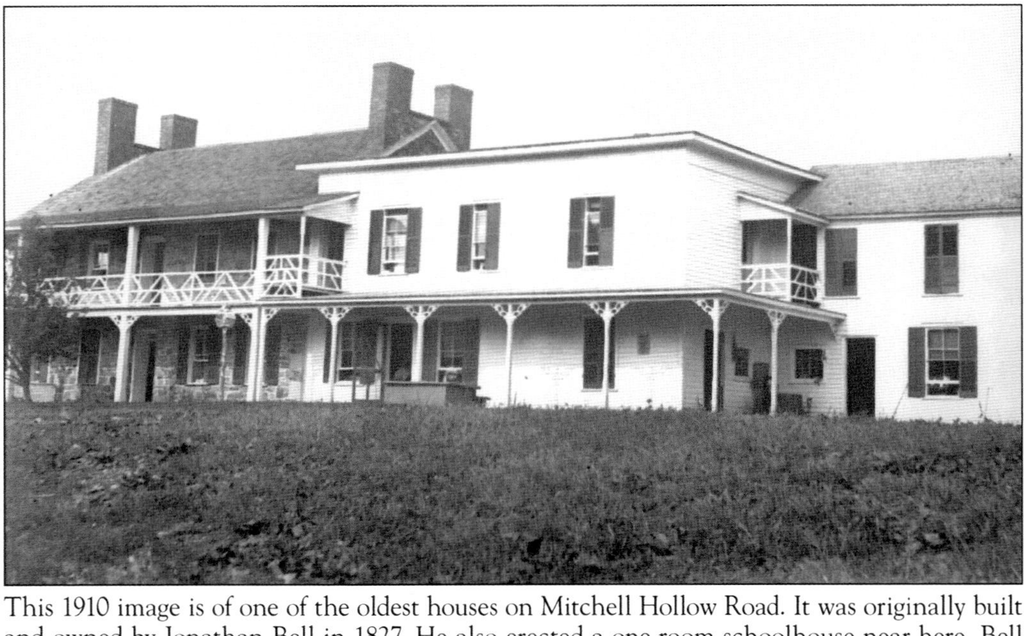

This 1910 image is of one of the oldest houses on Mitchell Hollow Road. It was originally built and owned by Jonathan Bell in 1827. He also erected a one-room schoolhouse near here. Bell and his wife came from England in 1810. Behind this house is one of the flood catch basins that were constructed in the 1960s.

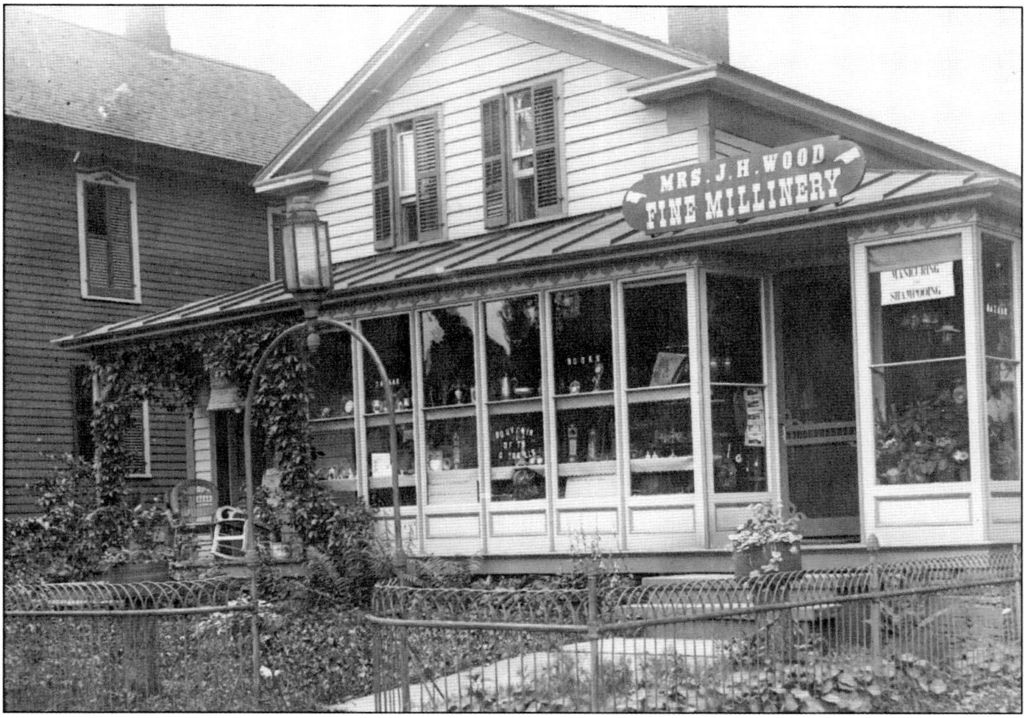

Mrs. J.H. Wood Fine Millinery shop did not just sell women's hats but provided other services as well. As the signs in the windows advertise, she offered shampooing and manicuring alongside the gift shop. Shops in Windham that catered to the summer vacationers were common, selling a variety of items such as books, postcards, and souvenirs. Today, this is a real estate office.

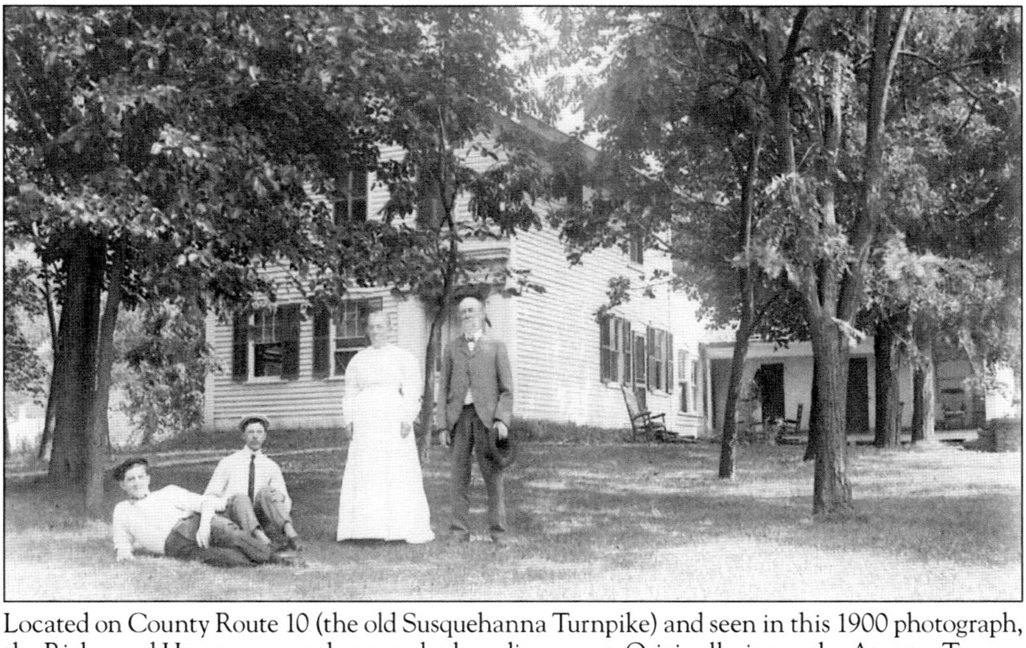

Located on County Route 10 (the old Susquehanna Turnpike) and seen in this 1900 photograph, the Richmond House was another popular boarding resort. Originally, it was the Atwater Tavern, a drovers' tavern on the turnpike. People in the photograph are identified only as "Dr. Dodge and group," who were most likely the boarders staying at the house.

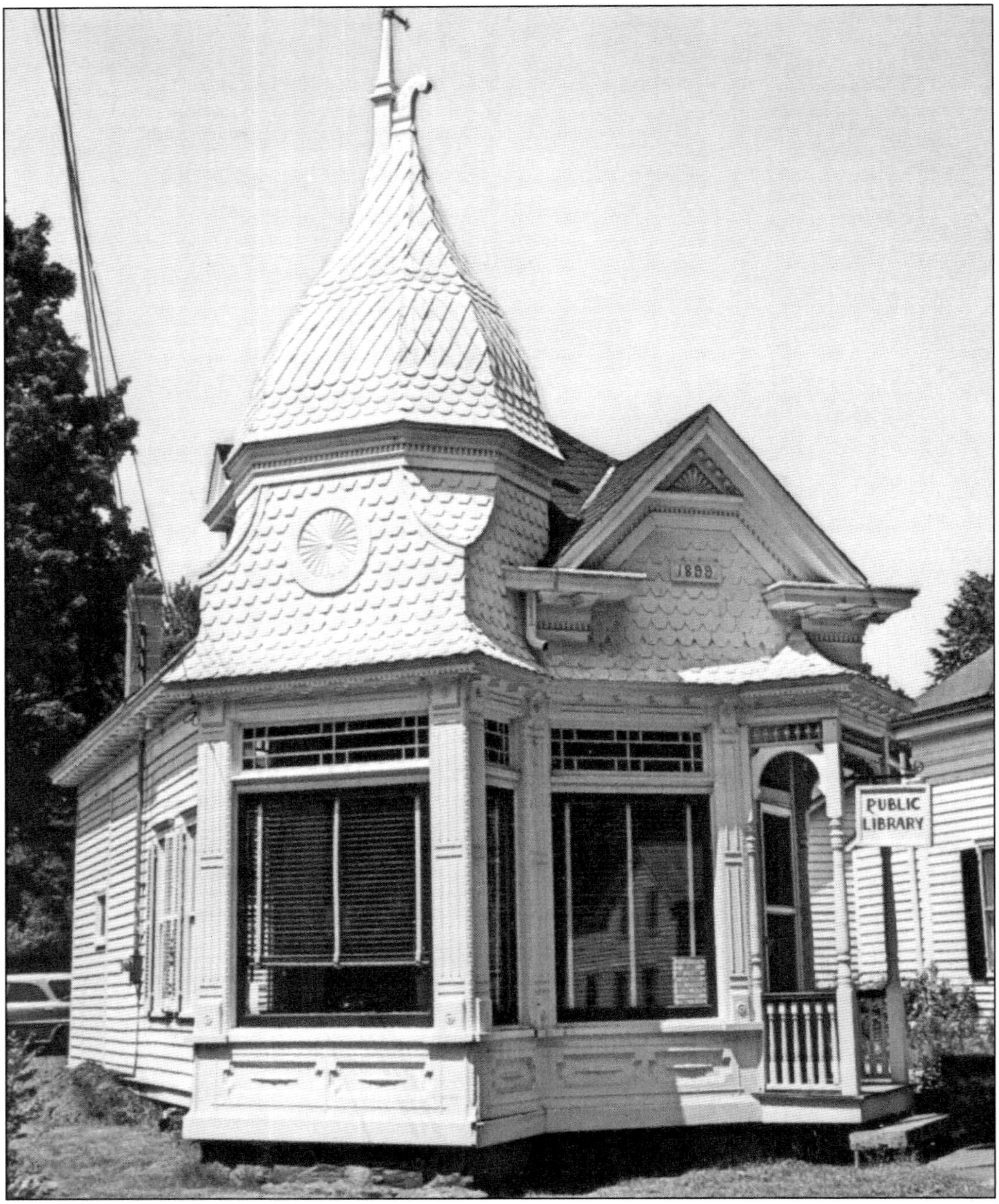

This unique building on Main Street Windham was originally a jewelry store constructed in 1899 by Prentice Mack. The intriguing Victorian architecture has captured many eyes of those visiting Windham. One was the famous Harry Devlin, a nationally renowned illustrator who worked for large magazines and newspapers in the mid-1900s. He created a beautiful illustration of this building, which is now famous as a coveted poster. Windham's economy was so prosperous in the early 1900s, the village had two jewelry stores, which seems incredible for a town with a population of only 1,500. When the summer tourists arrived, filling the innumerable boardinghouses in the town, the resident total easily tripled. At first, Windham was off the beaten path of tourism because it had no railroad access while other towns in the southern part of the mountains did. Consequently, it was not until the early part of the 1900s that it reaped the full benefits of the summer trade when the quality of highways and automobiles improved.

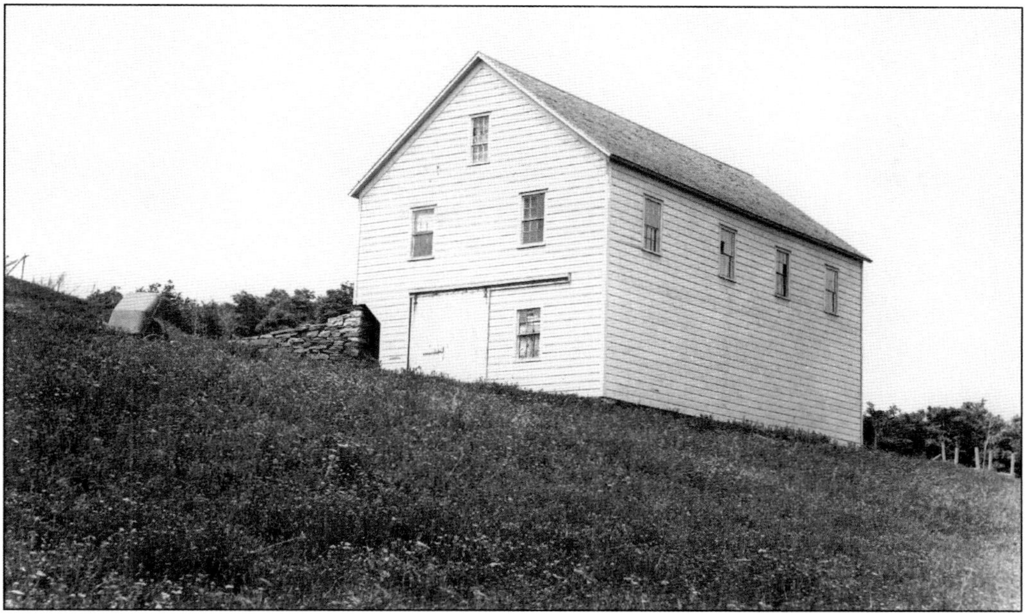

In the late-19th century, the Doolittle family built this barn on Mount Pisgah. Later, a large observatory tower was added to the end of the barn. From this panoramic view, one can see Albany 40 miles to the north, the Hudson Valley directly east and more than 3,000 feet below, the southern Catskill summits to the south, and the Delaware River Valley to the west.

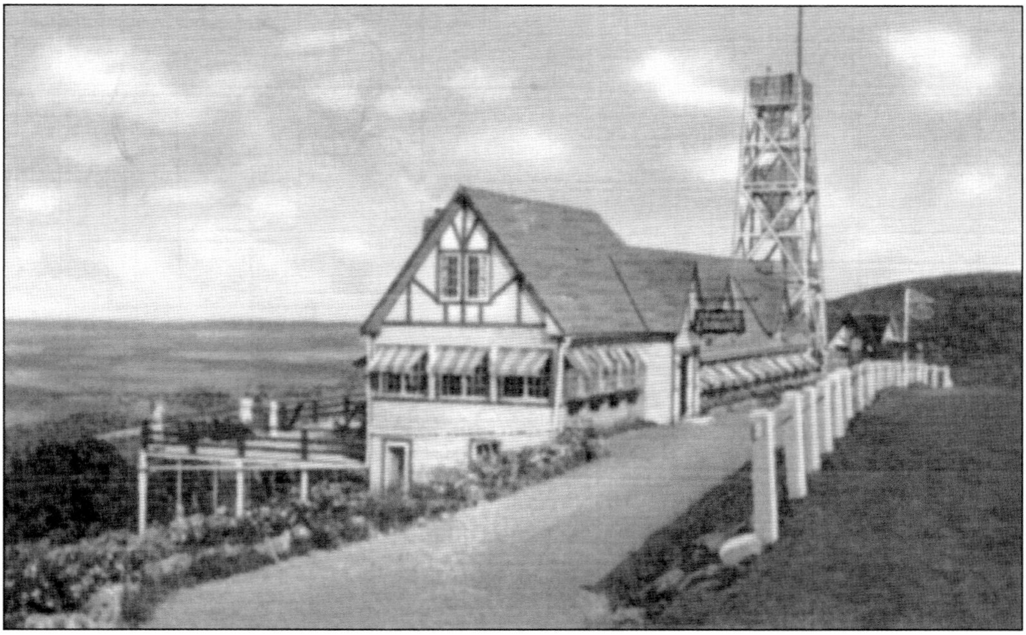

Point Lookout restaurant and hotel is situated on Route 23 in East Windham as the road reaches its high point of about 2,000 feet above the Hudson River Valley. Built in the early 1900s, it offered a five-state view from the tower. Looking east, visitors could see New York, Massachusetts, Connecticut, Vermont, and New Hampshire. This original structure burned to the ground in the early 1960s but was quickly rebuilt.

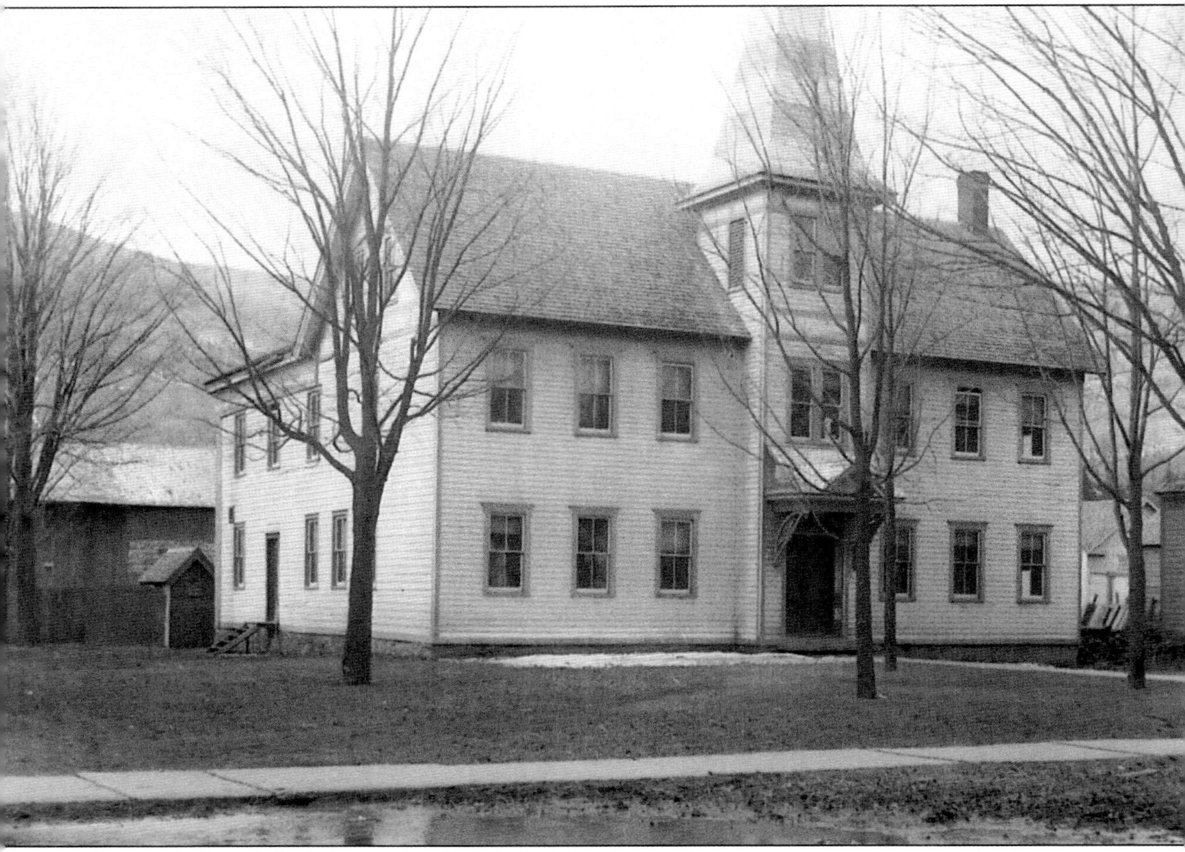

Originally on this site was the Windham Union Free School. In 1914, the Masons acquired the old school building and used it for their temple. After burning down in 1957, this building was immediately constructed and has been the Masonic Temple since. The Masons have had a lodge in Windham since they were first organized and held their initial meeting at the old Bump Tavern in 1804.

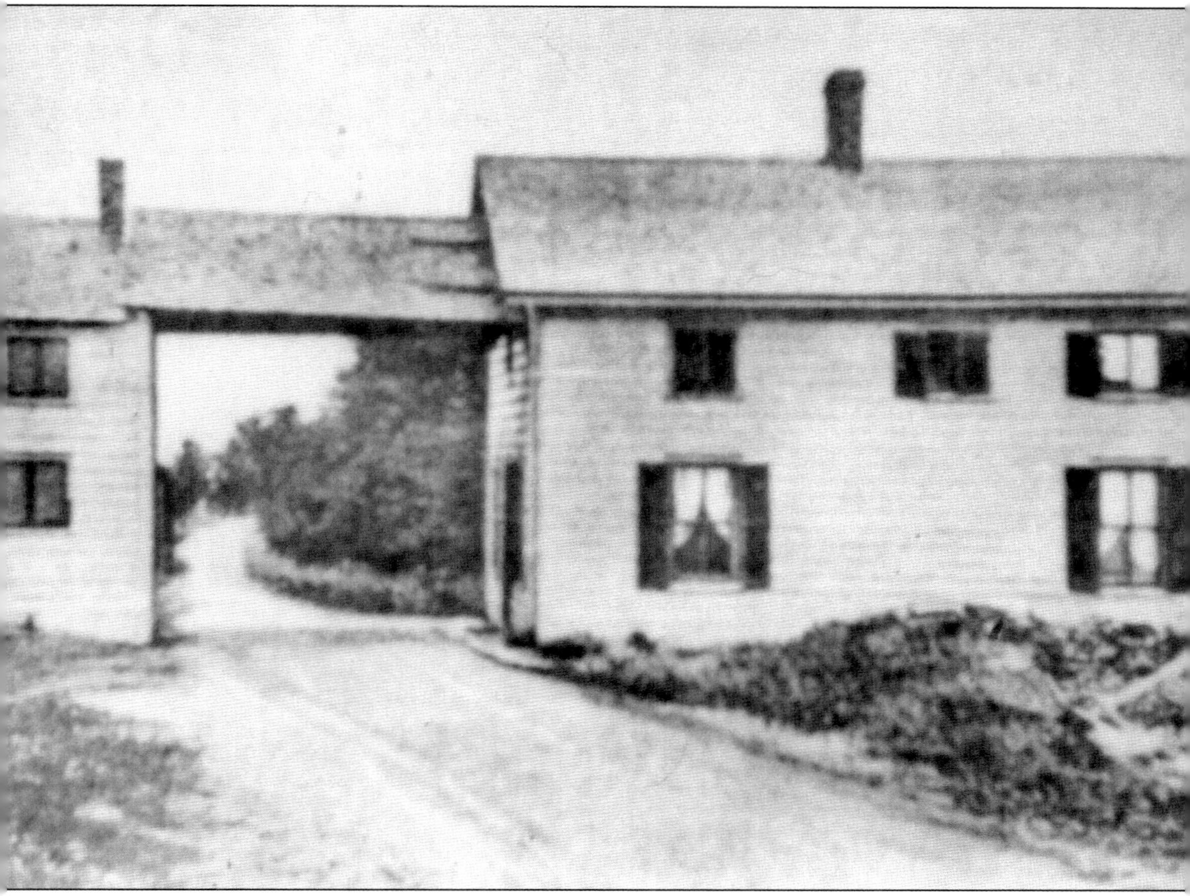

This 1890s tollgate, located between Windham and East Windham, was one of the last to be used. Money collected at these gates was used for maintenance of the road. After the Erie Canal opened, commercial traffic on the Windham roads all but ceased. Farmers and merchants west of Windham took their products north to the canal instead. Rates were reduced, and tollgates were removed, but the traffic never returned.

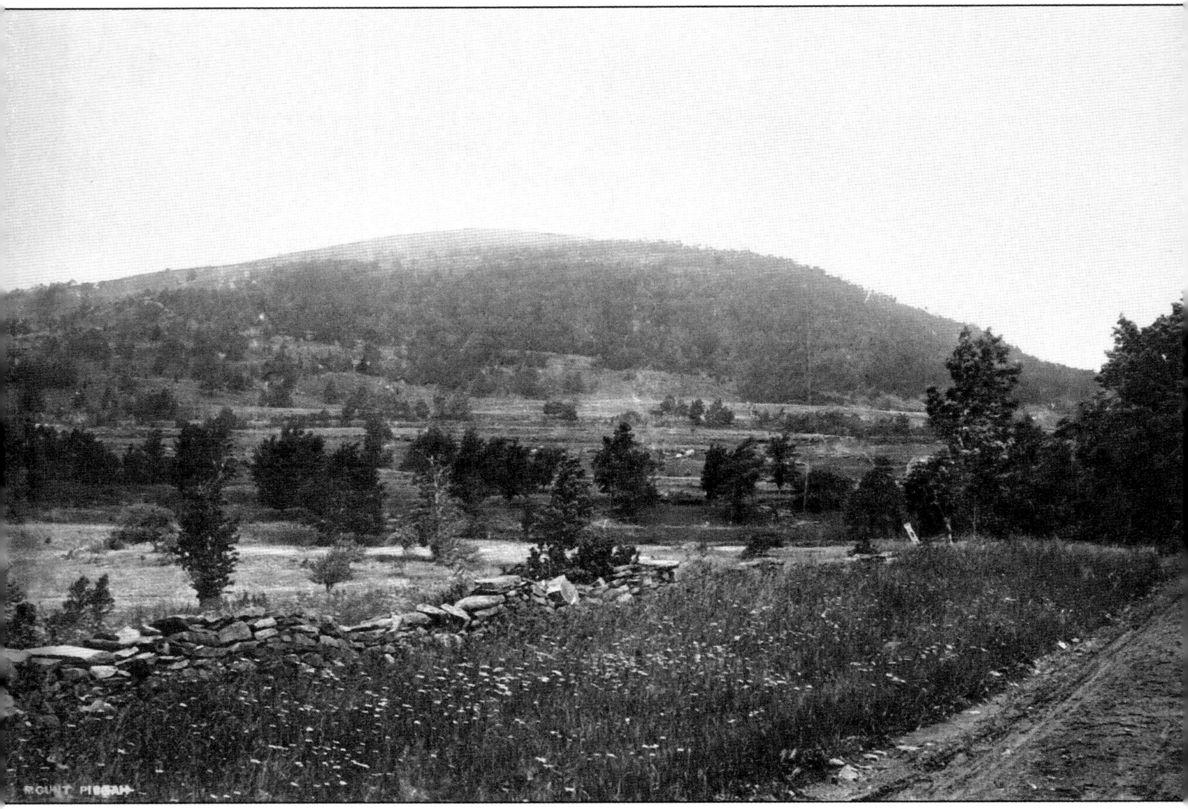

This c. 1900 view of Mount Pisgah was taken from Mitchell Hollow Road. Running across the center of the picture is the Susquehanna Turnpike, today's Greene County Route 10. The image is facing north toward the summit of the mountain, where the Doolittle barn can be seen. Today, the mountain is covered in pine trees planted by the Civilian Conservation Corps during the Great Depression.

Five

People, Places, and Events

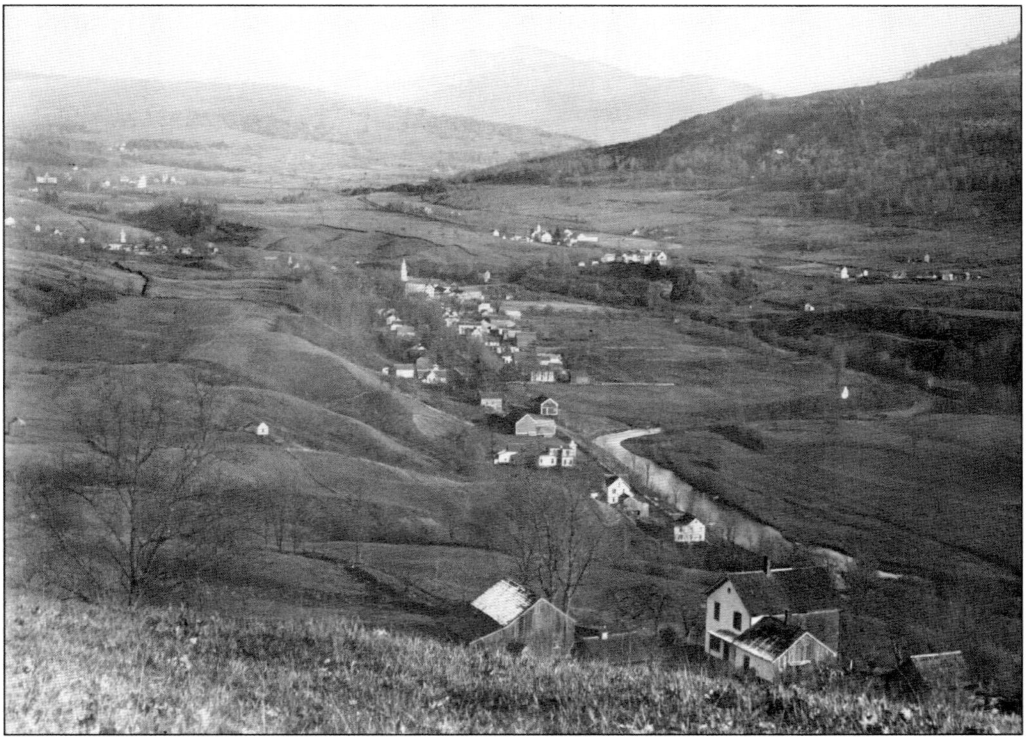

Looking east, Windham village can be seen tucked into the mountain valley in 1910. Batavia Kill flows parallel to the village and then makes two abrupt turns as it moves west toward Schoharie Creek. At the first bend in Batavia Kill, seen on the far right of the image was a favorite swimming spot known as the Corner Hole.

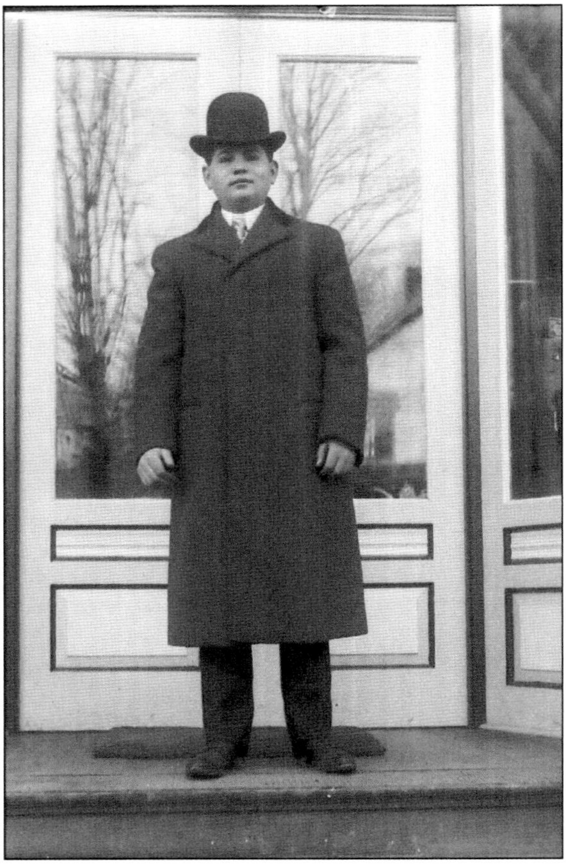

Harry Miller was one of the brothers who opened and operated Miller Brothers clothing store. Here, he stands in the doorway of his new building on Main Street in 1906. He was a generous, well-respected man in the community who never hesitated to help when needed. Harry also owned a hotel in East Windham and was instrumental in starting the Windham Country Club golf course in 1927.

Two summer guests staying at a local boardinghouse are enjoying a stroll and rest on a bench on Church Street around 1900. With such a concentration of boardinghouses around the village of Windham, the highways and country lanes were teeming with folks meandering about, enjoying the fresh air and enchanting mountains, especially after meals were served.

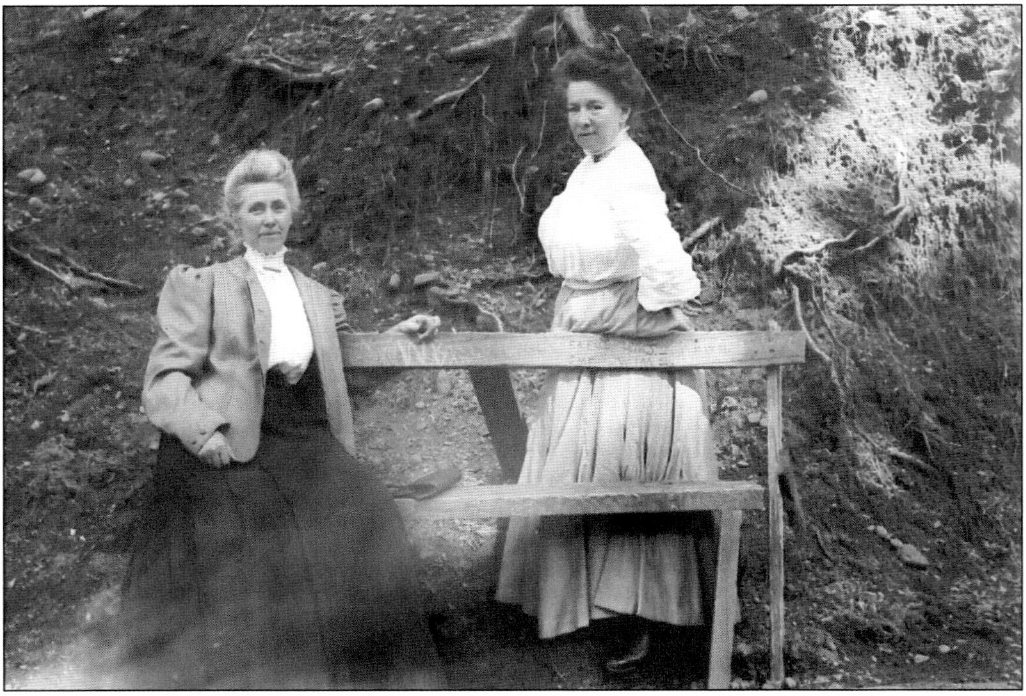

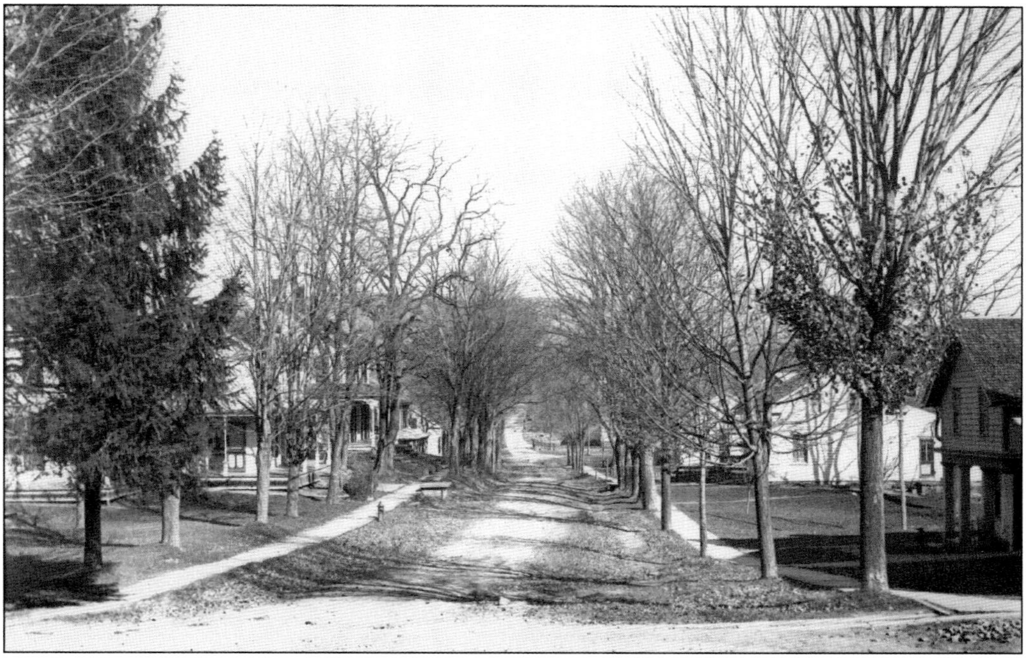

This is the intersection in Hensonville facing north on Brooksburg Road in 1902. Hensonville was originally called Bailey's Corners, but when John Henson became the postmaster, he renamed the village. Henson donated the cemetery east of here, and the first to be buried there was an Indian woman named Proctor. A woman named O'Brien, who drowned while trying to cross the flooded Batavia Kill, was buried there next.

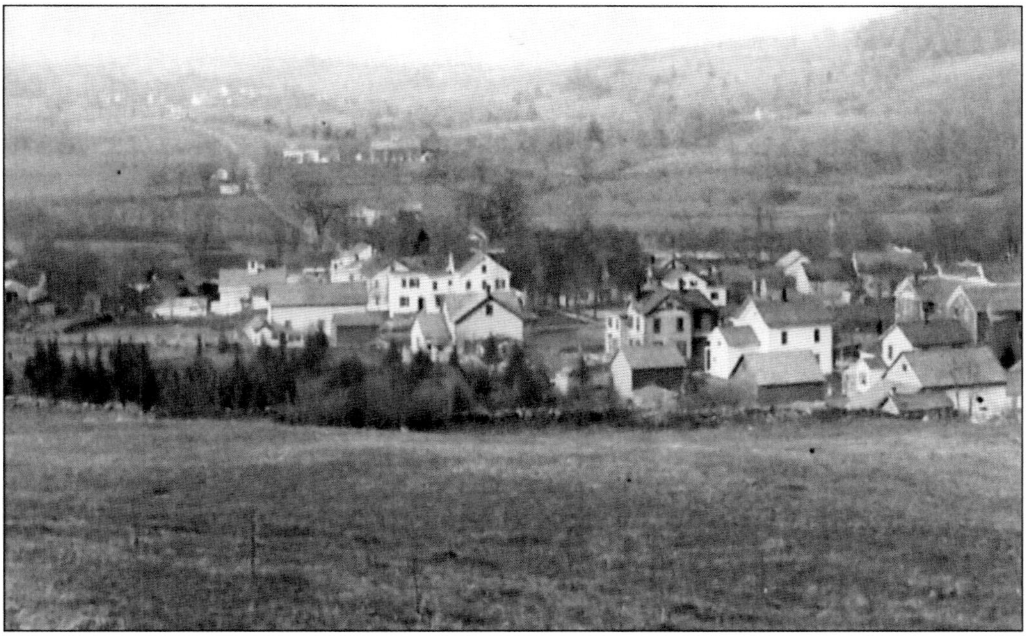

The view in this 1905 picture of Hensonville is looking north. Chase Flats lies beyond the hamlet with Elm Ridge on the right. Many Catskill Mountain towns in the mid-20th century became the summer destination for specific ethnic groups. Hensonville was no different, and the Greek American community became the primary summer visitors to the hamlet.

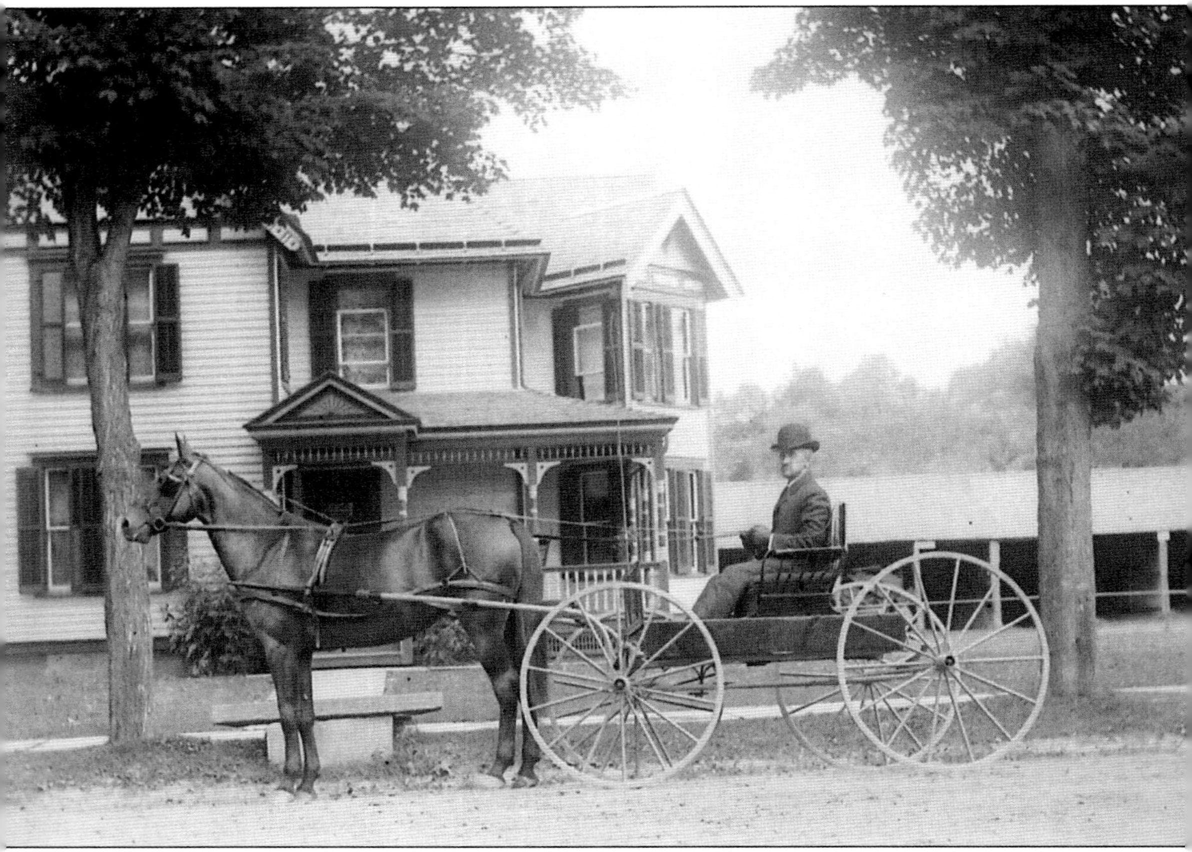

This is a beautiful example of a horse and carriage with Art Bresac at the reins in front of the Windham Methodist Church parsonage in 1904. The Windham United Methodist Church is to the right beyond the frame of the picture. Note the sheds in the background. These were a common feature at all the churches of the day. People who drove their carriages to the service on Sunday could park under the roof of the shed for protection from the weather. Note the stone carriage steps beside the horse. These steps can be seen in all the old pictures of the time. They were placed about every 200 feet on each side of Main Street and in front of homes on the back roads. Their use was so people could easily step off the carriage and onto the raised stone platform, thereby avoiding a very large step to the ground from the carriage.

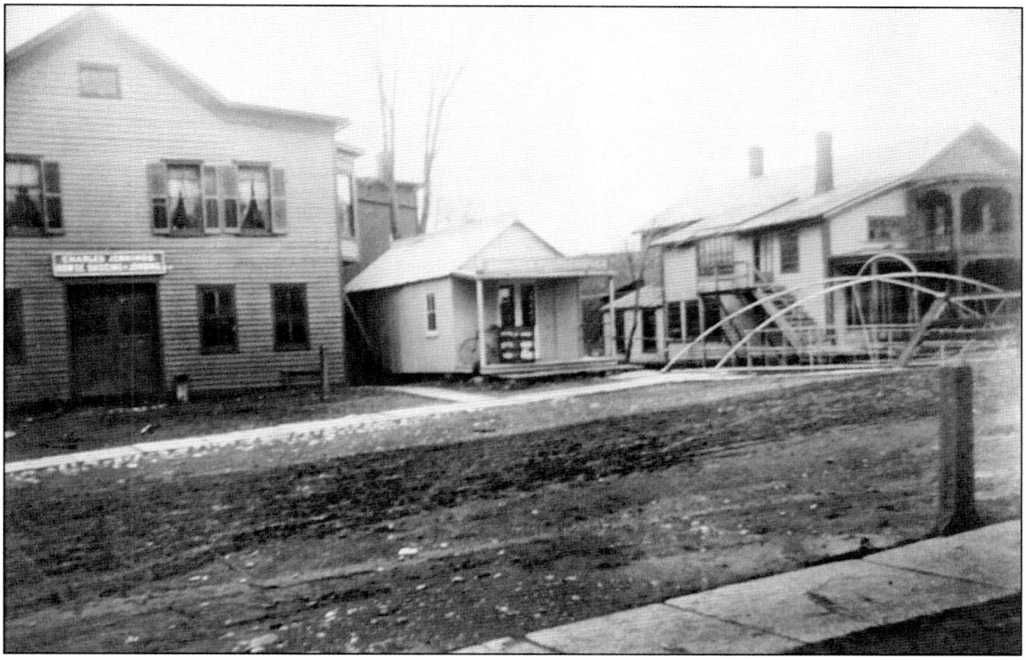

In this c. 1895 image are the Brandow Photography shop and Charles Jenning's horseshoe shop. Today, there is a larger building here on Main Street housing Roshkowska Galleries and Micha's Floor Covering. On the right today is Neapolis Pizzeria Grill. Note the vertical hitching posts by the sidewalk and in front of the building.

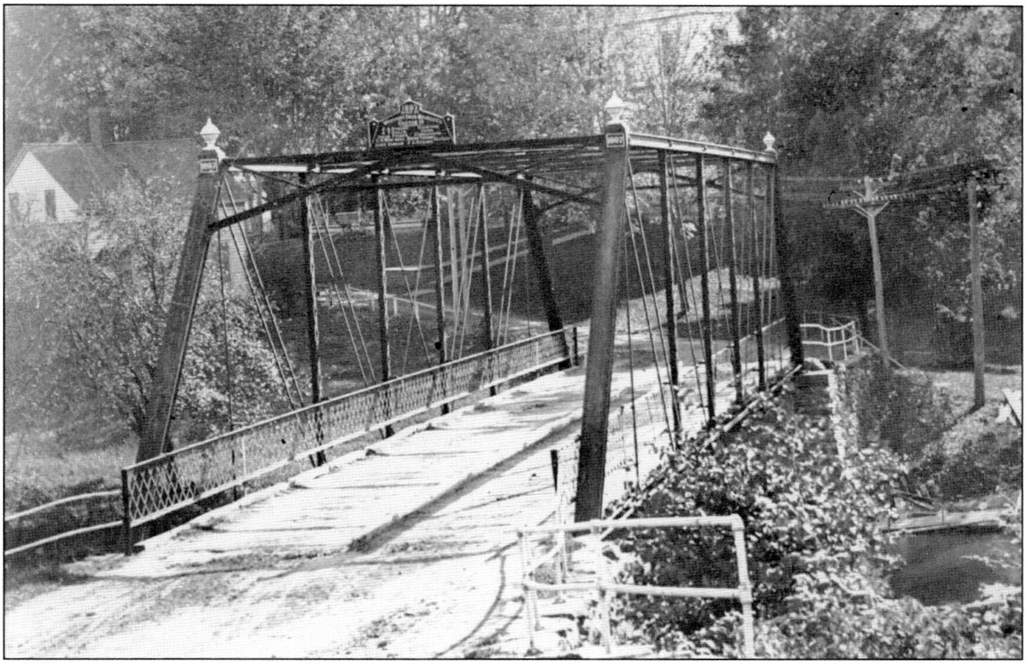

This is the old Brook Lynne Bridge, built in 1897, which crossed Batavia Kill at the intersection of Routes 296 and 23. This section of the stream was the location for several mills in the 1800s. Just 300 feet west of here is Reynolds' Creek, which had a schoolhouse and a mill driven by an overshot waterwheel affectionately called "Old Fiddle" because of the sound it made.

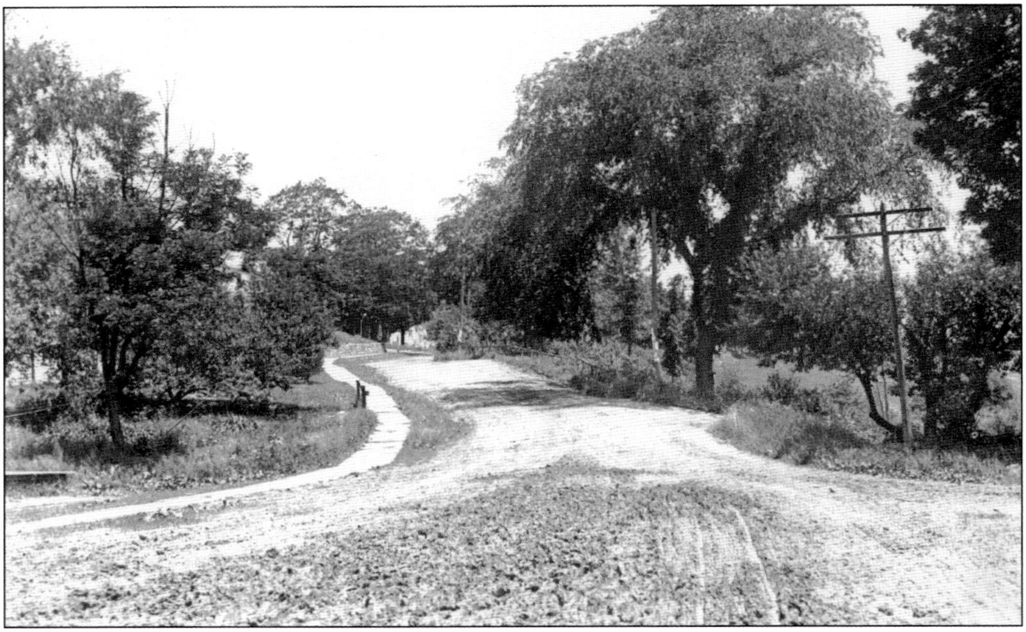

This 1905 view looks east on Main Street Windham from the front of the Windham Methodist Church. To the left side of the sidewalk is a small wooden guide rail that marks where the old millrace ran under the road and exited on the other side into the Creamery Pond, to the right of the image. This helped to divert some floodwaters coming down the hill but has since been covered over.

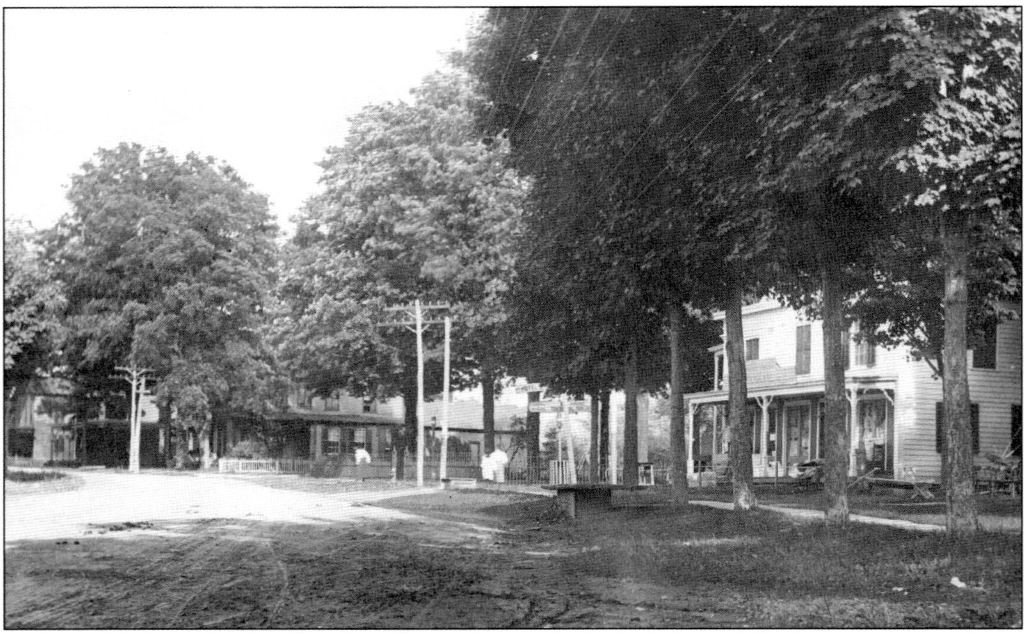

This c. 1904 view faces east from the corner of Church and Main Streets in Windham. The black wrought-iron fence in front of the Presbyterian church, now the Windham Civic Centre and Library, can be seen next to the pedestrians. The building on the right is Miller Brothers Clothiers, now a real estate office. The house at center is Woodbine Cottage, which is now Windham Country Store.

To the right is a letter sent by John Smith in the first airmail service from Windham in May 1938. John was the president of the National Bank of Windham. Below, John Garraghan stands beside his airplane in May 1938 at the Windham Airport on South Street, set to take off for the first Unites States Airmail Postal Service from Windham. Many felt this airmail connection was a giant step forward in the town's ability to prosper and grow. Before telephones, mail service was vitally important to the residents. Postcards were often used for communication between neighbors who lived far apart. (Right, courtesy of John and Carole Smith and Windham Historical Society; below, courtesy of Christopher Garraghan.)

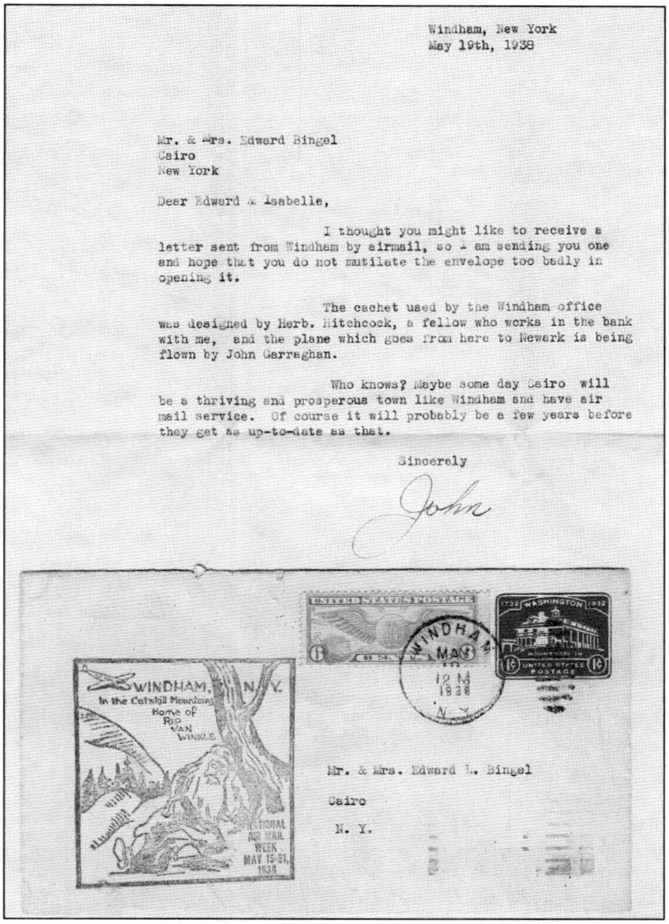

Windham, New York
May 19th, 1938

Mr. & Mrs. Edward Bingel
Cairo
New York

Dear Edward & Isabelle,

I thought you might like to receive a letter sent from Windham by airmail, so I am sending you one and hope that you do not mutilate the envelope too badly in opening it.

The cachet used by the Windham office was designed by Herb. Hitchcock, a fellow who works in the bank with me, and the plane which goes from here to Newark is being flown by John Garraghan.

Who knows? Maybe some day Cairo will be a thriving and prosperous town like Windham and have air mail service. Of course it will probably be a few years before they get as up-to-date as that.

Sincerely

John

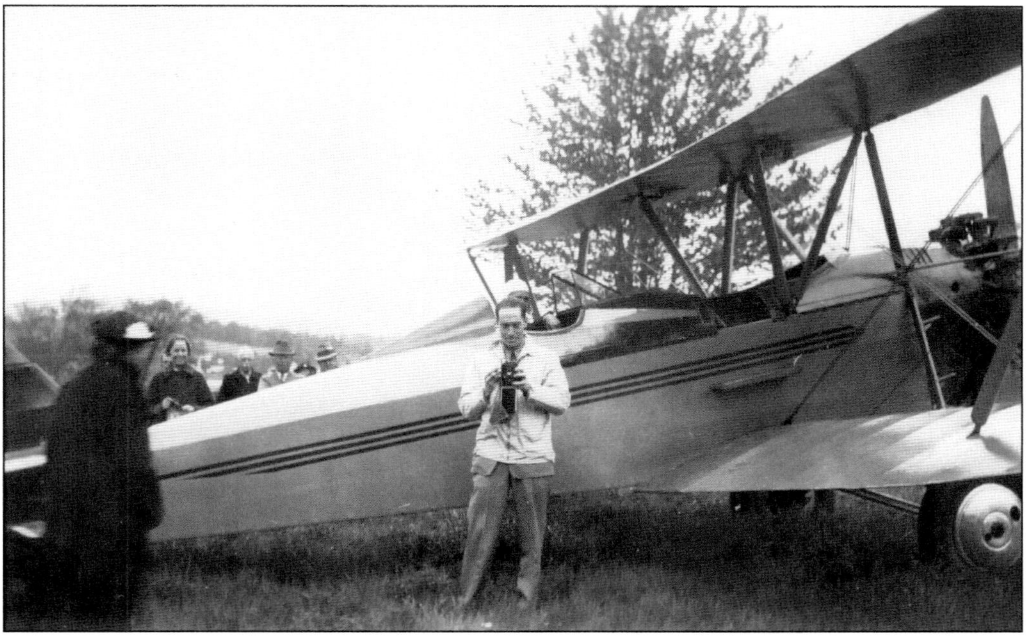

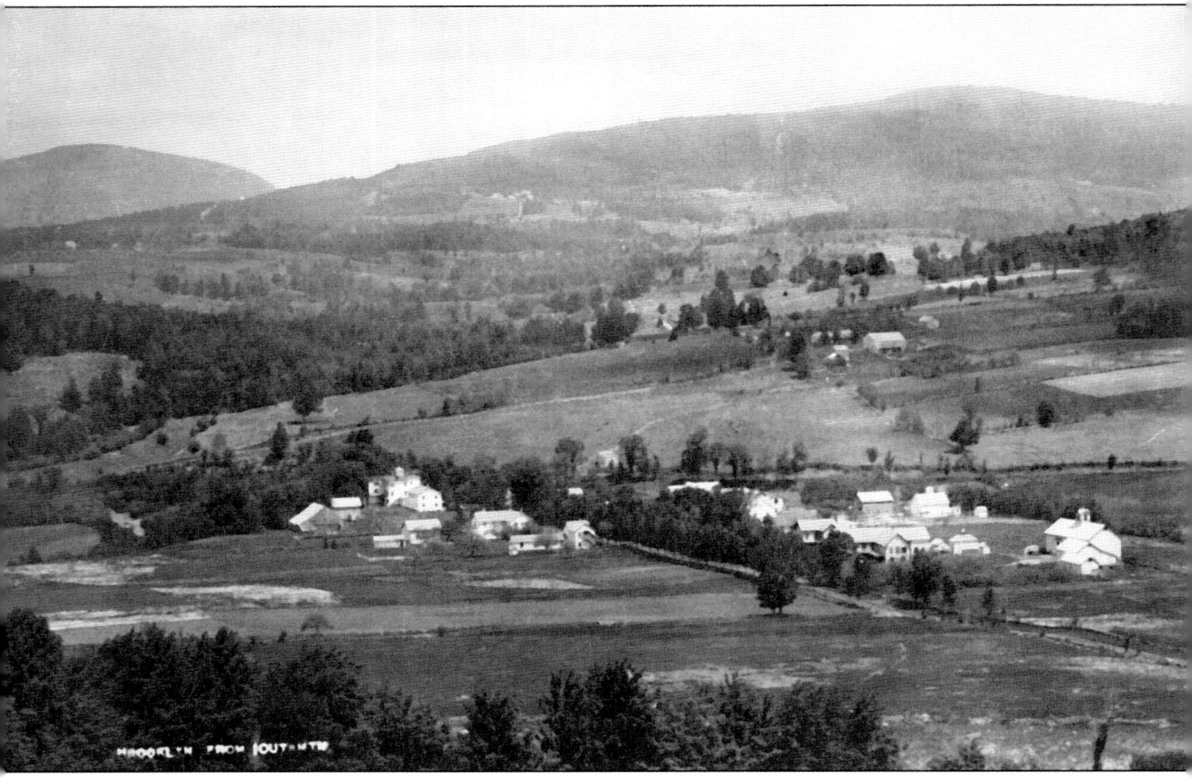

This view is looking north from Cave Mountain toward Brook Lynne. It can get confusing when reading historical records as to what this area was called. Several names were used over many years, referring to it as Brook Lynne, Brooklyn, Brooksburg, or Brooklyn Bridge. To add to the confusion, Brooksburg Road is three miles away in Hensonville, which did not help in trying to set a location in one's mind. The fields in the left foreground would later become the Windham Country Club's golf course. The large building left of center is Soper's hotel, which is now part of the Thompson House. To the right are the buildings of the Osborn House, and hidden among the trees is the original Thompson House. Mount Pisgah is in the left background, with Mount Hayden to the right. The empty land on the far right by the barn now has a strip mall with several small businesses, including Legacy Bank, Windham Pharmacy, and a Mobil station. The diagonal road is today's Route 296 going to Hensonville, and South Street is seen along the bottom of the picture.

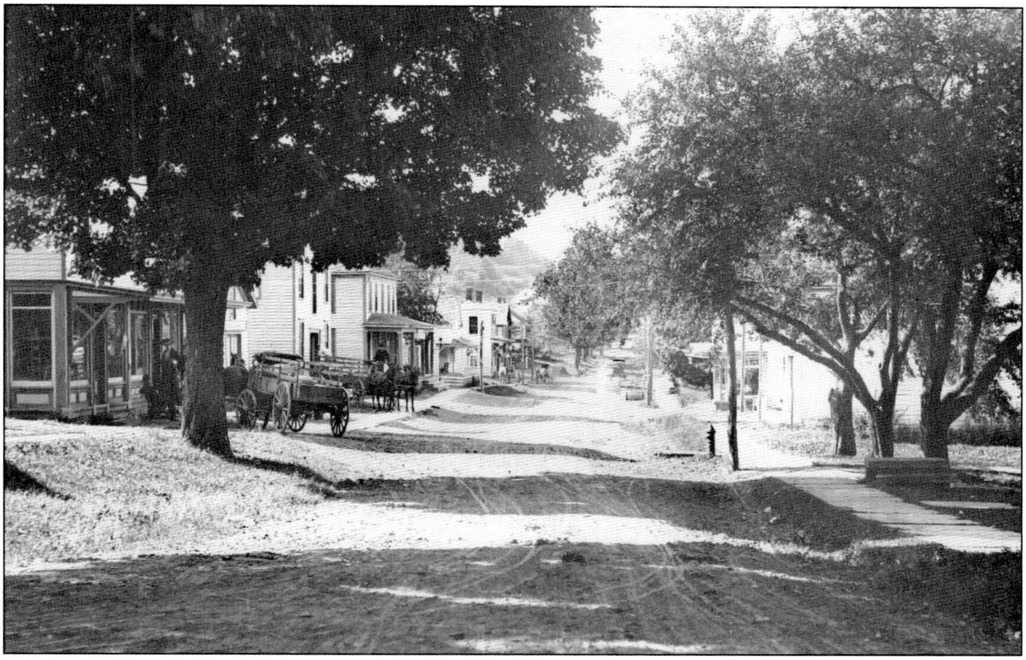

This c. 1900 picture of the bucolic hamlet of Hensonville looks west from the intersection of Route 296 and the Maplecrest Road. On the left is Winchell Brothers Choice Meats & Provisions store, the Hensonville Fire Company building, and Bloodgood's store, which also had the first telegraph office in Hensonville.

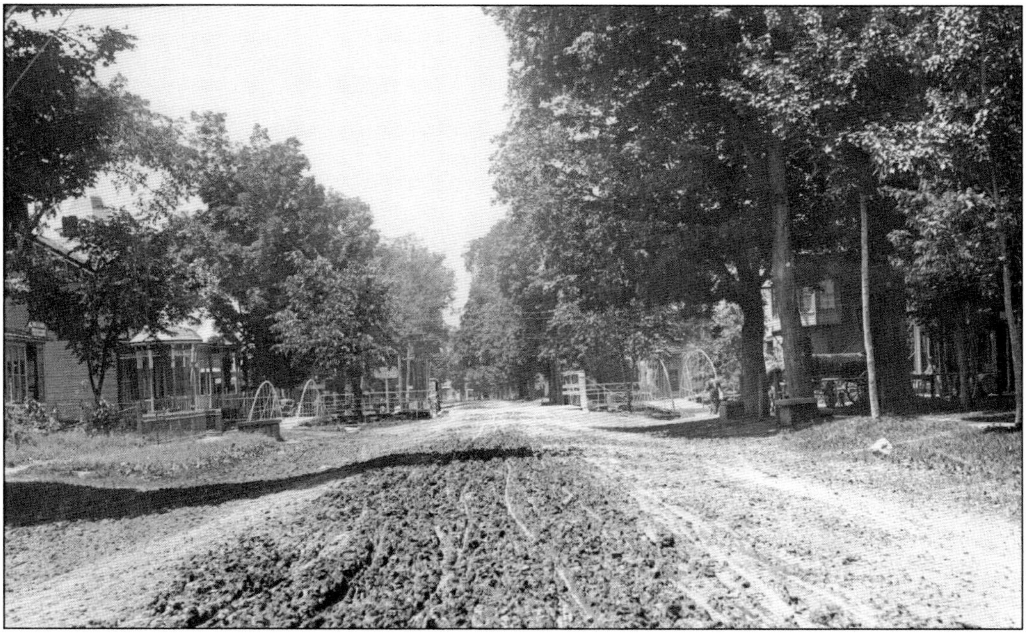

This 1905 view from the east side of Mad Brook Bridge looks down Main Street toward the west. The telegraph first came to Windham in 1875, followed by electricity around 1904. The Schoharie Kill and Stony Clove Telegraph Company ran its lines to Windham from Hunter. The Catskill, Cairo and Windham Telegraph Company came up the mountain at East Windham. Both lines were purchased by Western Union Telegraph Company in 1881.

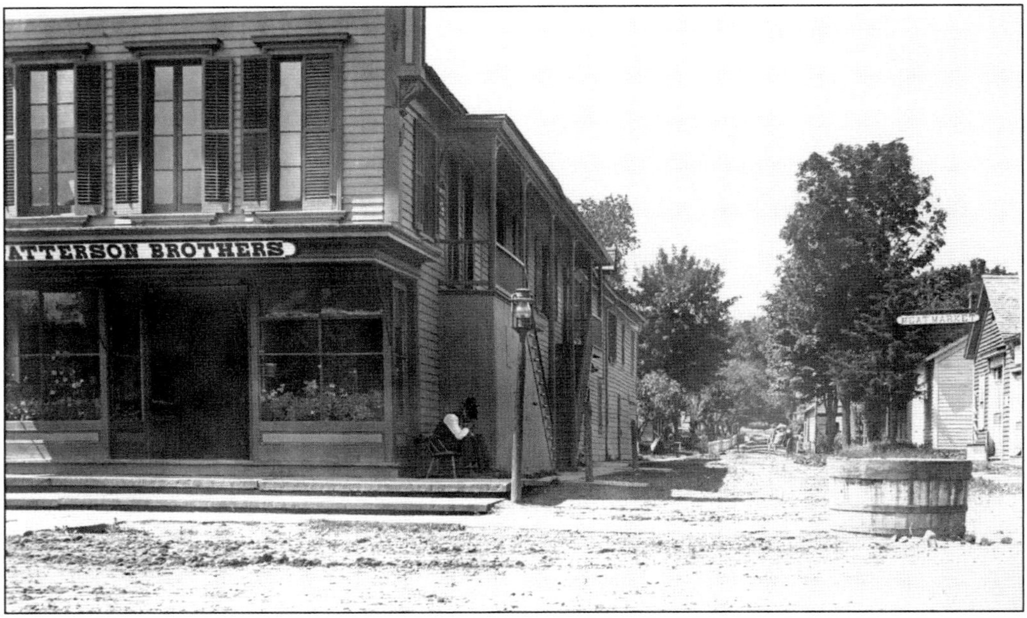

This c. 1900 photograph was taken looking up Mill Street from the corner of Main Street in Windham. The barrel in the intersection was for watering horses. The Patterson Brothers store had many owners over the years. There were attorney's offices on the second floor, and the building housed the area's first telegraph office. It burned to the ground in 1975, and today, Todaro's Salumeria grocery store is on this spot.

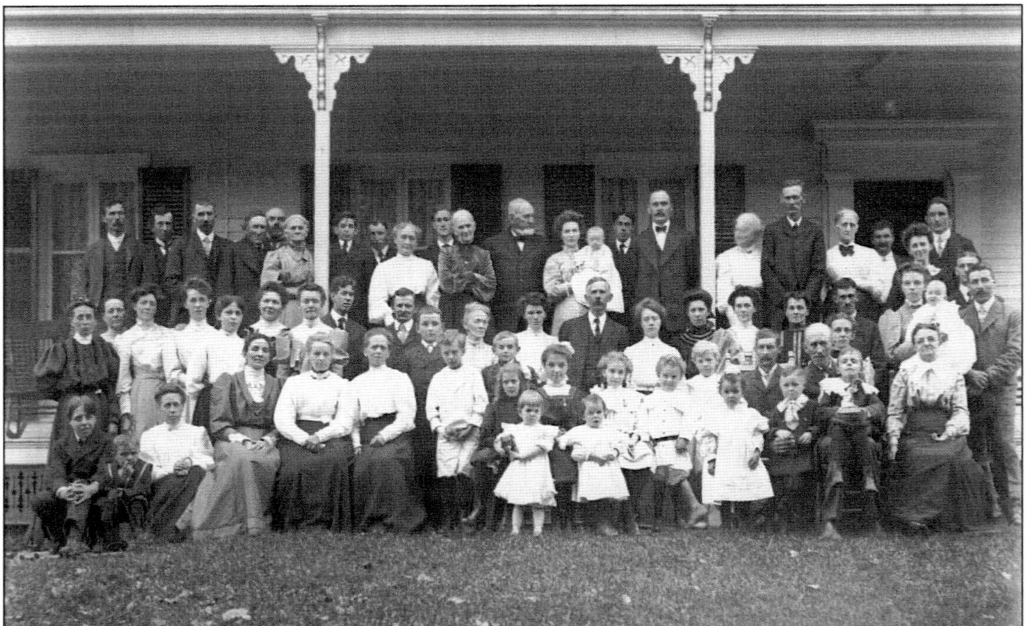

This is a typical family reunion in 1905, with the fourth generation of Windham Munsons. Solomon Munson was in his 70s when he came to North Settlement in 1798 with his 32-year-old son, Jairus. Solomon was killed while helping to build a neighbor's house in 1802. Silas Munson is seen center of the back row with his head turned, and his wife, Phebe, is to his right.

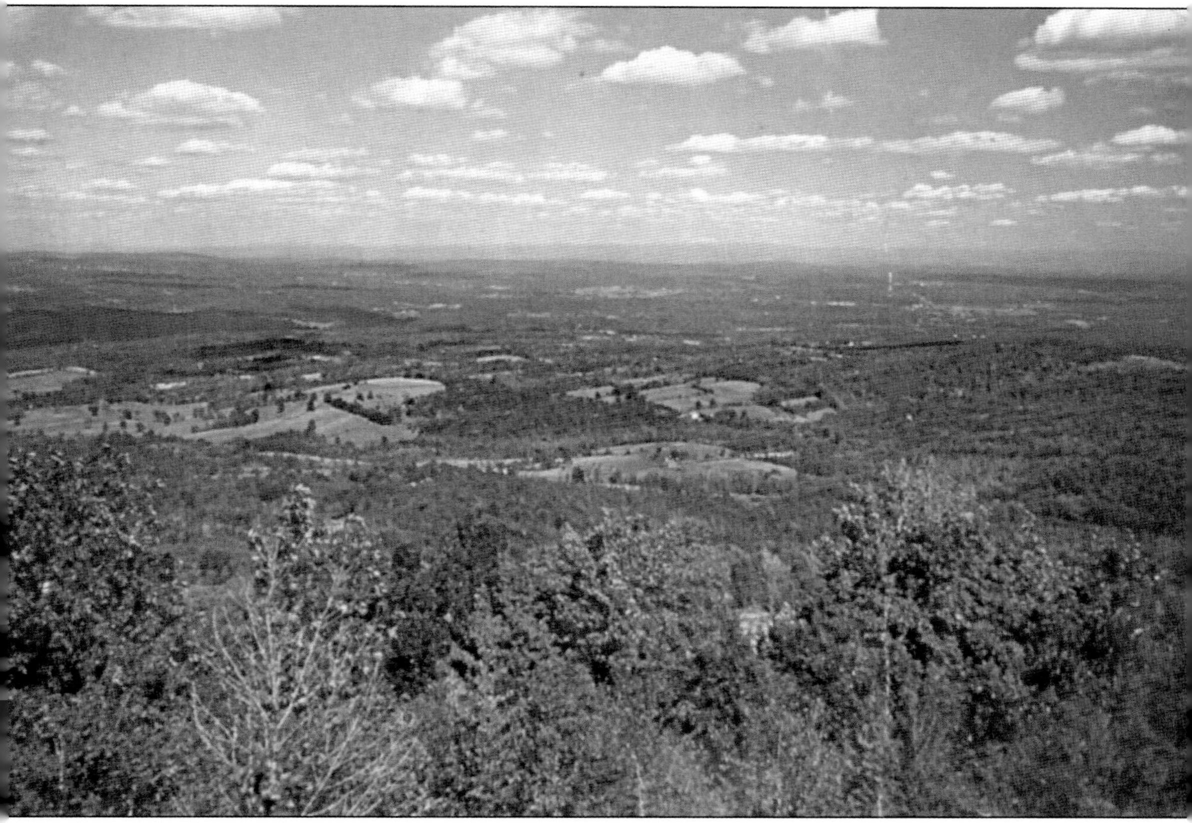

The breathtaking panoramic postcard image, captured from Point Lookout in East Windham, was probably produced in the 1950s. The view is looking northeast, with Albany to the left about 40 miles distant. Below the mountain in the bottom of this photograph is Greenville, and over to the right outside of frame is Cairo. In the far distance, the Berkshire Mountains in Massachusetts can be seen rising. The elevation here is about 2,000 feet above sea level and as advertised, on a clear day, one can see the five states of New York, Massachusetts, Vermont, Connecticut, and New Hampshire. Because of this steep eastern face of the northern Catskill Mountains, or the Wall of Manitou, as the Indians called it, there are only two roads that scale the mountains here—State Route 23 and County Route 10 (the old Susquehanna Turnpike). Ira Sherman ran a very popular hotel in East Windham from 1836 to 1875. He was the first postmaster of East Windham and a first cousin of Civil War general William Tecumseh Sherman.

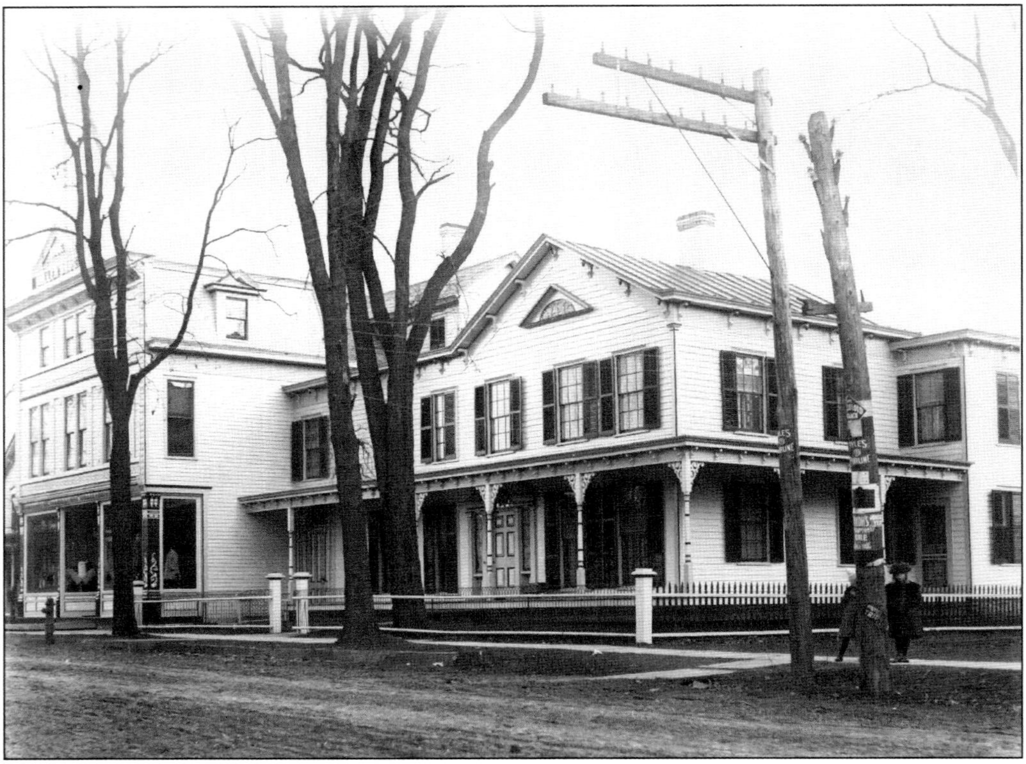

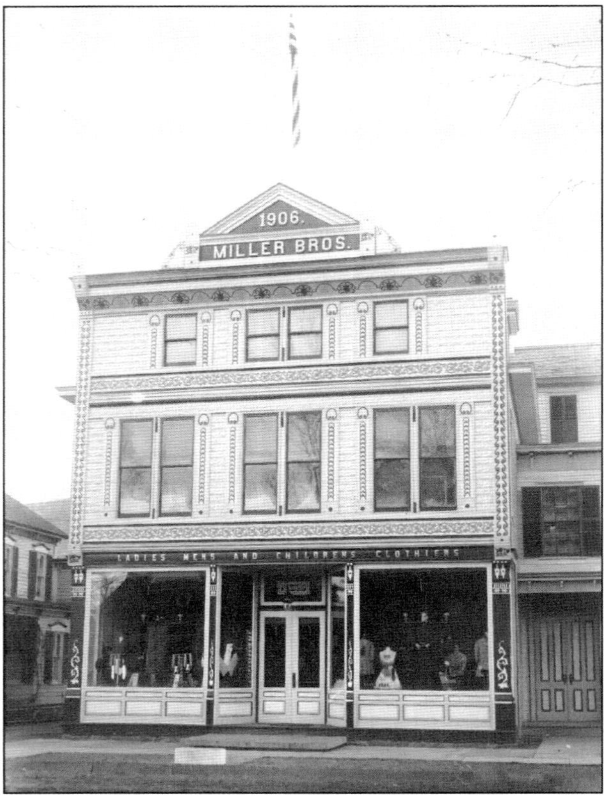

The Miller Brothers clothing store, built in 1906, was the showcase of the town in its day. In the 1930s, a bank was located in the attached building to the right of Miller Brothers store. Miller Brothers also sold jewelry, shoes, kitchenware, linens, household supplies, toys, and numerous other goods. The store was vital not only to Windham but to other surrounding towns as well. Today, the building has kept the same facade and houses the Cave Mountain Brewery, Urban Country gift shop, and condominiums on the second and third floors. Large porches, as seen in the photograph above, were very common on the front of homes built in the early 1900s. They were a social gathering place for guests at the boardinghouses in good and bad weather.

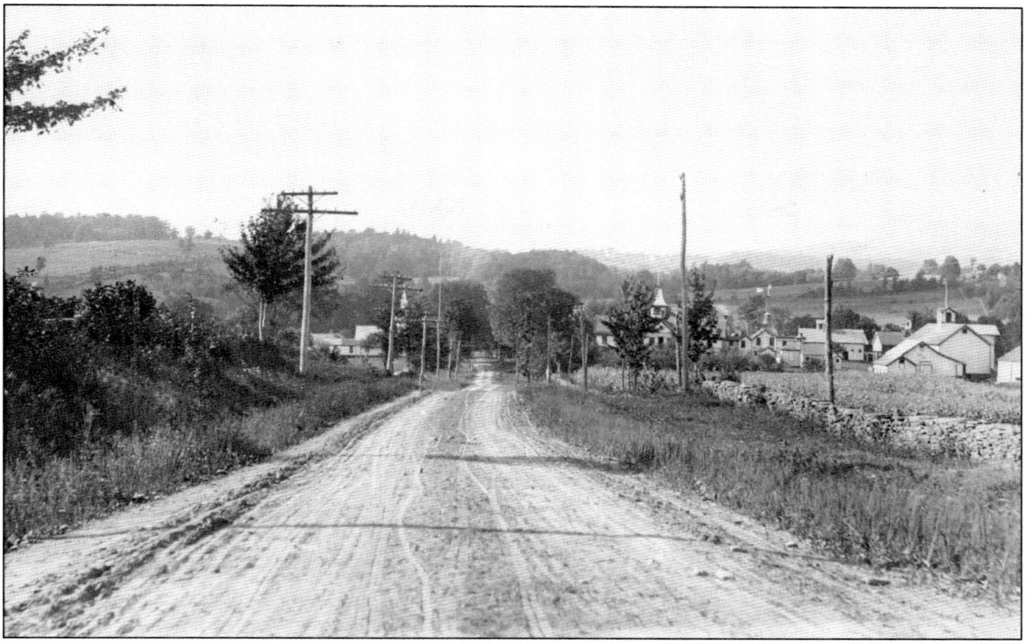

At the time this 1906 photograph was taken, the open land was all part of farms belonging to the Osborns and Thompsons. Today, the Windham Pharmacy, Chalet Fondue, a Mobil station, Legacy Bank, and other shops are to the right. For many years, the field on the right was where the Fourth of July fireworks were set off. Note the telegraph poles on the right and electric poles to the left.

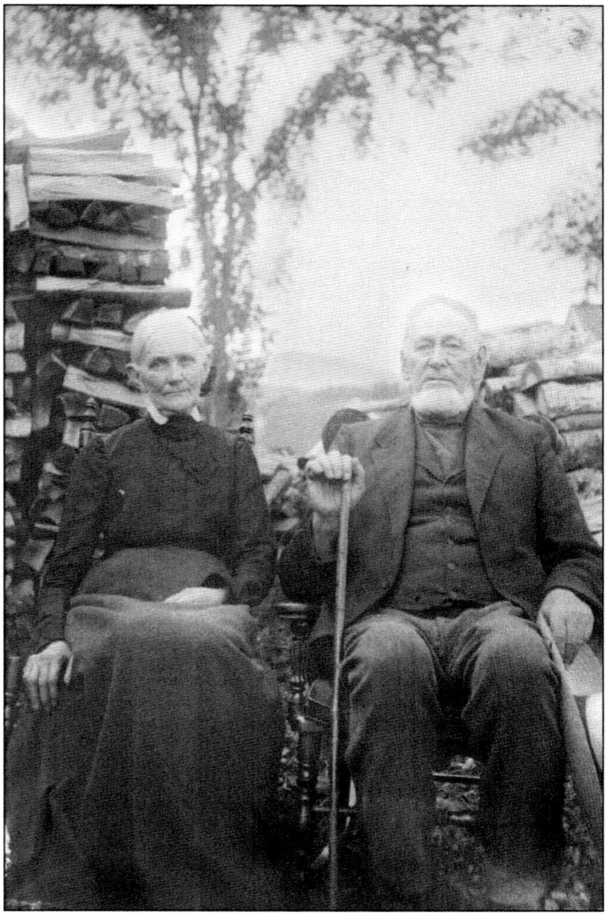

Silas and Phebe (Fuller) Munson pose at their home on the corner of South and Church Streets in 1904. Three of their sons—Alvah, Lewis, and Elmer—owned and operated three boardinghouses on South Street: Elsie's Cottage (now the Windham Mountain Inn), the Munson House, and Crest Park (the latter two are now both private residences).

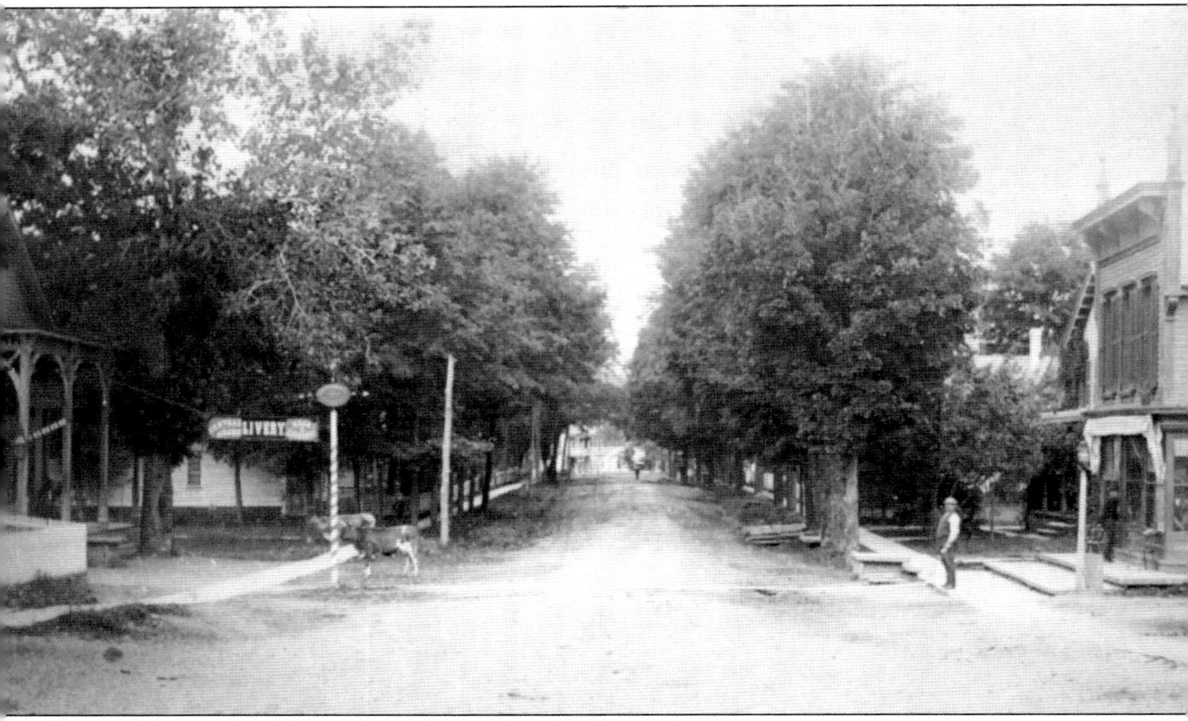

Omar Hitchcock stands in front of the Smith & Hitchcock dry goods store at the corner of Main and Mill Streets in this c. 1898 image. This photograph, taken from Mad Brook in the center of Windham village, is looking west. Livestock roving the streets of early villages was not an unusual sight, but they could be very destructive to gardens in their wanderings. Back then, picket fences were not just for decorative landscaping but also served a very practical purpose of keeping animals out of gardens and yards and keeping them penned securely in their yards. Town officials often had a designated fence viewer who inspected fences for security issues to prevent problems from arising between residents over any damage caused by animals. Gardens were not just a hobby because many people absolutely depended on them to supply food for the long winters. (Courtesy of Richard and Ruth Morse.)

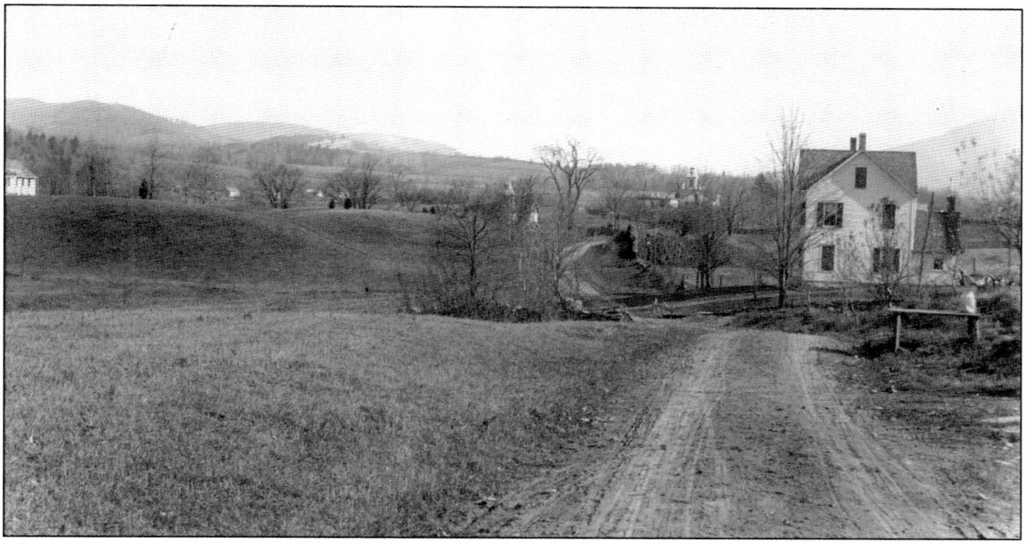

This 1903 view on South Street looks east toward the Church Street intersection in the center. The cupolas of Silas Munson's house and the Munson House can be seen in the center and center right of the picture, respectively. In the far left is a building that was part of the Crest Park boardinghouse.

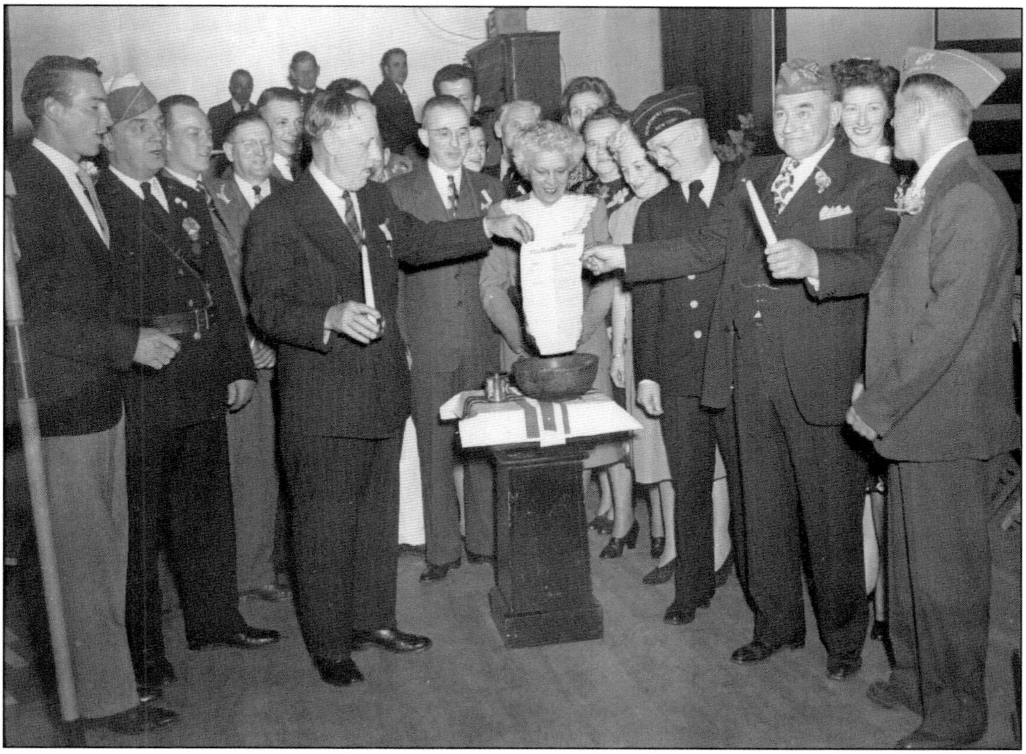

Windham established its Veterans of Foreign Wars post on February 21, 1928, with the name Catskill Mountain Post No. 1545, renamed in 1929 to Sgt. James F. Carty Post No. 1545 VFW. That year, the group purchased Kelly's Saw Mill with donations and a mortgage for its hall. The smiling people seen here on May 21, 1948, are happily burning the paid-off mortgage. (Courtesy of Richard and Ruth Morse.)

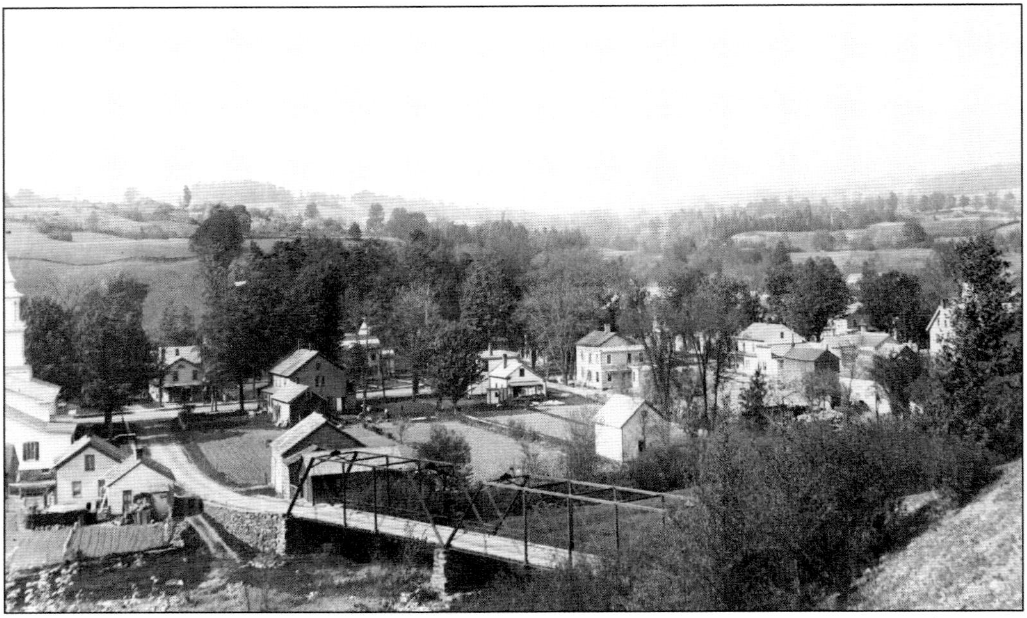

This view looks down on the Church Street Bridge and the Windham Centre Presbyterian Church in 1905. Note the neatly tended gardens at each home, which were absolutely essential for supplying the family with food. Fences surround each garden to protect crops from damage by wandering animals.

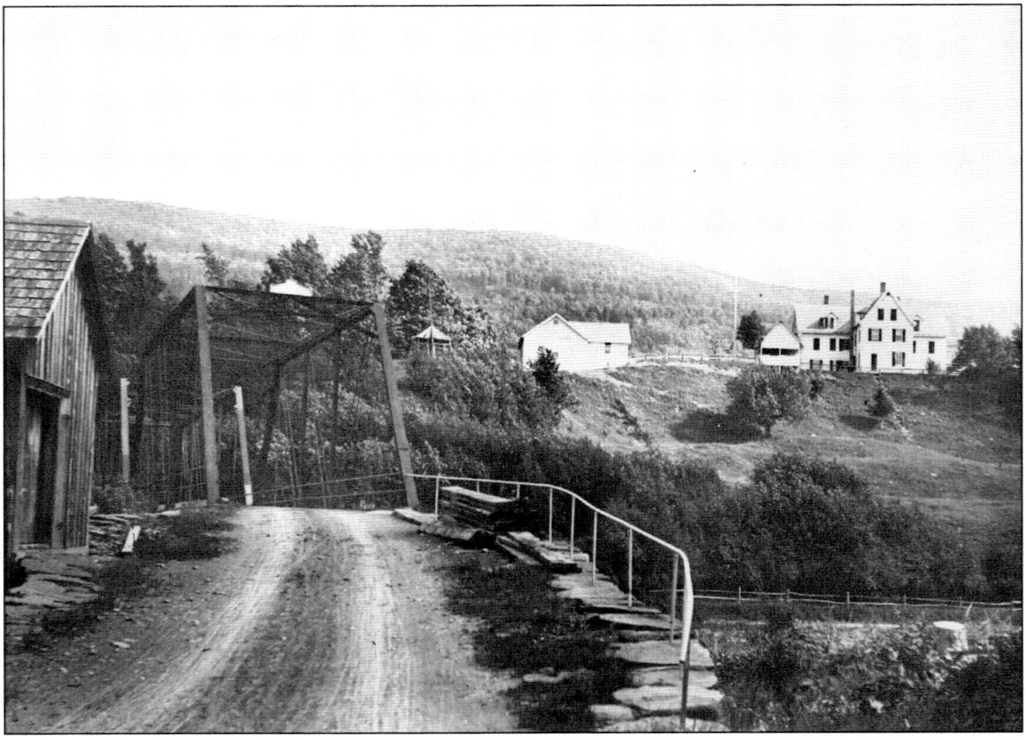

Crest Park boardinghouse is on the right as seen from the Church Street Bridge in this 1910 photograph. Cave Mountain, seen in the background, is today the home of Windham Mountain ski slope, which attracts tens of thousands of visitors to the town during both winter and summer.

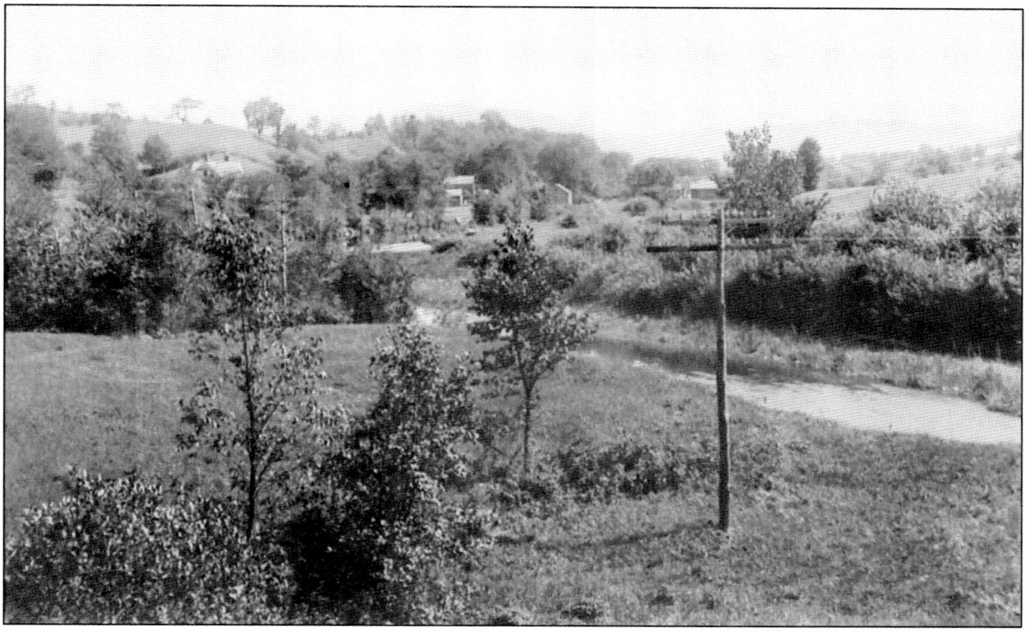

This 1910 view was taken from Kelly's Saw Mill, where the Veterans of Foreign Wars Hall sits at the west end of Windham, looking east toward the village along Batavia Kill. The barn in the center right is where GNH Lumber now stands. Route 23 is center left behind the trees.

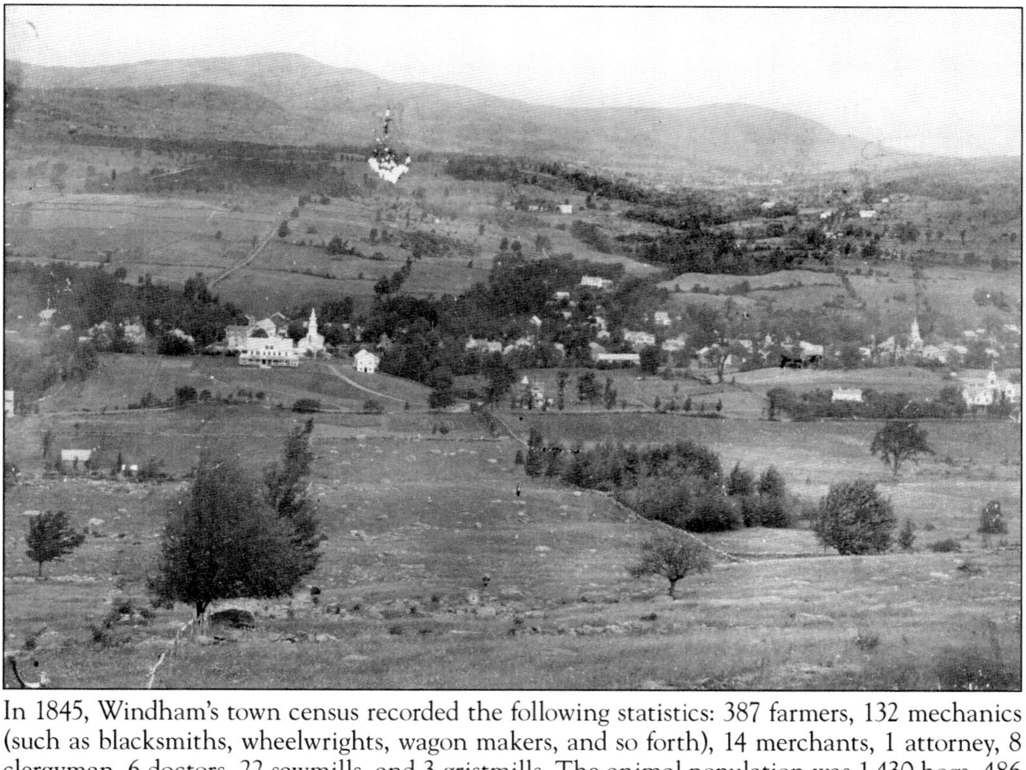

In 1845, Windham's town census recorded the following statistics: 387 farmers, 132 mechanics (such as blacksmiths, wheelwrights, wagon makers, and so forth), 14 merchants, 1 attorney, 8 clergyman, 6 doctors, 22 sawmills, and 3 gristmills. The animal population was 1,430 hogs, 486 horses, and 3,174 cattle. In this 1905 photograph, Windham village can be seen nestled among the trees lining Batavia Kill.

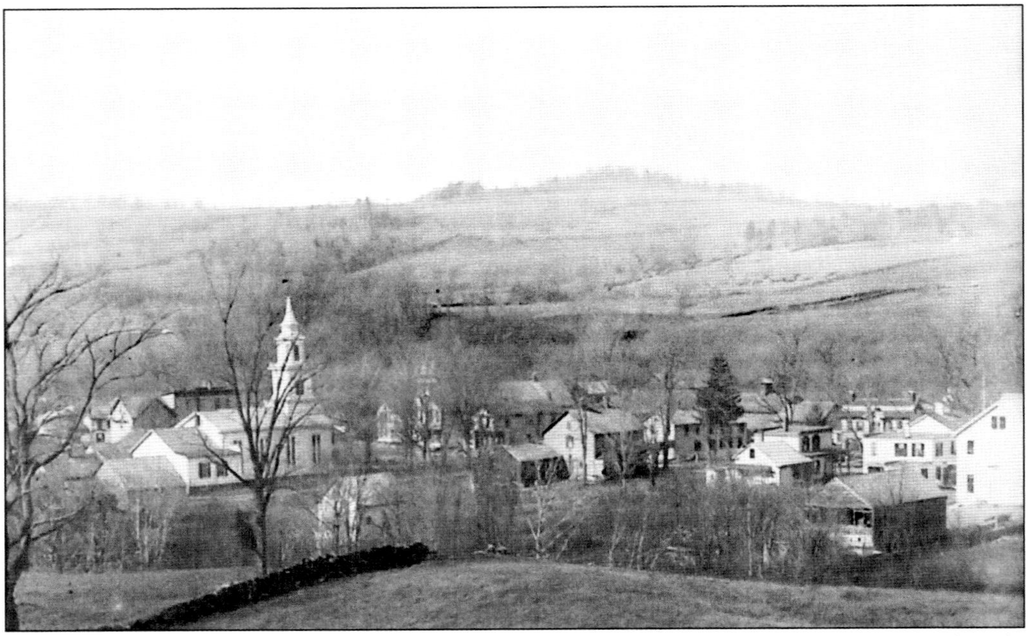

This 1902 photograph is looking northwest toward the Windham Centre Presbyterian Church. In the foreground and on the distant hills are the ever-present stone walls that added a natural-looking, yet man-made, element to Windham's bucolic scenery. Most of these walls have been reclaimed by forests, which grew back with the decline of farms. They stand like shaded monuments to the hard work that created them.

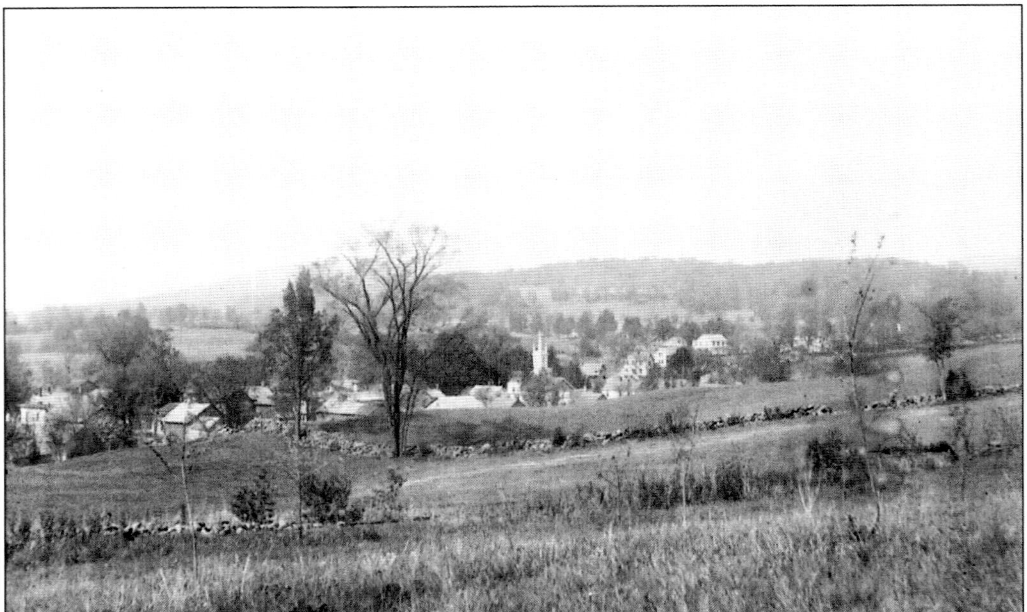

This c. 1902 view is looking northeast toward Windham village from the south side of Batavia Kill. The Methodist church's bell tower and steeple in the center were added to the front, along with a clock and vestibule entrance, in 1866. A tradition started with the addition of the bell. When a resident died, the bell was rung the number of times equal to the deceased's age.

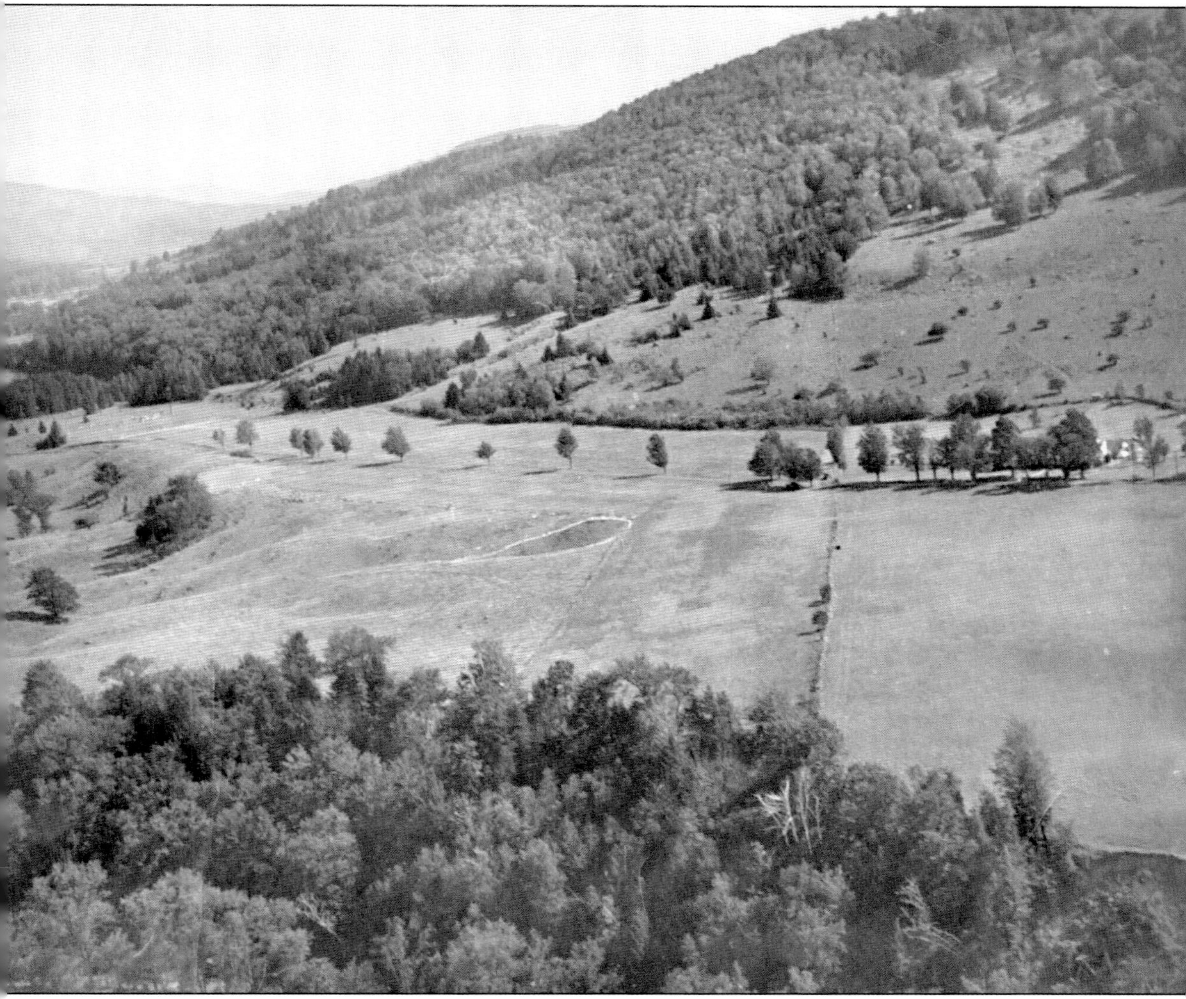

In this 1937 photograph is the runway at the east end of South Street when John Garraghan used it as the Windham Airport. Behind the trees, in the center right of the picture, is the boardinghouse known as Elsie's Cottage. This eventually became the Westmere, and today, it is the Windham Mountain Inn. In the center, John built a hangar that became a garage for his oil business, followed by a bowling alley, and is now the home to radio station WRIP. In 2011, to the left of center near the white oval fence, are the Little League Field and several private residences. The Windham Country Club purchased the remaining land in the bottom of the photograph in the 1960s to add nine holes to its already established golf course. In the bottom center of the photograph is the spot where the Garraghans built their house in the early 1950s. Flowers by Kaylyn is located there in 2011. The annual Fourth of July fireworks were held here in the 1950s and 1960s. (Courtesy of Christopher Garraghan.)

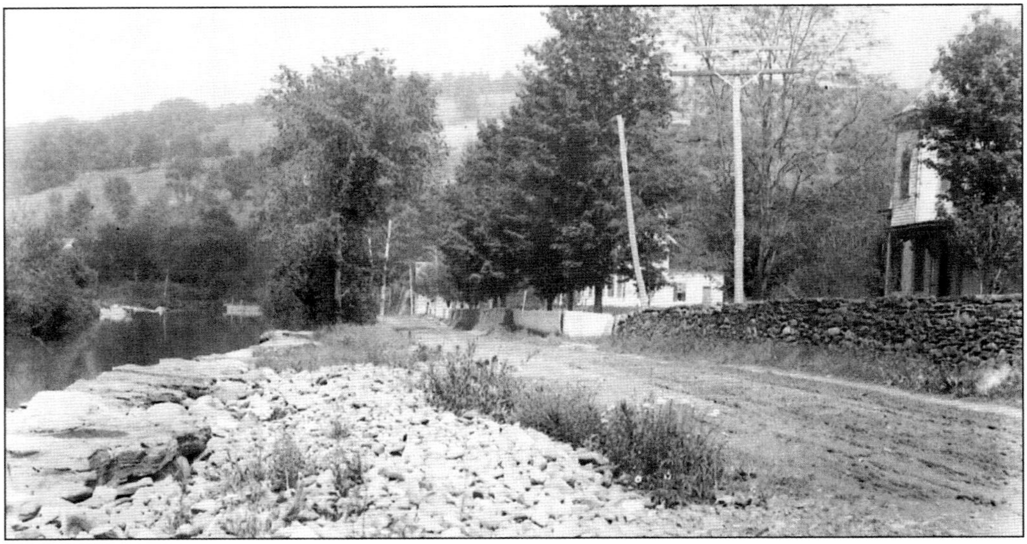

This 1906 view looks west toward Hickory Hill on Route 23. In its day, this was the Windham Turnpike, which was highly traveled by drovers from the west as they brought their livestock to market at the Catskill docks. The high volume of animal traffic accounts for the stone and wood fences necessary to keep the livestock from destroying gardens while en route.

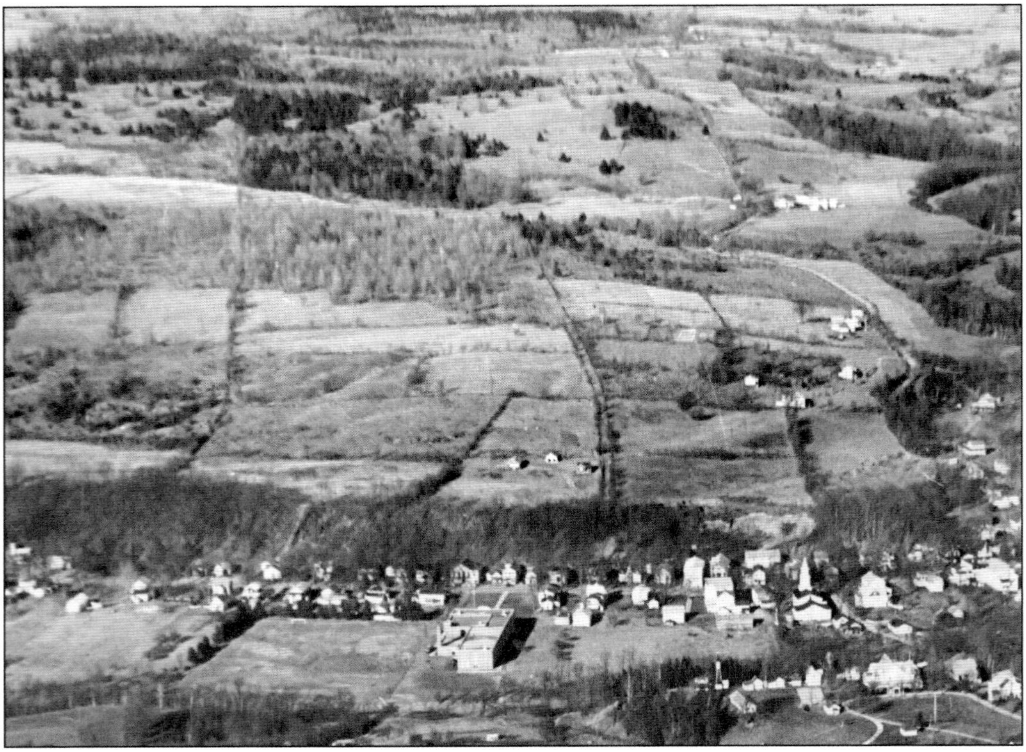

This is a late-1930s aerial photograph of Windham village taken by John Garraghan. The new Windham-Ashland-Jewett Central School is visible in the bottom center of the image. Mill Street is the road that starts in the bottom right and meanders to the top. A large portion of the vacant land seen here is now covered with condominiums and second homes for skiers. (Courtesy of Christopher Garraghan.)

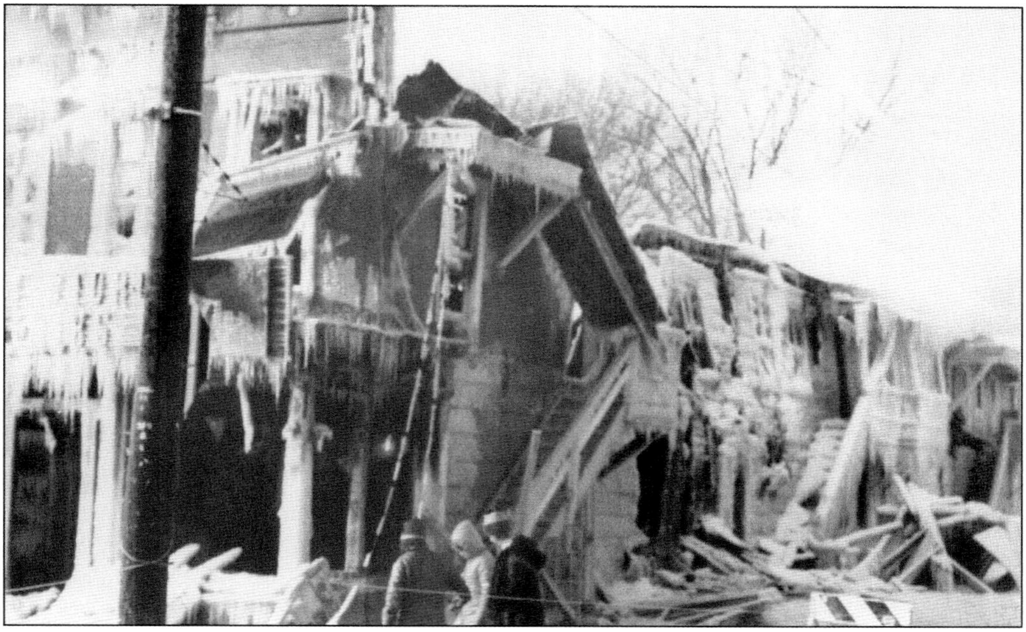

On a bitterly cold winter night in 1975, the Blue Moon gift shop and restaurant was consumed by fire and completely destroyed. This old building was a fixture in Windham at the intersection of Mill and Main Streets for 100 years. In that time, it had many owners and occupants—from a grocery store with lawyer's offices on the second floor to apartments and a restaurant. (Courtesy of Leonard Bell and Windham Historical Society.)

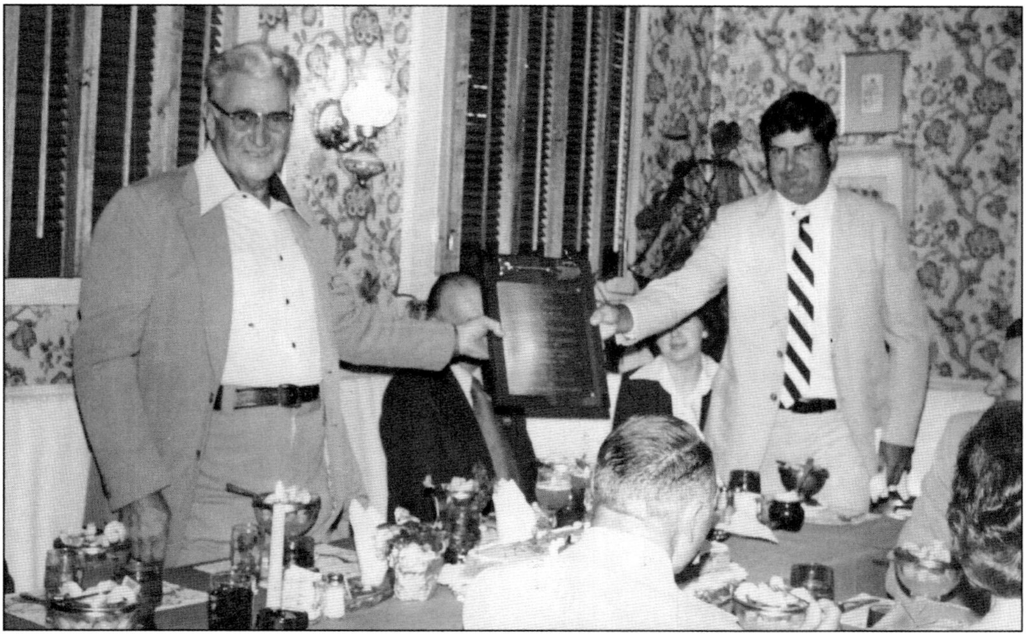

Pat Meehan (right) is handing a 20-year retirement plaque to Windham highway superintendent Cliff "Biff" Andrus in 1977 at Seeley's Inn in Hensonville. Pat was Windham's town supervisor from 1971 to 2009 and had just been elected to his 20th two-year term when he passed away. His steady, competent leadership guided Windham through turbulent economic times during those years. (Courtesy of Regina Kazman.)

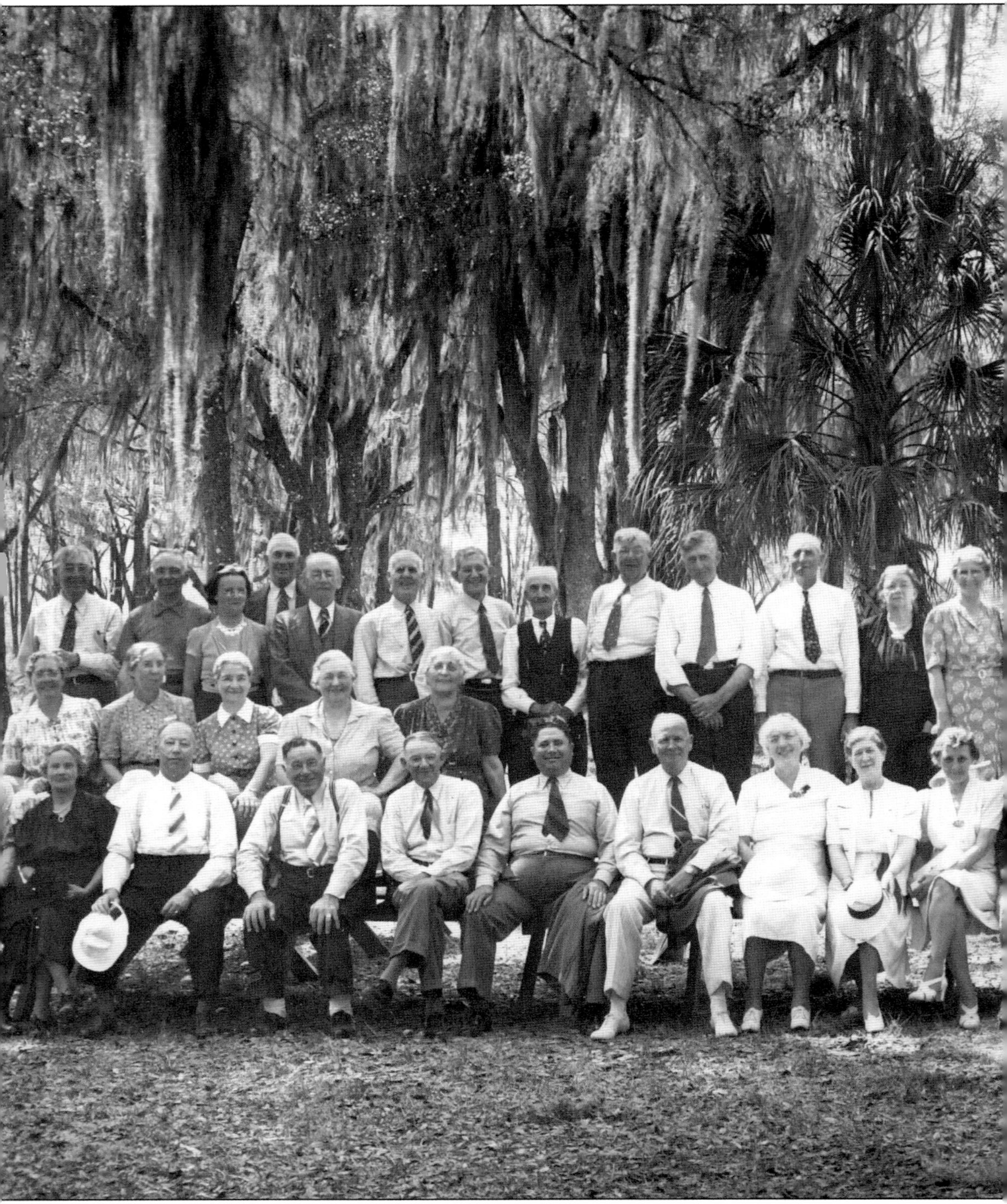

In this March 23, 1940, image, residents and business owners from Greene County, New York, pose at their annual picnic in De Leon Springs, Florida. The boardinghouse industry was so popular and profitable for Windham that even in these early years, the owners could afford to go south for the winter. They were probably the first generation of Windham snowbirds that could indulge in escape from winter's icy grip after the crush of the summer trade. One boardinghouse in

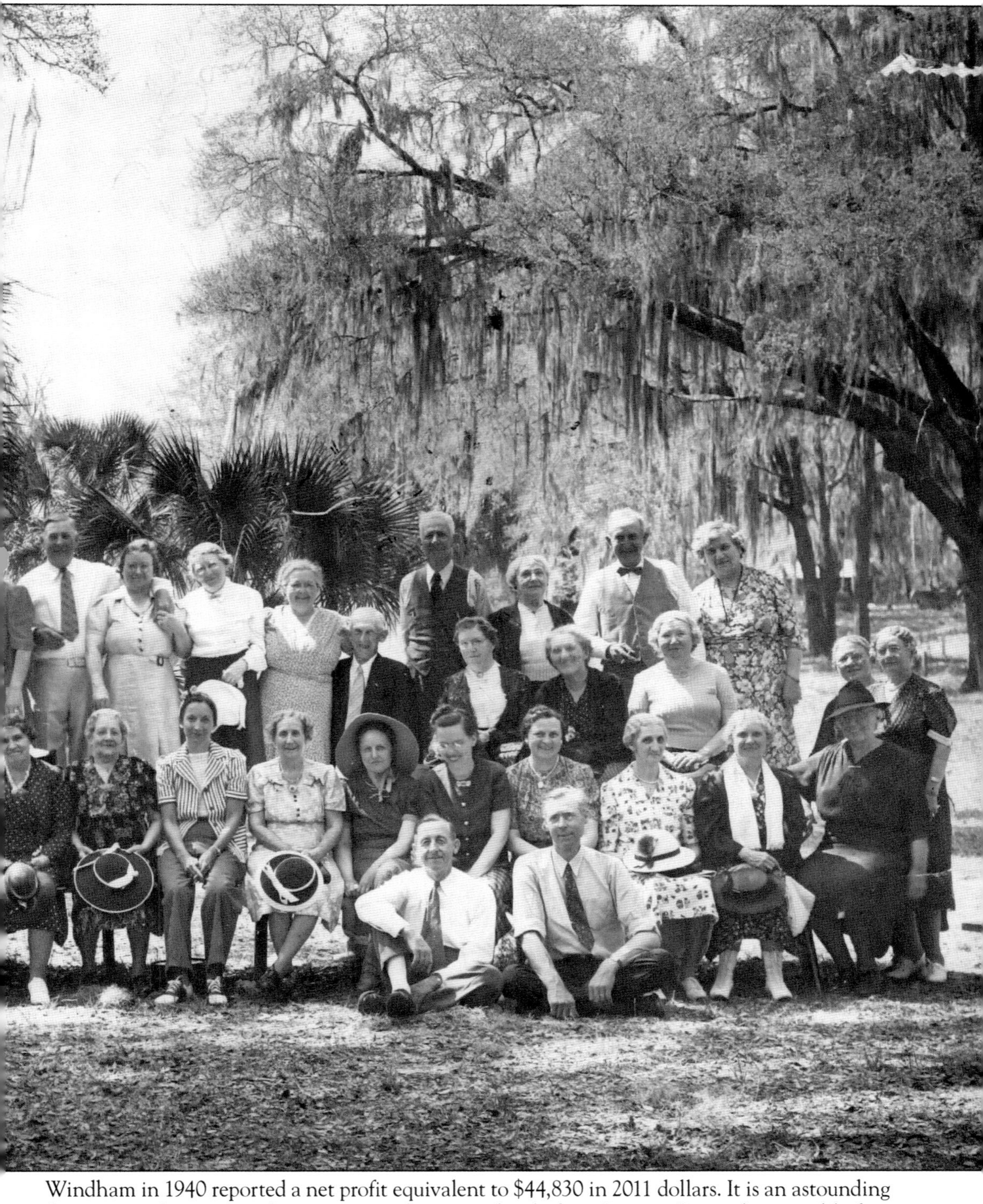

Windham in 1940 reported a net profit equivalent to $44,830 in 2011 dollars. It is an astounding figure, considering that the summer trade spanned only from June to September, roughly four months. That is about $11,000 net profit per month, and economically speaking, it would be very difficult for any kind of new business in Windham to generate that kind of prosperity for so many local residents.

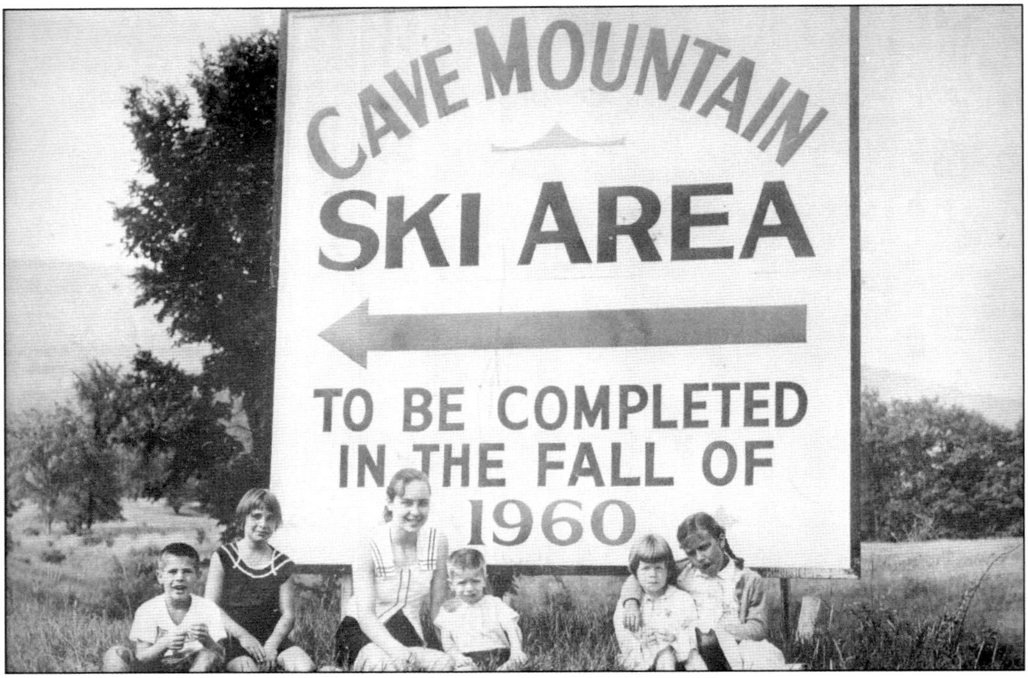

Originally called the Cave Mountain Ski Area, the facility opened for business in 1960. It was a modest start with comparatively few trails and a small geodesic dome for a base lodge. As would be expected in any start-up, results were slow, and the operation struggled for many years. From left to right are Roger Lane, Claudia Lane, Sandy Lane Mattice, Kenneth Lane, ? Macomber, and ? Macomber. (Courtesy of Eleanor Lane.)

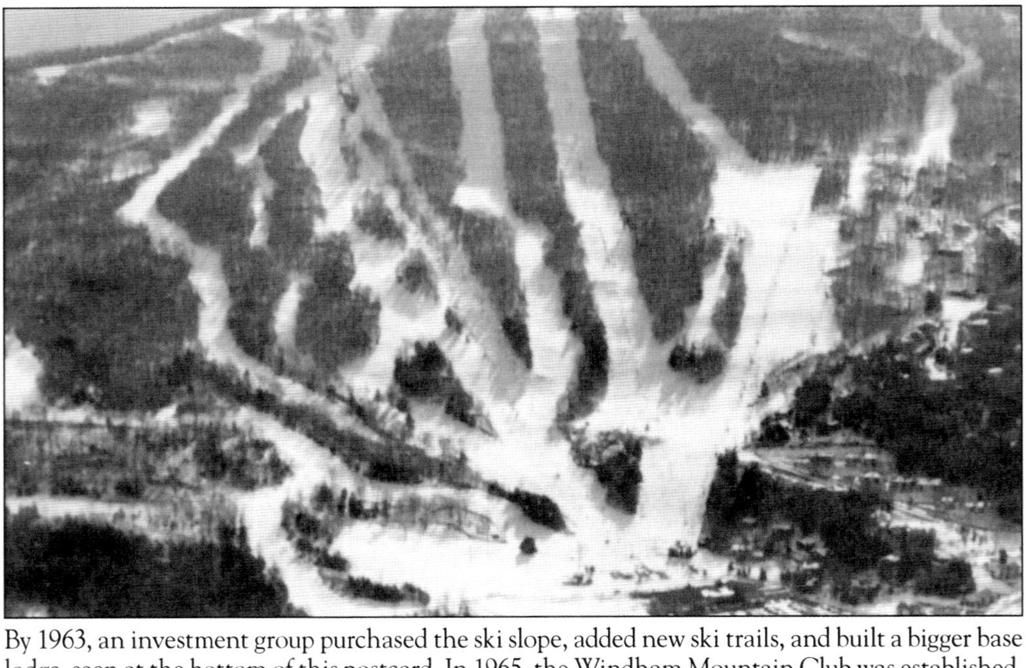

By 1963, an investment group purchased the ski slope, added new ski trails, and built a bigger base lodge, seen at the bottom of this postcard. In 1965, the Windham Mountain Club was established, turning the entire ski slope operation into a private club. In 1981, it was sold, made public, and renamed Ski Windham. Resold in 2005, it was renamed Windham Mountain.

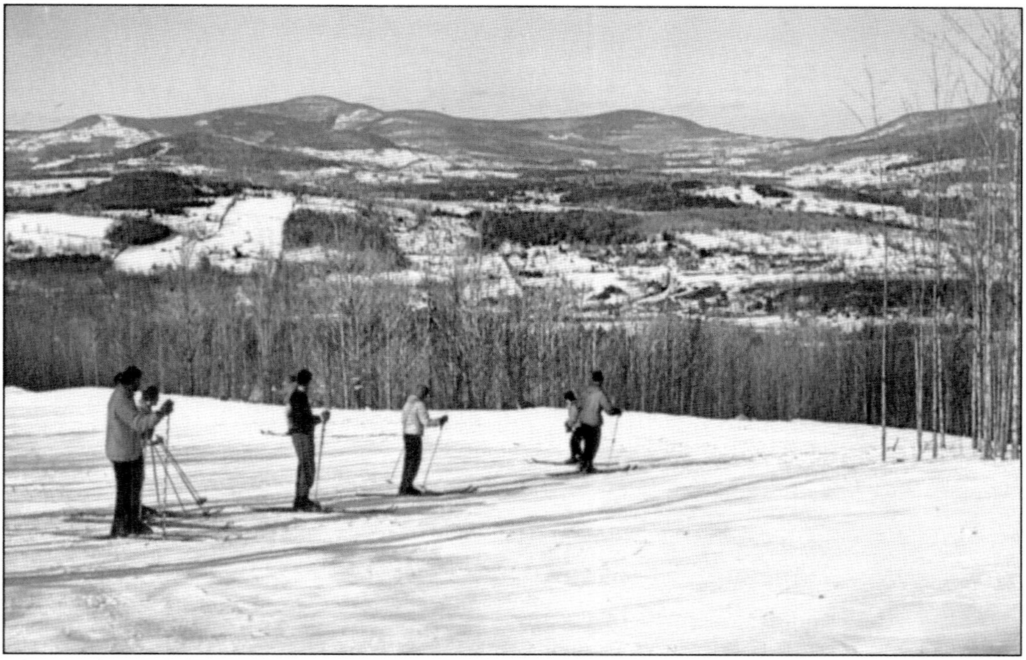

This is a beautiful c. 1969 view from Windham Mountain ski slope looking out over the Windham Valley. In the far distant center right of picture is Mount Pisgah with North Settlement to its left. Windham village is at the bottom of the picture, hidden behind the trees. Before the ski trails, the mountain was used as pasture for livestock and a woodlot by the Munson and Brainerd farms.

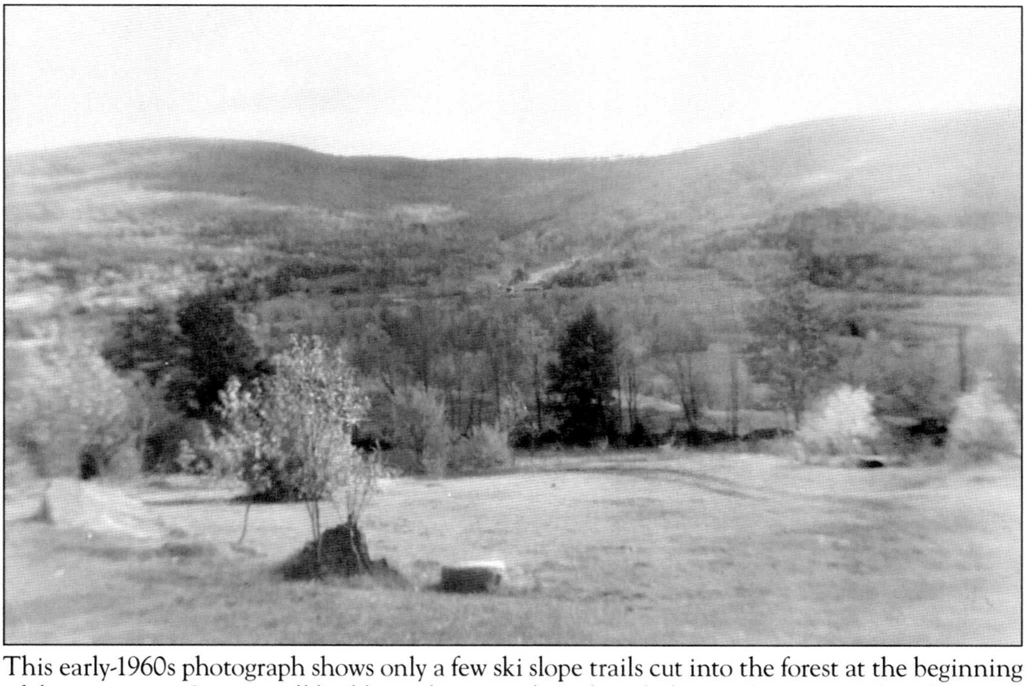

This early-1960s photograph shows only a few ski slope trails cut into the forest at the beginning of the operation. Some small buildings that served as a base lodge can be seen. Today, the entire mountain has numerous ski trails from top to bottom. In addition, there are condominiums and homes built almost to the top of the mountain and spanning its width.

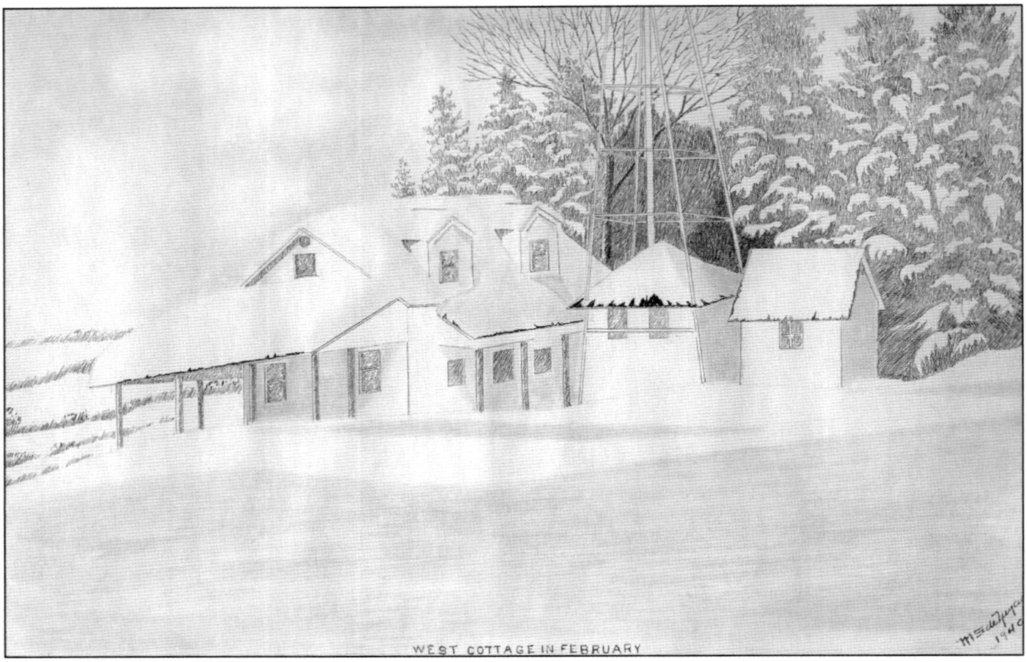

Marius de Zayas (March 13, 1880–January 10, 1961) was a world-famous Mexican artist and New York City gallery owner in the early to mid-1900s. He vacationed at the Crest Park boardinghouse and drew these pen-and-ink pictures. The winter scene above is of the west cottage, and below is a picture of the main house in summer. Windham has inspired many artists to create beautiful paintings and drawings.

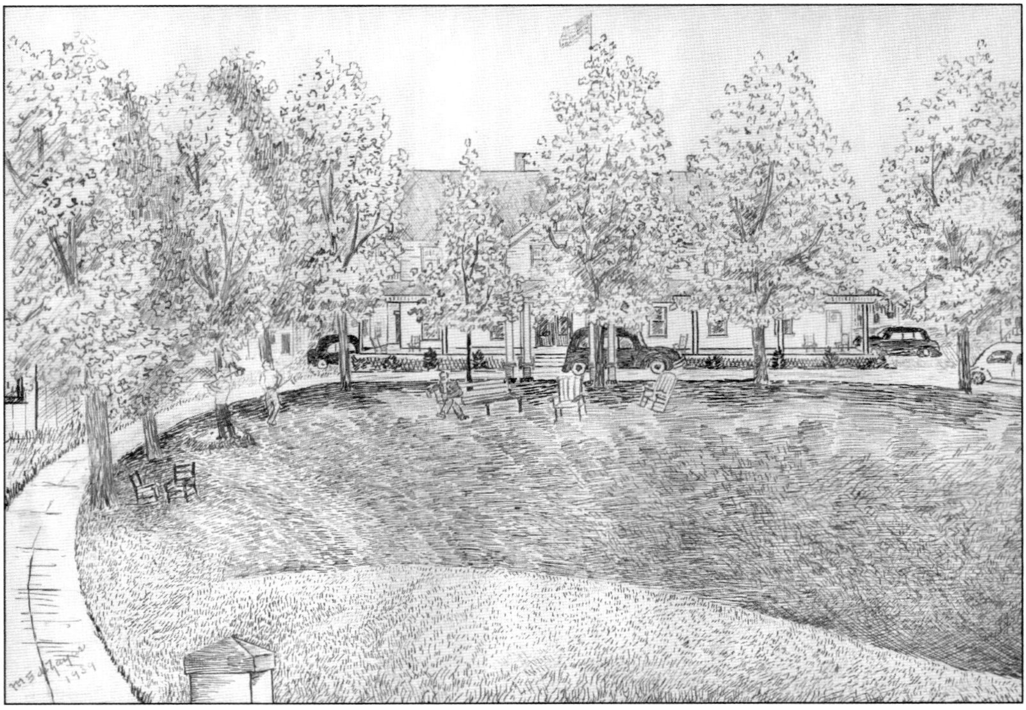

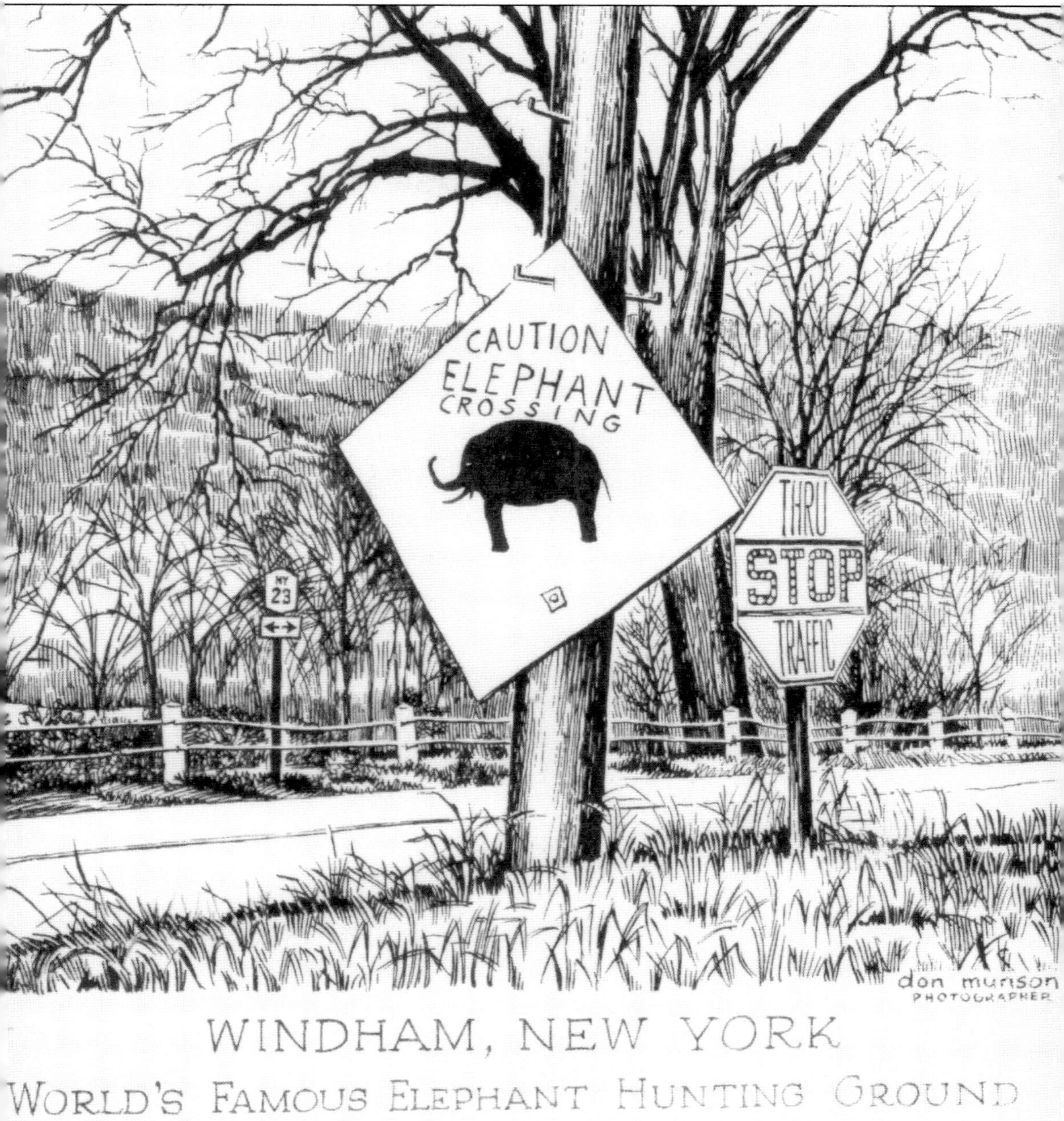

Siam, a 4,500-pound elephant, was owned and kept by the Vidbel family on their farm off of Mitchell Hollow Road. Siam was one of many animals the family had as part of its circus business. At the end of traveling in the summer, they brought their animals to the Windham farm before taking them to Florida for the winter. In October 1957, Siam broke her hobbling chains and disappeared into the forest, which by now had shed its leaves. Incredibly, despite extensive ground and aircraft searches by hundreds of people, Siam was seen only once in 12 days before she was finally found in a stone quarry. The cold night temperatures had fallen to 20 degrees, and it was feared she was not going to survive. After a thorough examination, she only had a cold and was taken home. In the course of those 12 days, Siam had traversed the mountains and descended 2,000 feet to Cairo, 15 miles away.

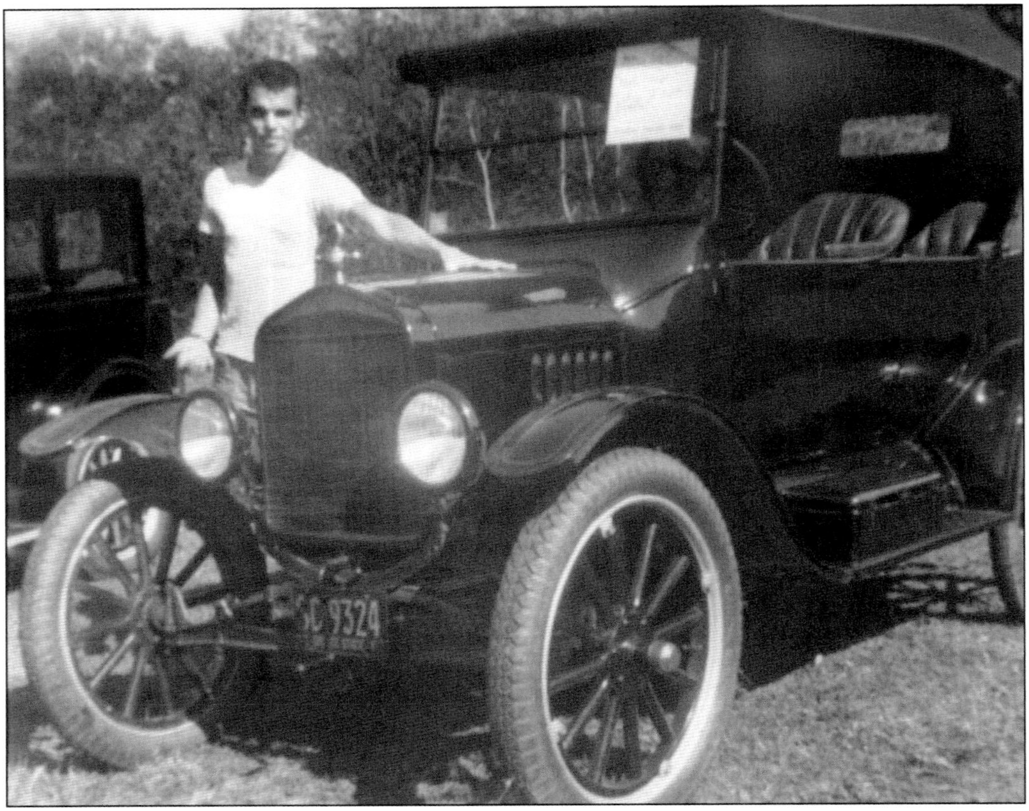

Windham town officials, civic groups, and businesses (especially the boardinghouses) made sure there were always frequent events during the summer months. These 1950s photographs are of an antique car show being held in the field across from Cole's Pleasant View boardinghouse. In the image above, Chris Garraghan is standing next to one of the beautiful cars on display. Below is a view of the many cars lined up for exhibition. This field is located west of Old Road on the south side of Route 23. All of the buildings from Cole's are gone. Summer guests, as well as local residents, thoroughly enjoyed such events, which drew people to Windham from miles around.

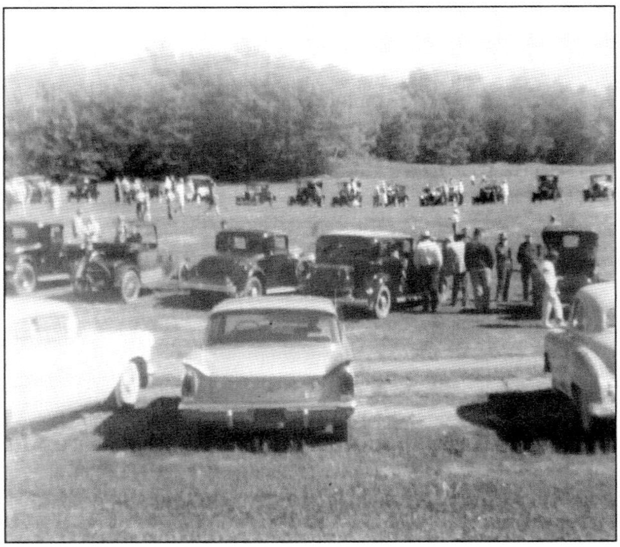

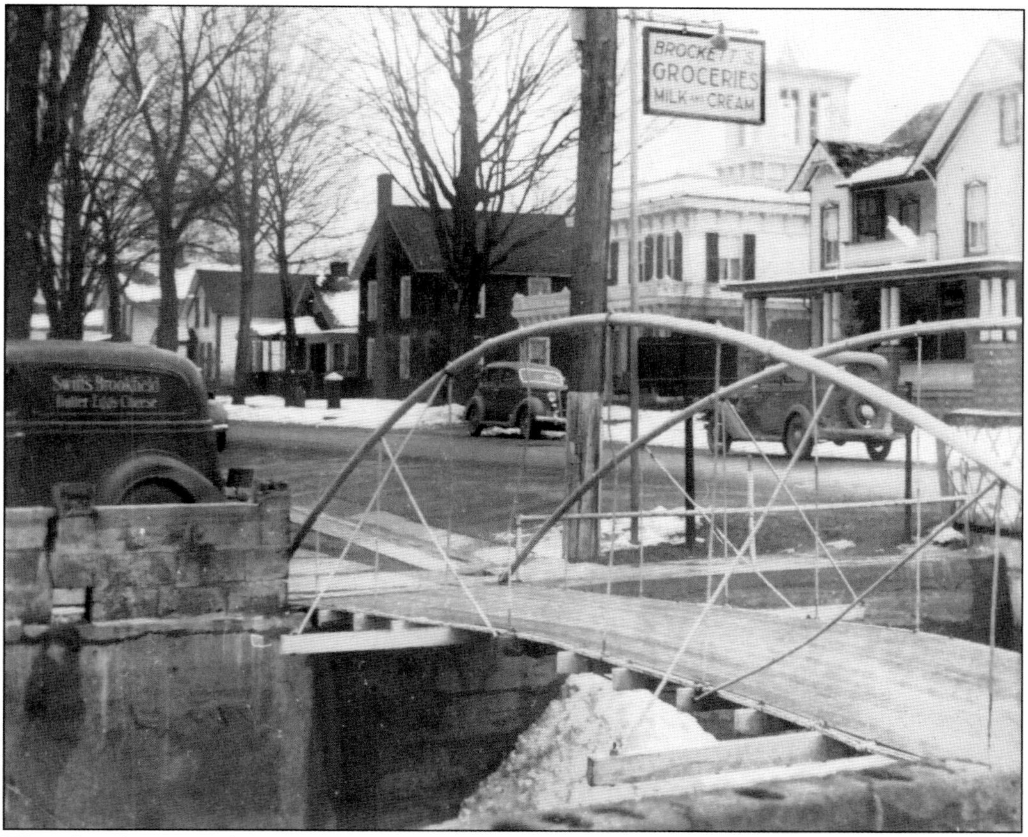

The white house in the center of this 1930s photograph is known locally as the Wedding Cake House because of its layered flat roofs, which resemble a wedding cake. It was built in 1836 for Col. George Robertson. The dark-colored house to its left, built in 1886, is owned by Stephanie Sullivan Brown and her brother Phillip.

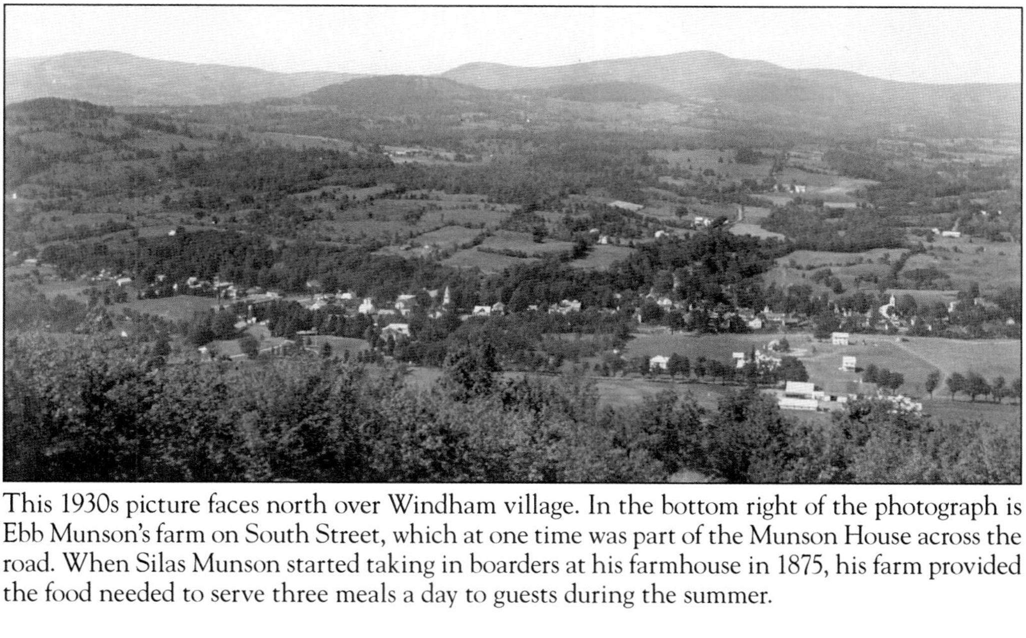

This 1930s picture faces north over Windham village. In the bottom right of the photograph is Ebb Munson's farm on South Street, which at one time was part of the Munson House across the road. When Silas Munson started taking in boarders at his farmhouse in 1875, his farm provided the food needed to serve three meals a day to guests during the summer.

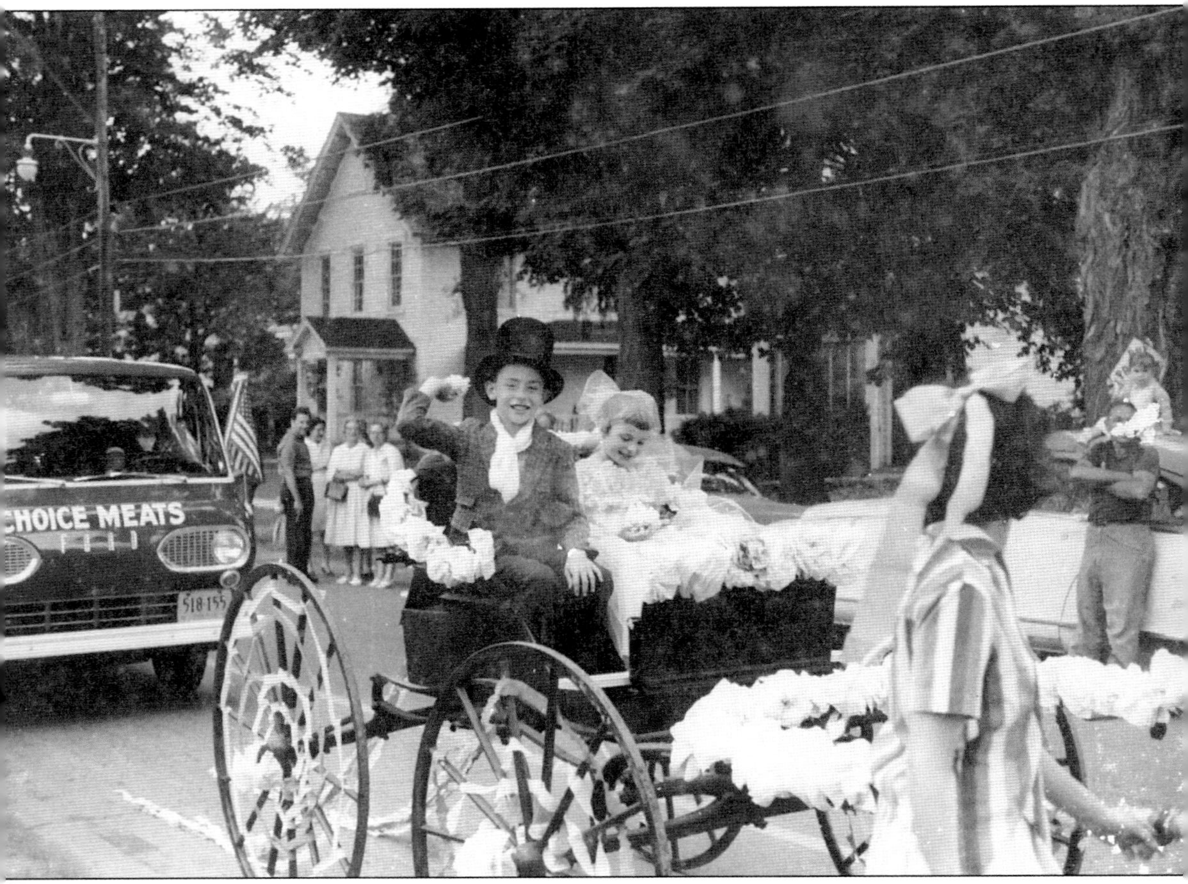

One popular town-wide event held was Old Times of Windham, which included a parade, games, and vendors in the village. This 1963 photograph shows Pat Knefley (left) and Phoebe Davis in a carriage being pulled by waitresses from Crest Park. This event was one of many that various local civic groups sponsored for the summer festivities in Windham.

Six

CHURCHES AND SCHOOLS

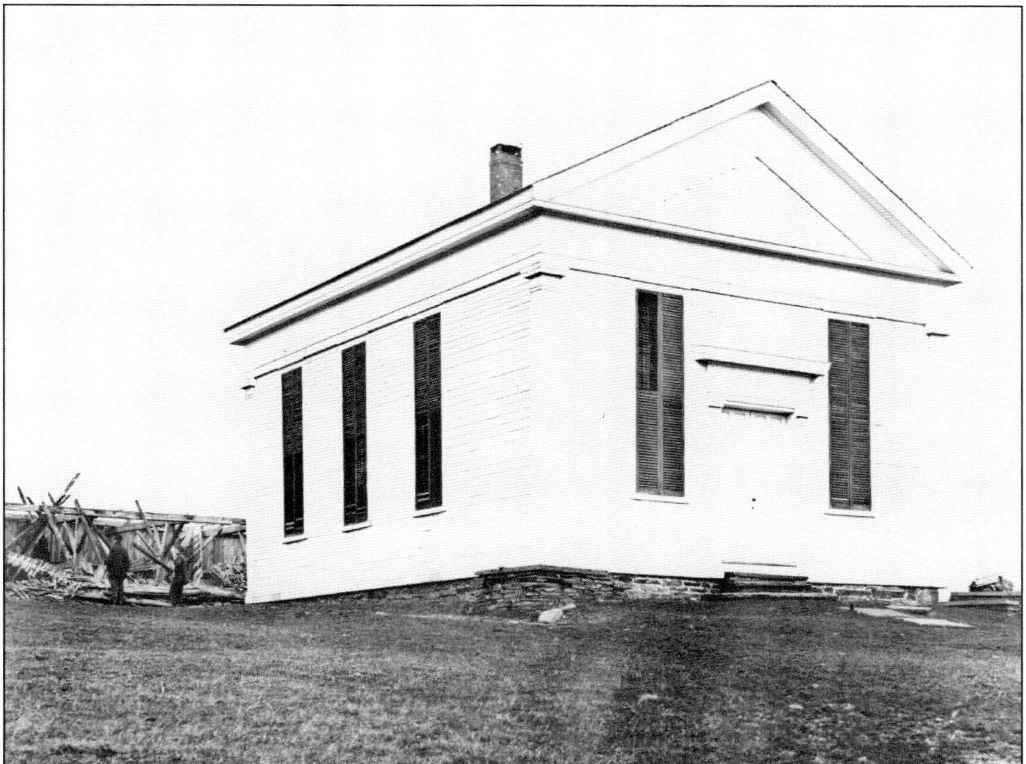

The North Settlement Methodist Church is one of the oldest churches still standing on the mountaintop. Built in 1826, limited services are still held here. Originally, it was within the boundaries of Old Windham, but it is now in Ashland's borders. In this 1910 photograph, workers are dismantling the horse sheds in the back. At the time, Greek Revival architecture was used on all the Methodist churches built on the mountaintop.

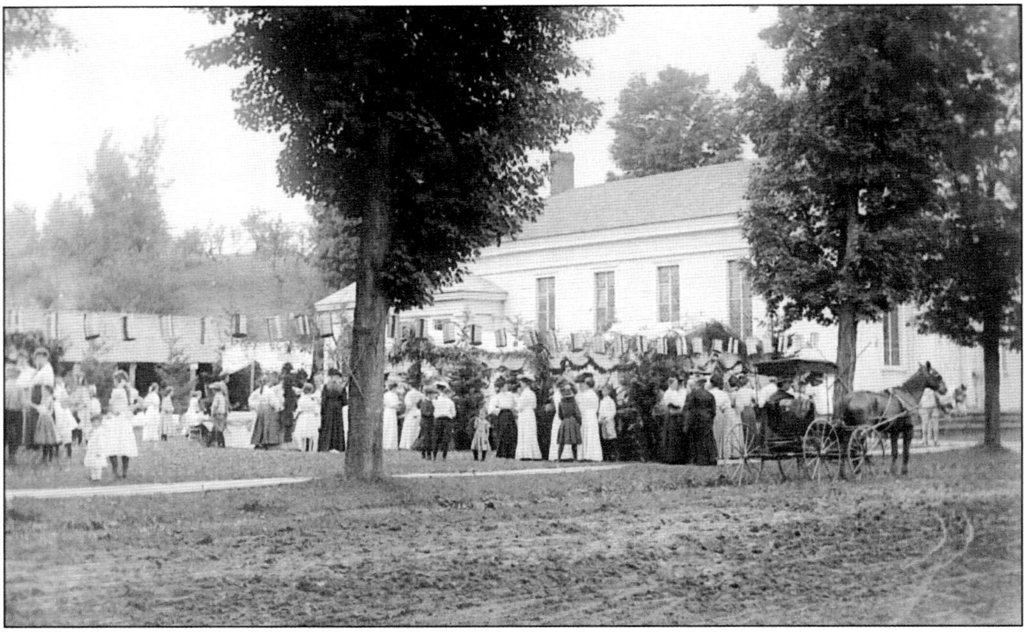

Churches were a very important part of Windham in the early settlement years. Church fairs, such as the one seen here at the Windham Methodist Church in 1904, are just one example of many events held throughout the year. The denominations of the very first settlers were Presbyterian, Episcopalian, Baptist, Dutch Reformed, and Methodist, and all worshipped together in 1800 at the Old Meeting House.

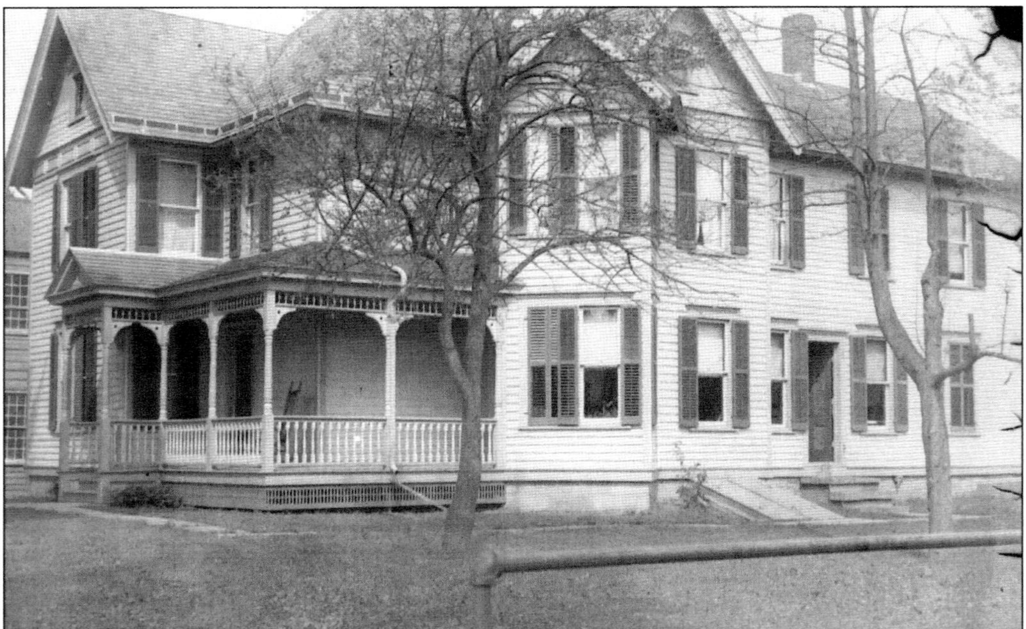

This 1903 photograph is of the Windham Methodist Church parsonage built the year before. Previously on this spot was the old Osborn Hotel, which was built in the early 1800s and deeded to the Methodists around 1870 to be used as a parsonage. The hotel/parsonage was dismantled in 1901. The parsonage seen here is still standing next to the Methodist church.

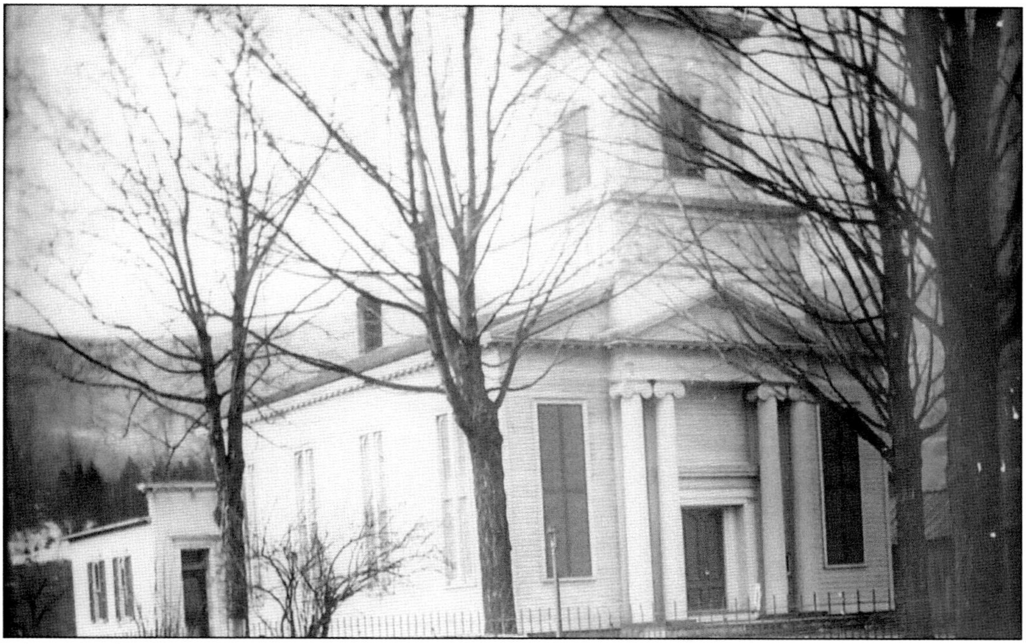

The Windham Centre Presbyterian Church in this 1900 photograph was built in 1834 and was active until it closed due to declining membership in 1970. The descendants of the original donors of the land turned the building and property over to the town. Today, it has been beautifully restored and is now the Windham Civic Centre and Library. Cultural events and concerts are held here throughout the year.

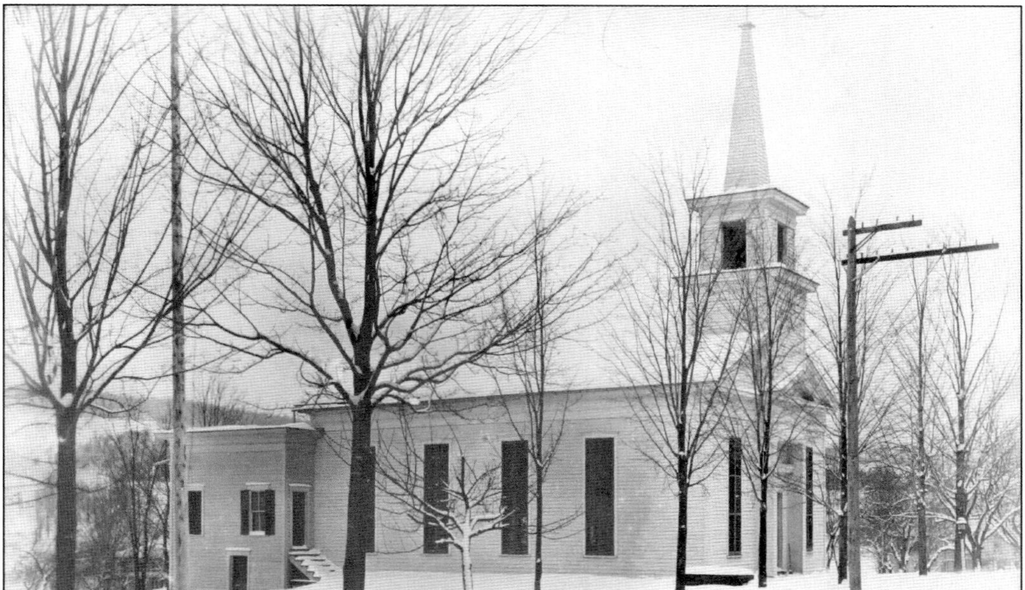

The Hensonville Methodist Church in this 1905 photograph was built in 1874. Throughout the 19th and 20th centuries, churches thrived in hamlets. With local population declining and social changes, many of the churches in Windham closed or combined with others. This church closed in 2007 and merged with the Windham Methodist Church. The building has been converted and now houses the Fitness Concepts exercise center.

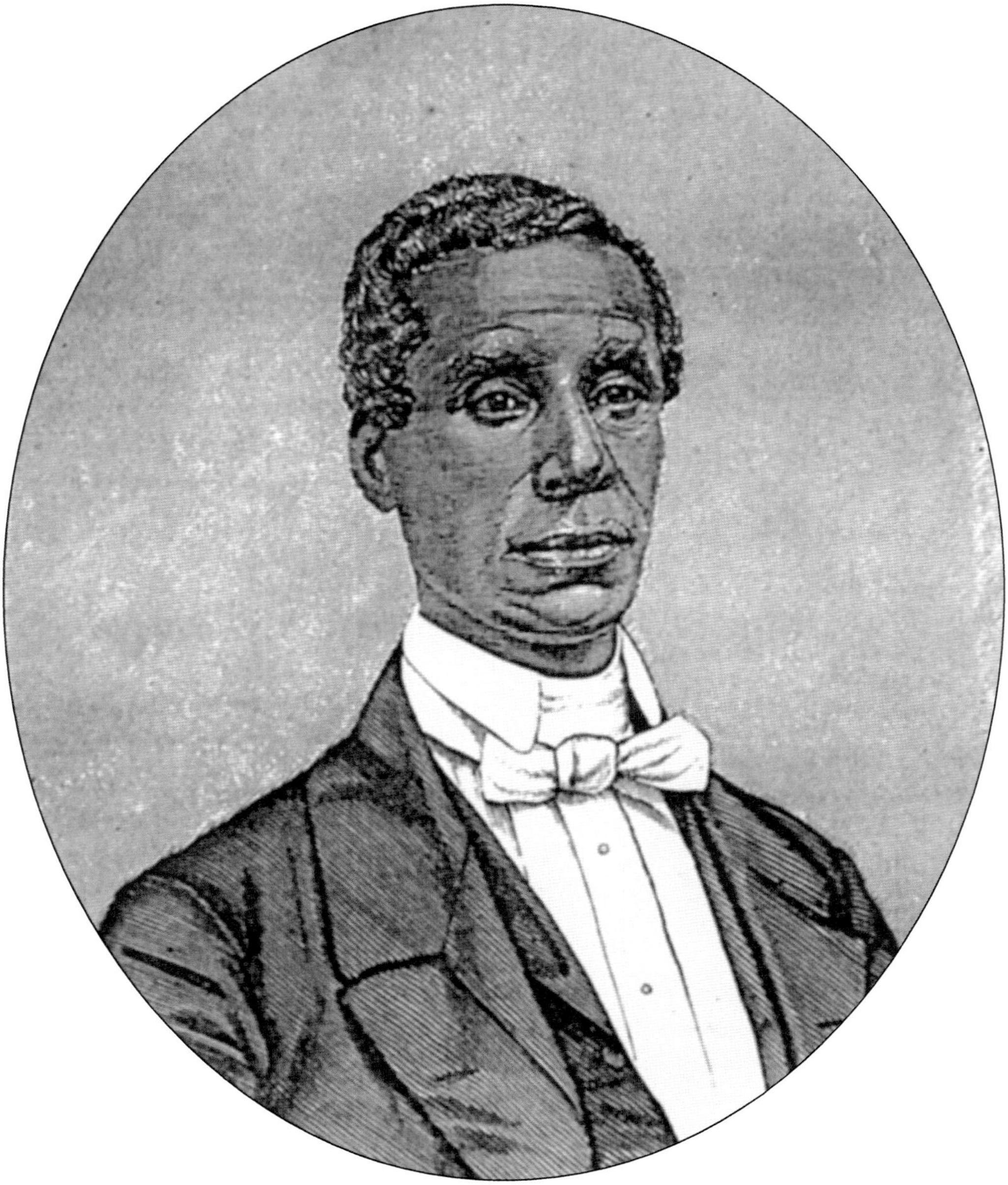

Francis Burns was an African American born in Albany on December 15, 1809. Bennet Atwood was a Windham farmer in North Settlement on Route 10. Atwood went to Albany on business in 1813 and asked Burns's parents if their four-year-old child could accompany him as an indentured servant until the age of 21. In return, Atwood promised to feed, clothe, and educate Francis. The parents agreed, and Burns came to Windham. The Atwoods were devout Methodists and did as promised. Francis's life was filled with accomplishments that had not been achieved by any other African Americans at that time: he attended an all-white public school system in Windham and excelled in his studies; at 17 years old in 1827, he became an ordained Methodist minister and preached at local Windham churches; in 1834, he became America's first black missionary and was sent to Liberia; and in 1858, he became America's first ordained African American bishop. Francis suffered from malaria during his entire 29 years in Liberia and died in Baltimore in 1863.

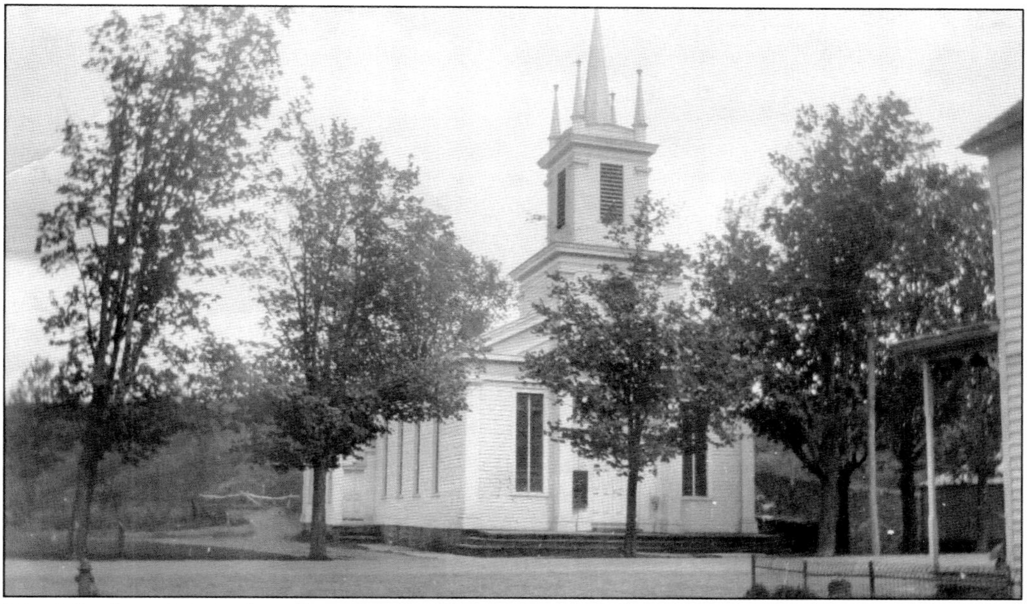

The Windham Methodist Church was built in 1843, and the bell tower, clock, steeple, vestibule, and fellowship hall in the back were added in 1866. The tradition then when a resident died was to ring the bell a number of times equaling the deceased person's age. The Methodist revival that swept America during the colonial times explains why the area had eight Methodist churches at one time. In the late 1800s, Greene County had 32 Methodist churches with over 9,000 attendees. The four small spires around the base of the steeple were removed in the 1920s. In the photograph below, a 14-member children's choir gathers outside the Windham Methodist Church after services in 1955. There were also an adult choir and a large Sunday school class at the time.

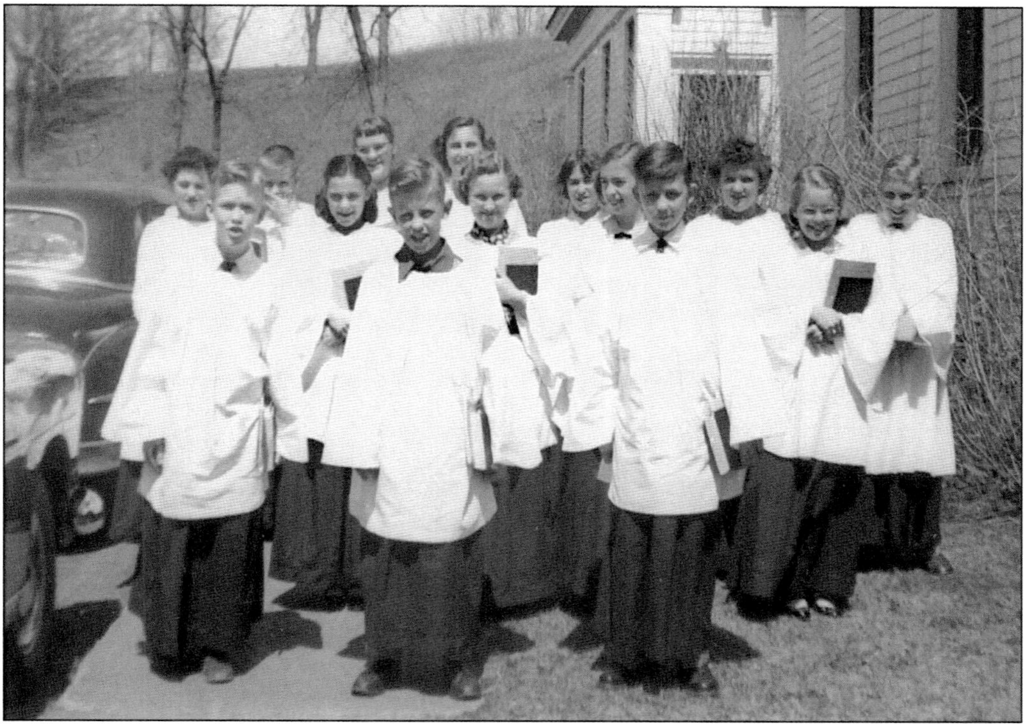

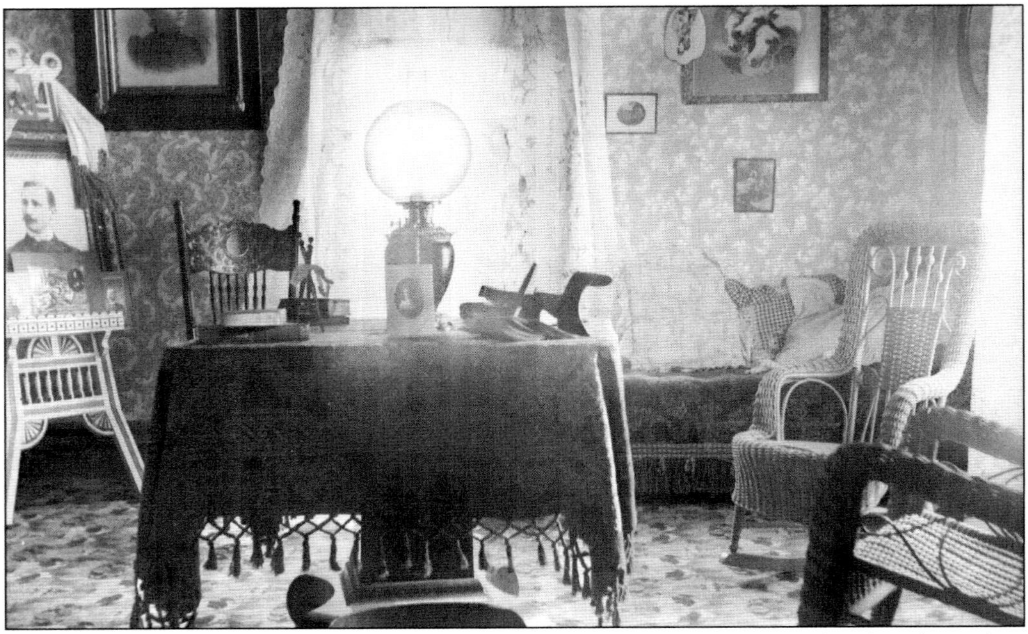

When the new Windham Methodist Church parsonage was built in 1902, the church's Ladies' Aid Society worked diligently to make it "one of the best equipped parsonages in the Kingston District," according to the *Windham Journal*. They immediately started fundraisers to purchase the newest appliances and furniture of the day and succeeded in very short order. The 1904 picture above is of the parsonage back parlor, with the gas lamp on the table and fine furniture throughout. The dining room below shows that their work had produced the desired results. Note the gas lamp mounted on the doorframe at the top of the picture below. The lamp is gone, but the gas line and mounting hole can still be seen today. Back then, gas lines were built into the walls and framework at locations where lamps would be mounted for lighting.

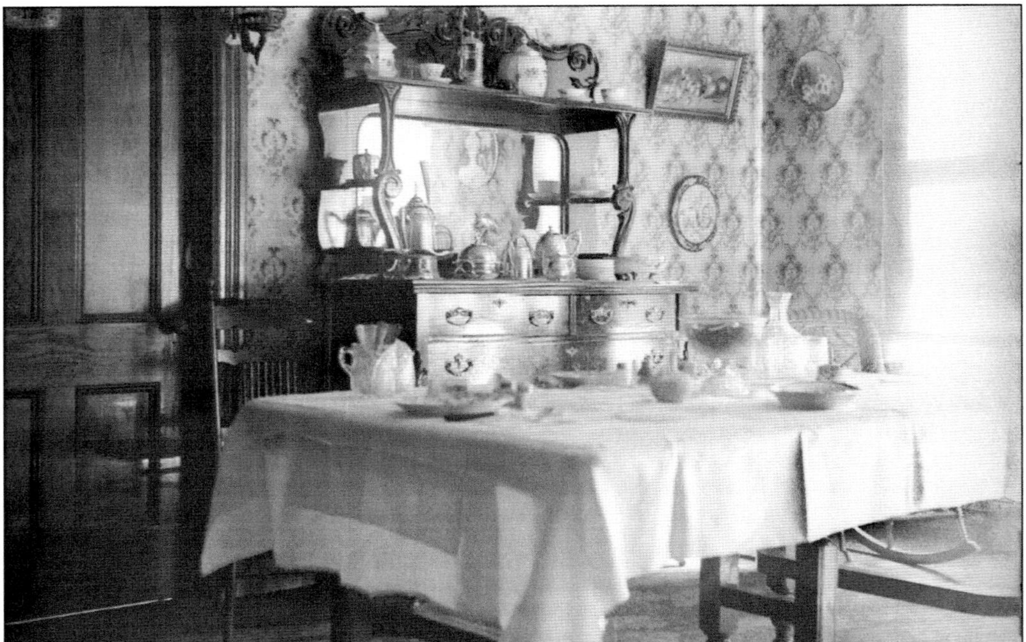

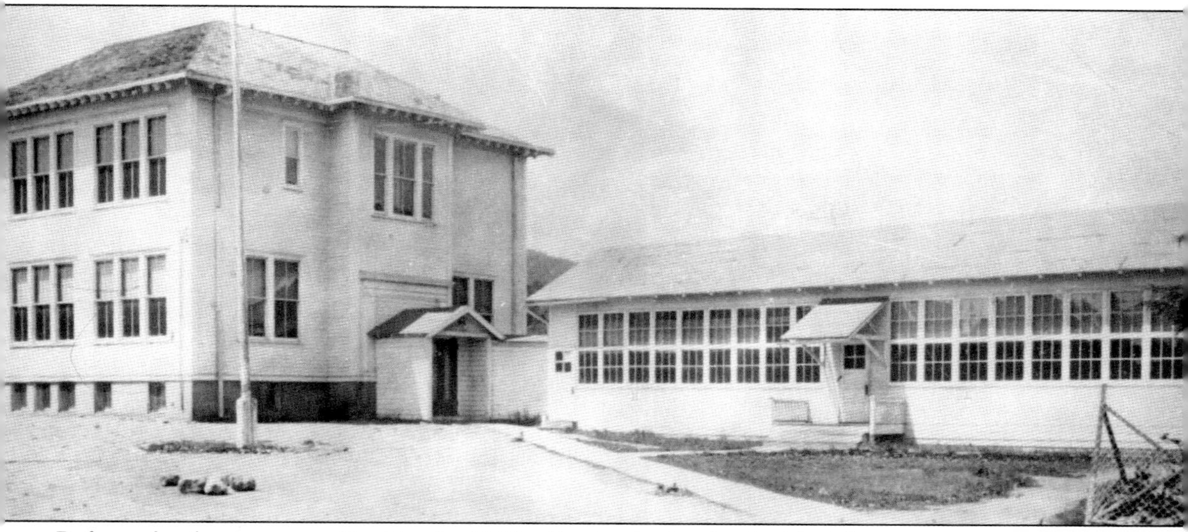

Before schools were centralized in the 1930s, districts had individual buildings most commonly referred to as one-room schoolhouses. In 1882, Windham had 10 school districts: East Windham, Upper Big Hollow (Maplecrest), Windham, Hensonville, Lower Big Hollow, Stump Hollow (Nauvoo Road area), Mitchell Hollow, Big Hollow, Bell District (Mitchell Hollow Road), and Pelham District, which was most likely the Union Society area at the east end of Old Road. There were 386 school-age children living in Windham, but only 301 attended school. No doubt, the missing 85 children were older and working on their family farms. A teacher's weekly pay ranged from a low of $3.25 in Upper Big Hollow, with 15 children, to a high of $14 in Windham, with 86 children. The monthly wage of $13.28 in 1882 was up from $9.58 in 1844. This schoolhouse stood on the site of the present Windham-Ashland-Jewett Central School.

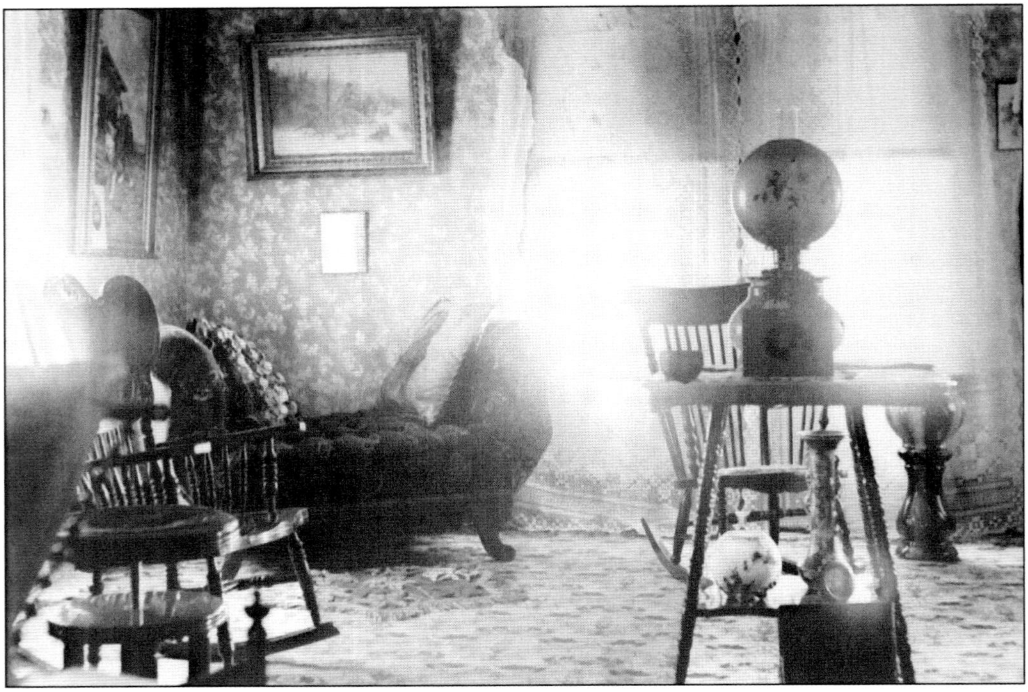

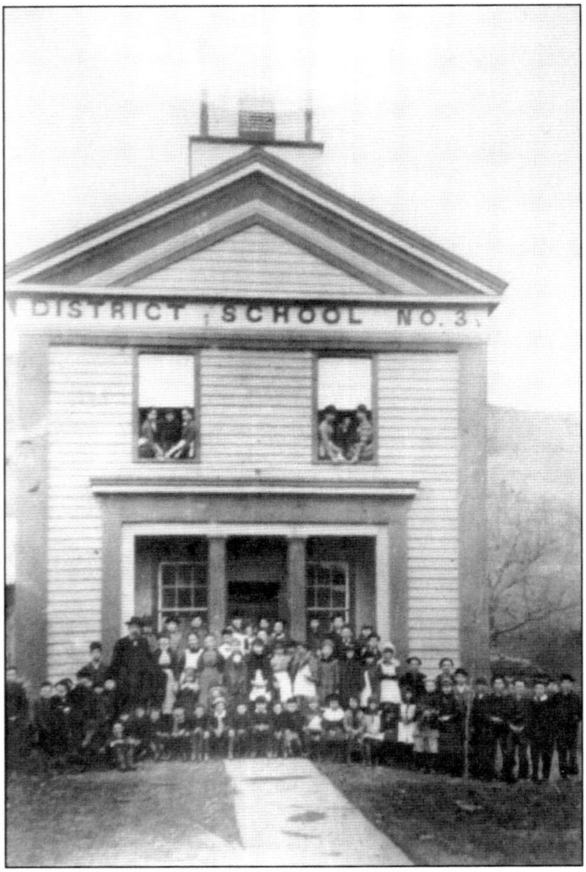

This 1904 photograph of the Windham Methodist Church parsonage living room illustrates how well the Ladies' Aid Society furnished the house for the pastor and his family. They bought the best items available, and when it was completed, they had a showcase home. The table in the foreground right is the only piece of the original furniture still in the house today.

The first settlers in Windham knew how important education was and built many schoolhouses around the mountainsides. This early-1900s picture is of Windham's District No. 3 School, which was on the site where the current Masonic Temple is. Windham village had the largest school building, but there were as many as 12 school districts within the town's boundaries at one time before it was centralized.

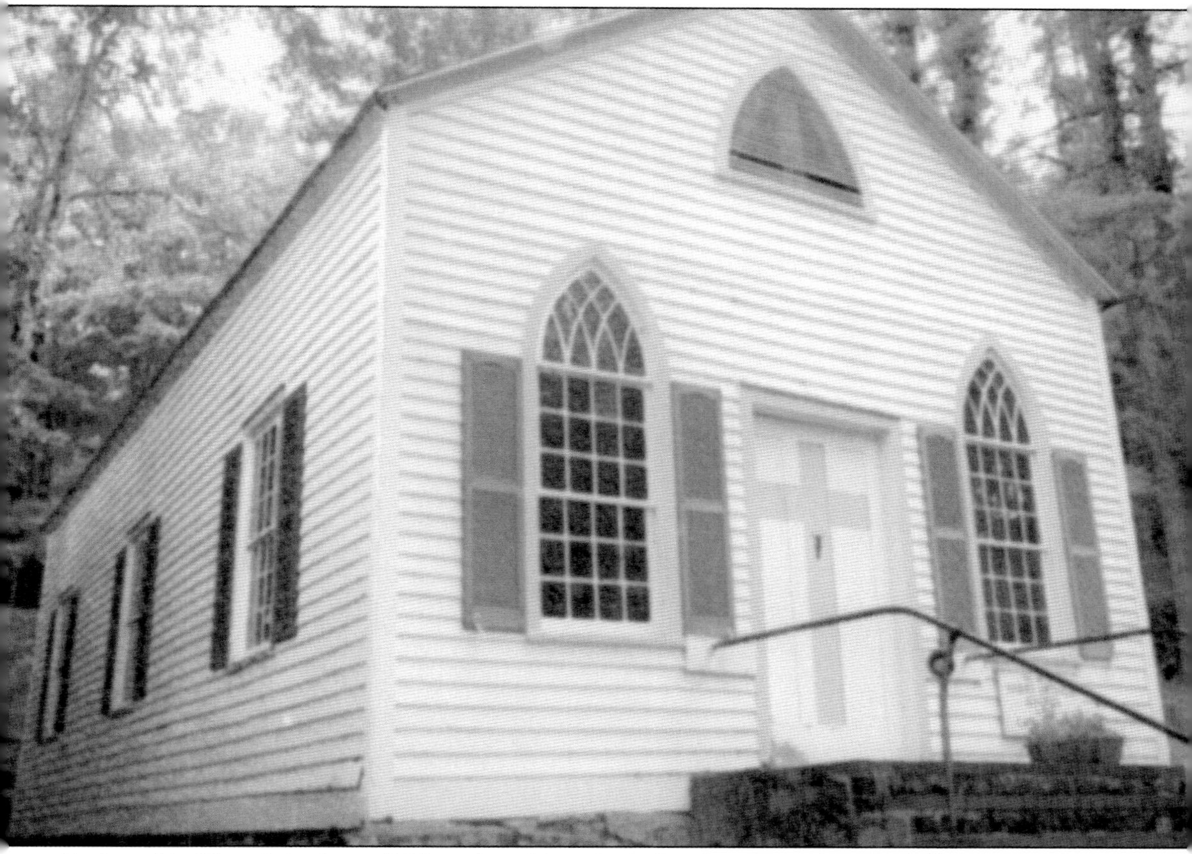

St. Joseph's Chapel, built in 1830, is the oldest Catholic church in the Catskill Mountains. Originally in old Windham, it is now within Ashland's borders. The second Catholic church in Windham was St. Theresa of the Child Jesus, built in 1926; it burned down on February 6, 1962. A new structure was quickly built as a replacement and stands today. The very first churches in Old Windham were Old School Baptist Church in Lexington (established October 25, 1790), Dutch Reformed Church of Windham, later named Prattsville (1798), Trinity Episcopal Church (1799), First Congregational Church (1799) at the Old Meeting House, and Big Hollow Congregational Church (1802). Eventually, the Presbyterians, Episcopalians, and Methodists left the Old Meeting House to build their own churches as the various towns were established. Many of those churches built in the early 1800s are still standing. Other, later churches include Big Hollow (Maplecrest) Free Methodist Church (1871), Mitchell Hollow Chapel (1899), Greek Church of the Assumption, Hope Restoration Christian Fellowship, and Mitchell Hollow Mission Church.

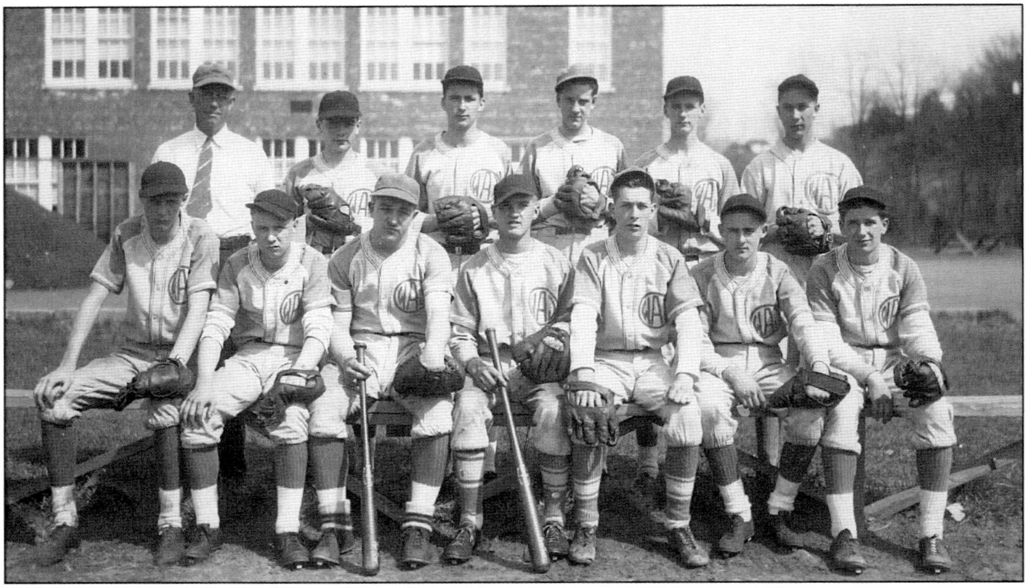

The 1945 Windham-Ashland-Jewett Central School baseball team poses for the camera outside the school on Main Street. The enrollment for kindergarten through 12th grade has remained steady at around 500 students from its opening to the present day. The sports and music programs, along with academic achievements, have always been an important part of the community.

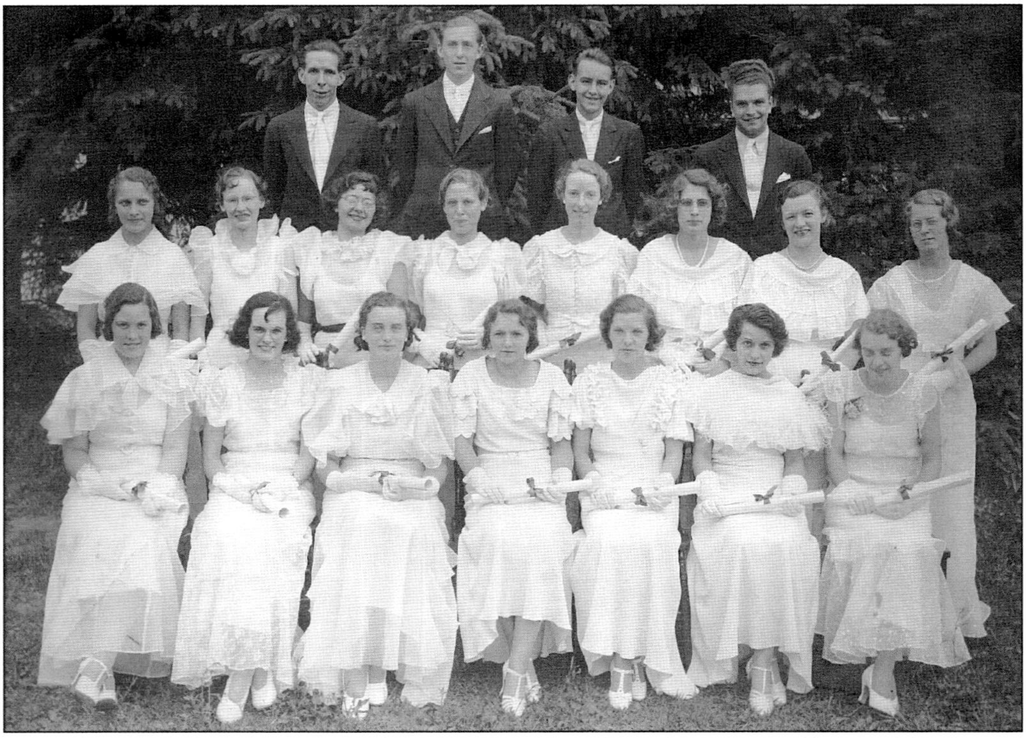

Seen here, the class of 1934 was the first to graduate from the new Windham-Ashland-Jewett Central School building in Windham. Previous to the centralized school district concept, the proverbial one-room schoolhouses dotted the countryside in each town. Combining the three towns into one school district merged resources and led to greater efficiency.

Seven

SUMMER FUN

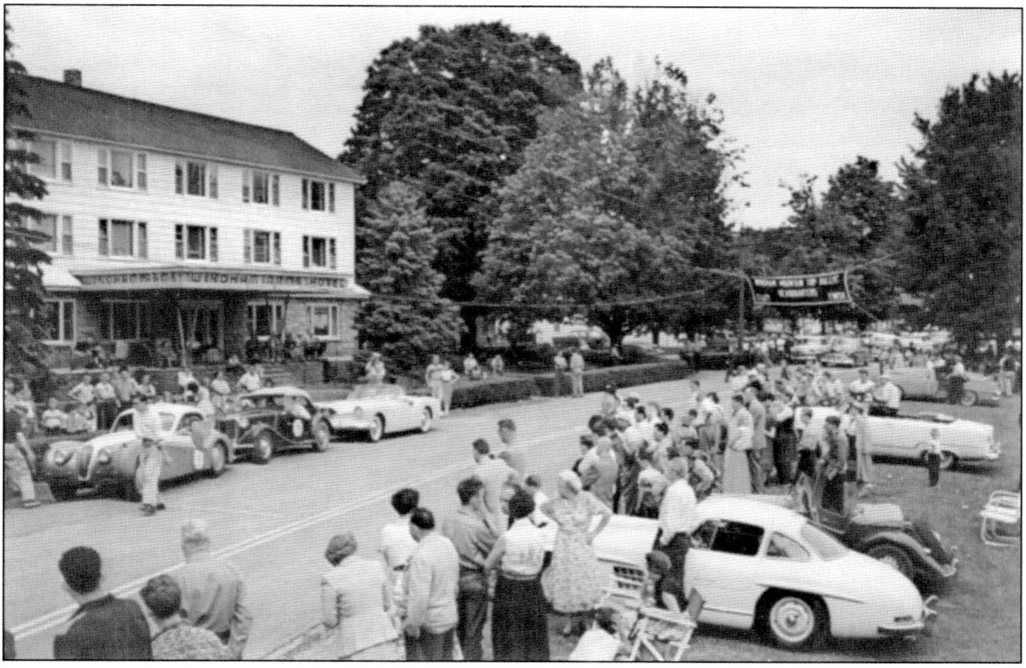

In the late 1950s, Windham made a name for itself in the sports world with competitive sports car rallies through the challenging mountain roads. In one national magazine article, the sportswriter commented, "Windham was so beautiful it should have been painted by Grandma Moses." Seen here is the starting point in front of the Windham Arms Hotel.

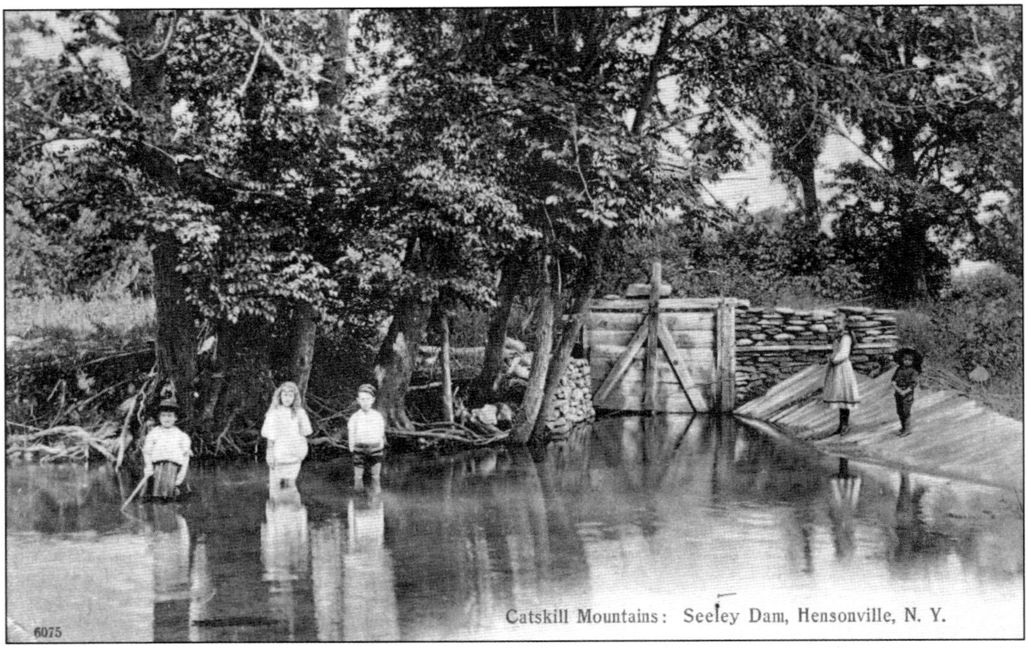

In this 1908 postcard, the Seeley Dam in Hensonville created a swimming hole on Batavia Kill for children of all ages to enjoy. Secret swimming and fishing spots were shared with the summer boarders when they arrived. Many dams were built for waterpower as well as recreation. All too often, the poorly built ones would fail in high water, sending a torrent downstream that caused severe damage.

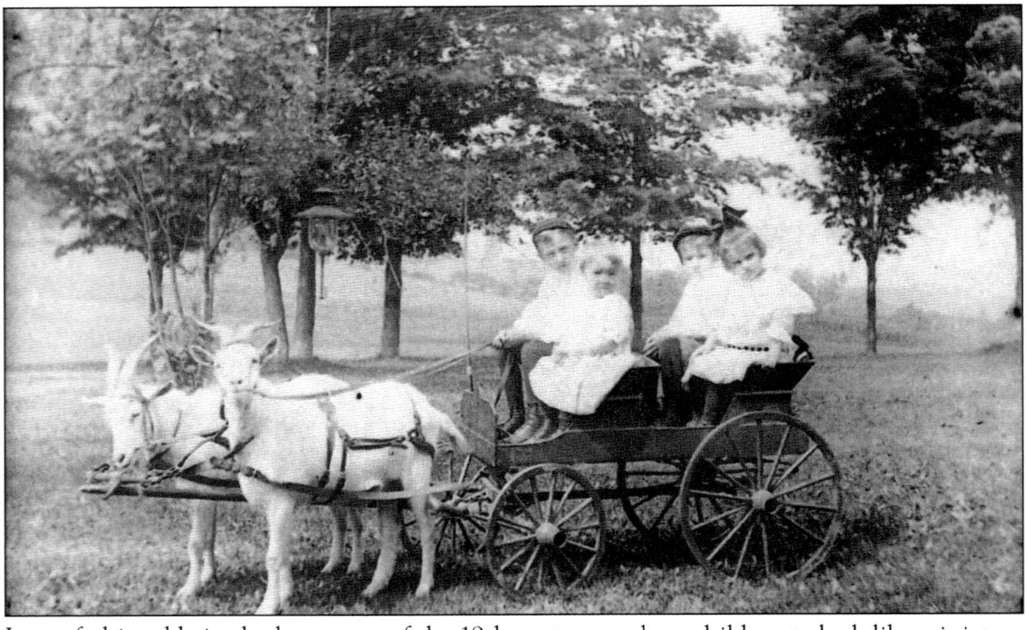

It was fashionable in the latter part of the 19th century to dress children to look like miniature adults, even to the point of outfitting them with equally miniature paraphernalia, such as the wagon seen here. But some things could not be duplicated, and since there were no horses small enough, goats had to be used. It was an imitation of a popular practice in England during the Victorian era.

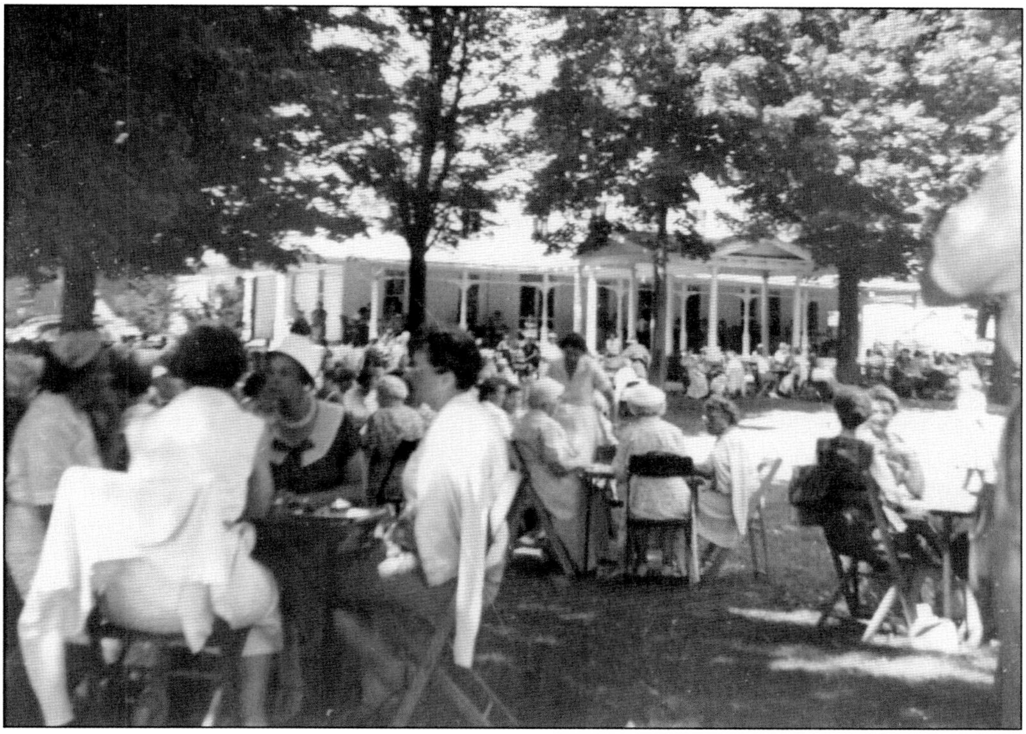

Events for boarders in Windham were organized by the hotels, businesses, or the town to entertain the guests throughout the summer. In the photograph above, tables set up in the cool shade on Crest Park's lawn provided comfort for all to enjoy a card tournament sponsored by the Catholic church. This was done each week at different hotels, and the guests loved the affairs. Other events such as bingo, golf tournaments, softball games, shuffleboard, Fourth of July celebrations, road rallies, and antique car shows were all part of the Windham resort experience. The town had two movie theaters, a theme park, and horse-riding ranches, as well as countless gift shops and restaurants. Many of the guests themselves would organize the events, which added to the entertainment, as pictured below.

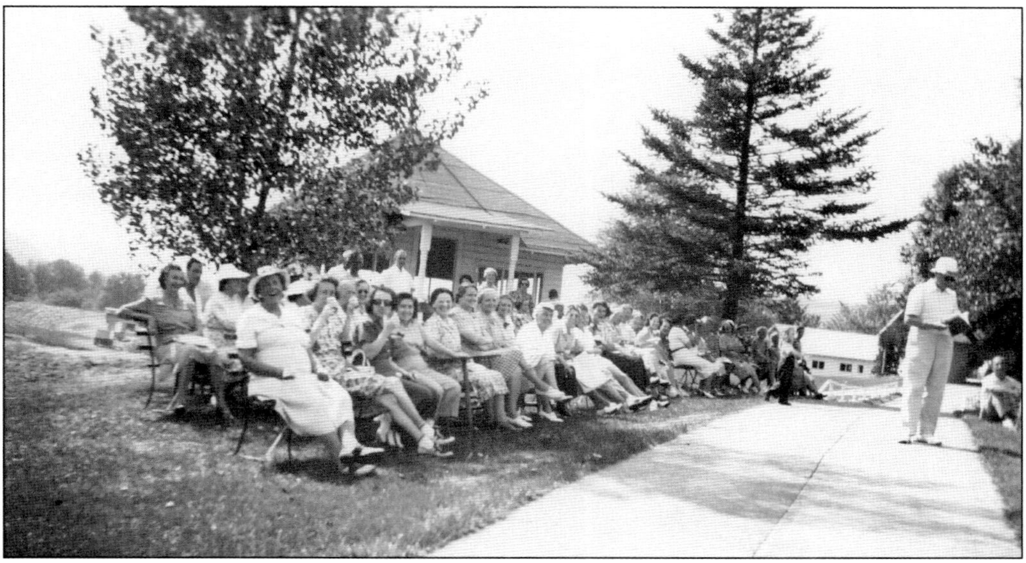

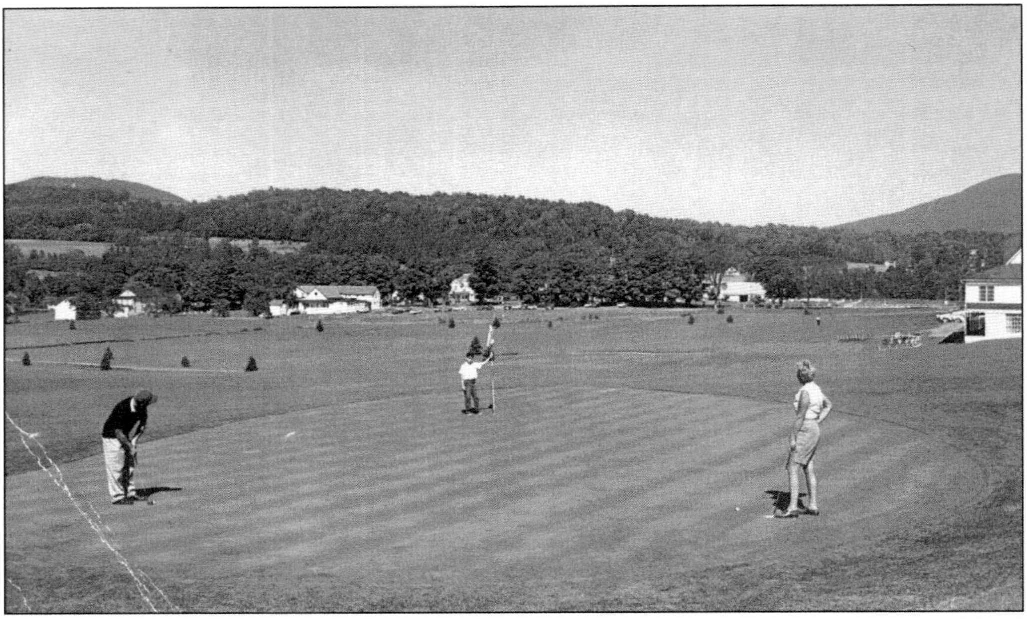

The Windham Country Club was formed on 75 acres on South Street in 1927 by several local businessmen. The nine-hole golf course and clubhouse became one of the most popular summer attractions in Windham. In the 1960s, it was expanded to 18 holes, and today, it is one of the most picturesque golf courses found in the Catskill Mountains.

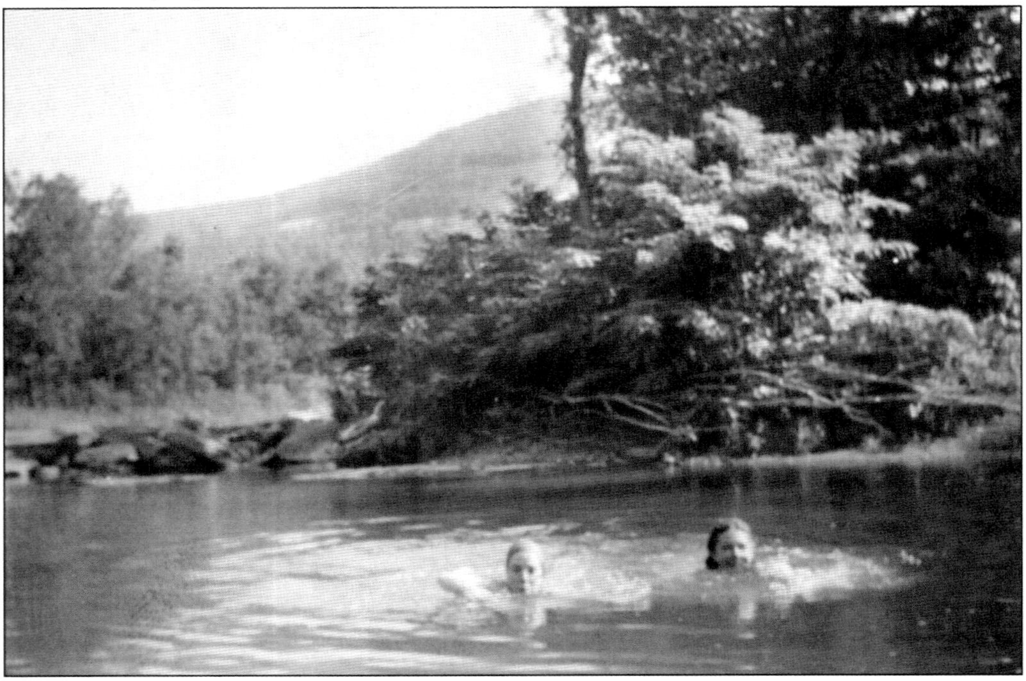

Local swimming holes, such as this one on Batavia Kill, were attractions for Windham residents. The summer guests, especially children, would seek them out to enjoy the entire summer. In this 1938 photograph, Harriett Munson (left) and Marge Usher enjoy the cool water. Deep pools perfect for swimming were common along the stream until it was leveled and widened in the 1960s for flood control.

It is hard to imagine the tenacity of people who were willing to drive up the primitive dirt road to the top of Mount Pisgah for entertainment and the panoramic view of the Hudson Valley and Catskill Mountains. The photograph above shows the road used to climb more than 1,000 feet, which must have taxed them and their horses to their limits. Nevertheless, the view from the summit of Mount Pisgah was second to none, drawing thousands every summer when it was operated by the Doolittle family. In 1883, there were 2,500 names recorded in the sign-in book at the summit with an estimated 1,000 more that had not signed. A picnic was a common venture while enjoying the view, as demonstrated in the photograph below. Today, the mountain is owned by New York State and is part of the Catskill Mountain State Park.

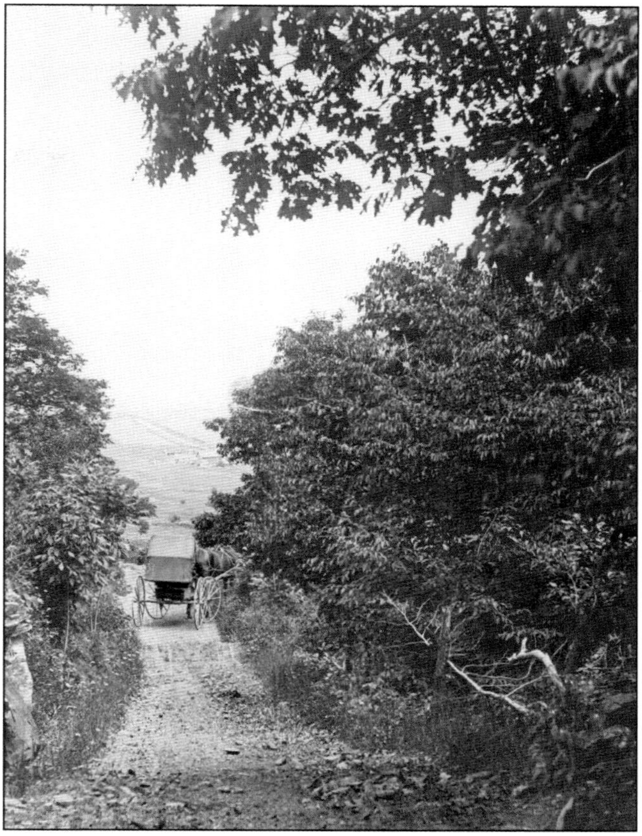

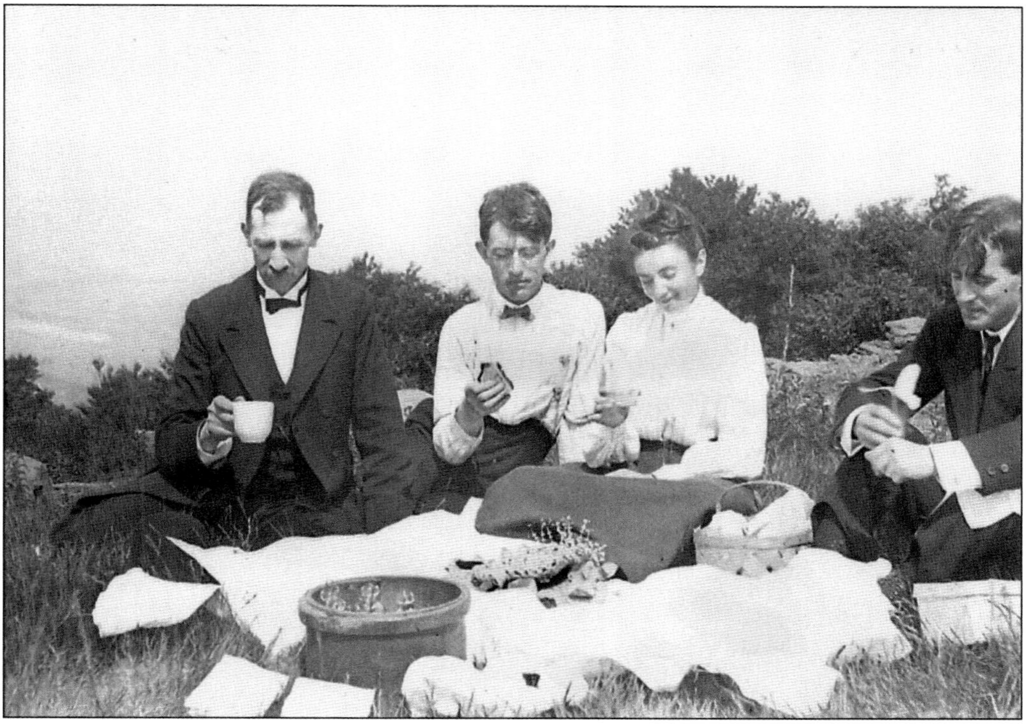

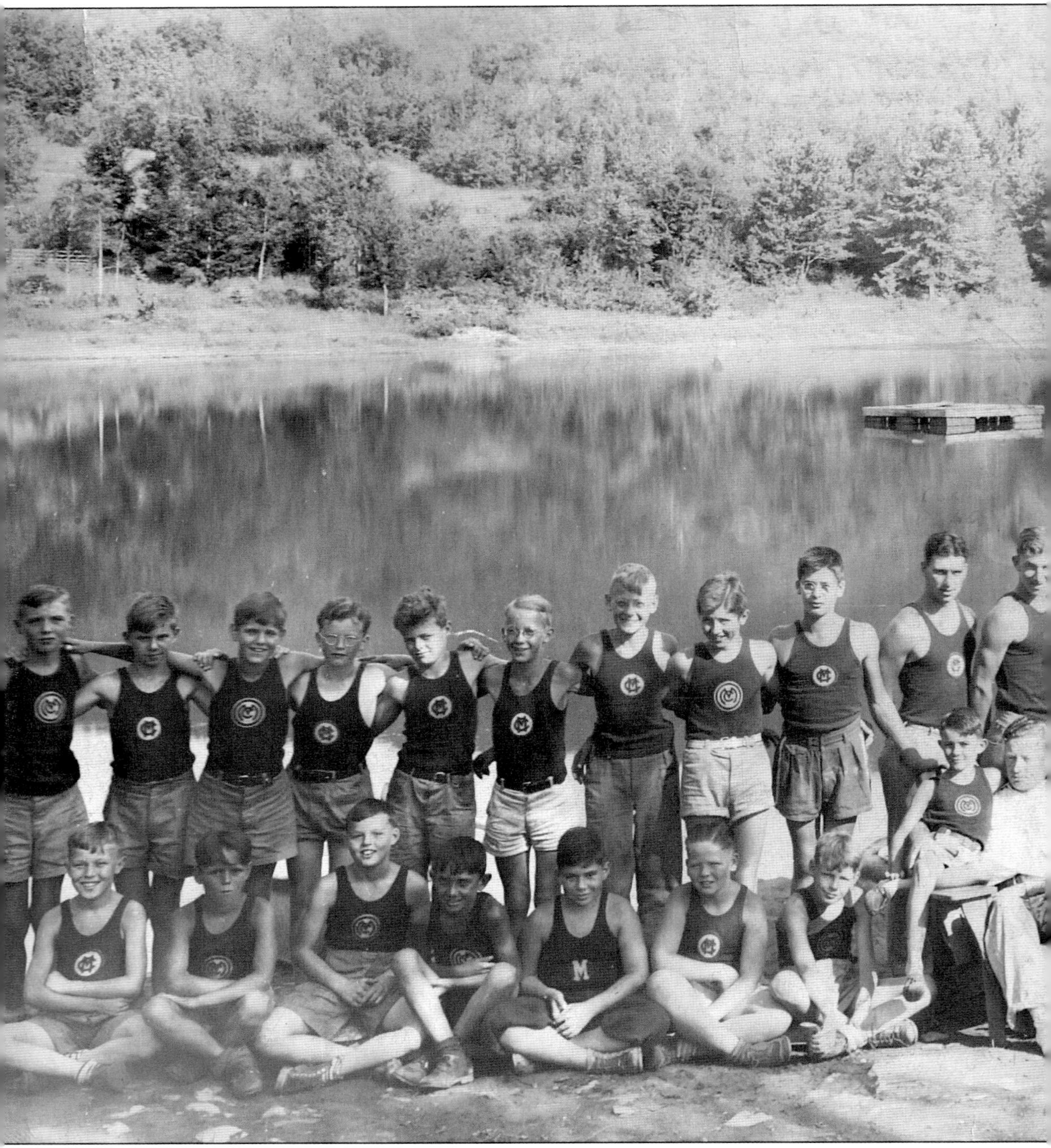

Camp Mohawk brought boys from the New Jersey area to Windham for summer recreation, as seen in this late-1930s photograph. Beautiful Lake Heloise is located at the end of Nauvoo Road, which is surrounded by Ginseng Mountain and Mount Hayden. It is not a natural lake but was created by a large dam built on the south side in the late 1800s. Ted Davis married Opal Seeley,

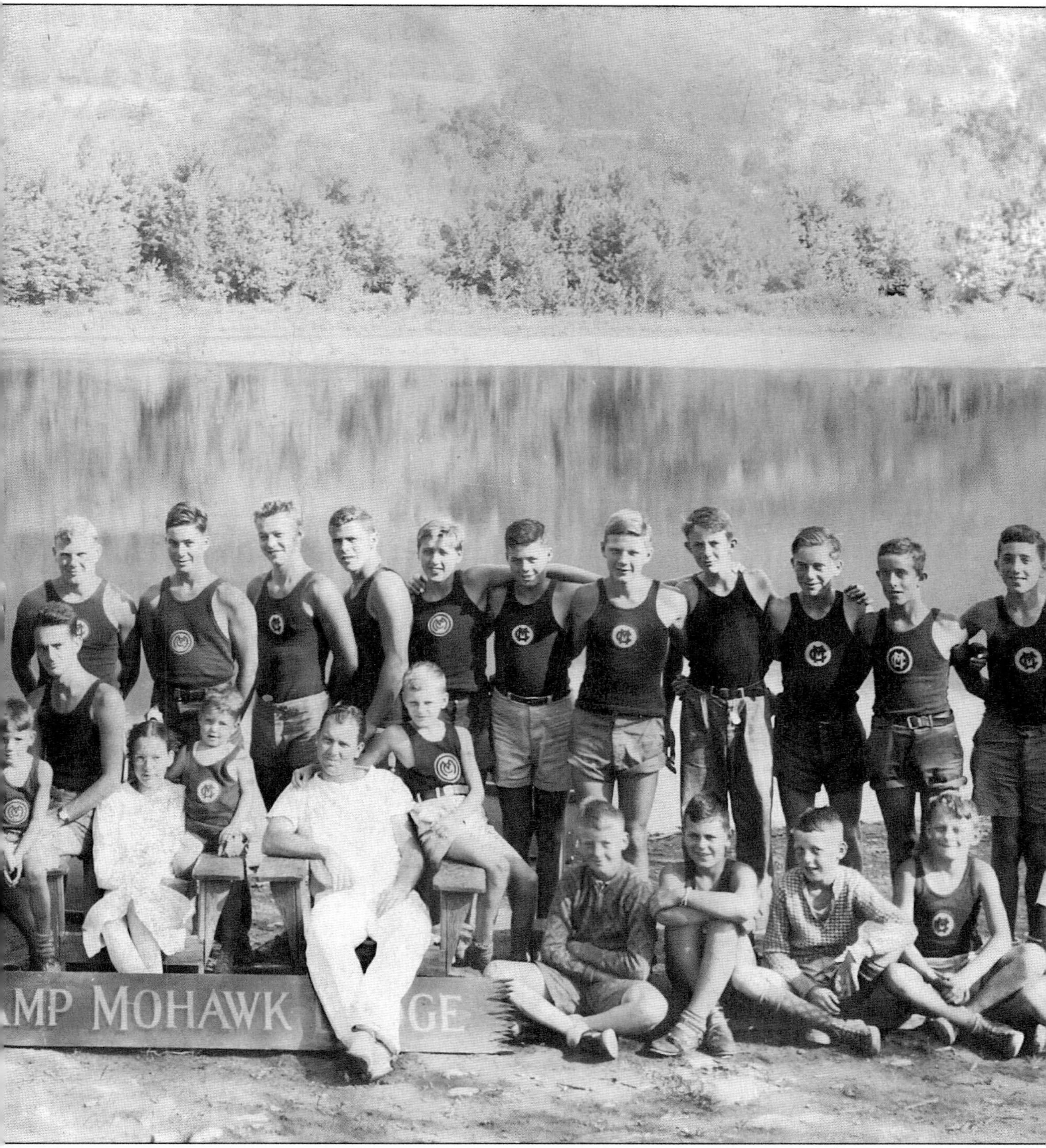

whose family owned the lake. By the mid-1900s, campsites were built in the woods on the east side of the lake and operated for many years as White Birches Campground. Ted is seated on the right in white clothes with Phoebe Munson seated in center. Also in the photograph, in the second row, are Ted's brothers Donald (10th from left) and Bill (12th from left).

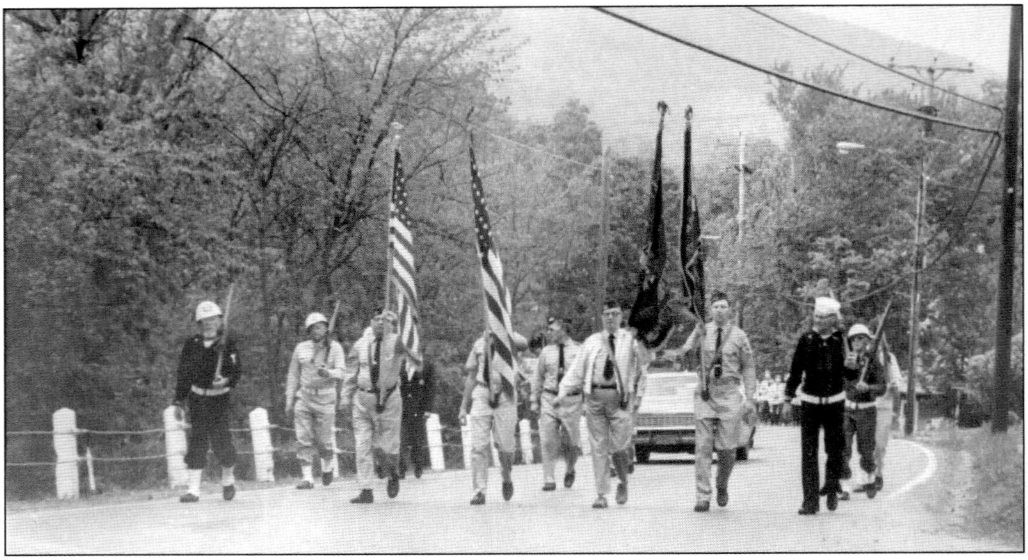

The parade colors lead the march through Windham in this c. 1963 image taken during the annual Fourth of July celebration of a parade and fireworks. The Windham Hose Company sponsors the event, which draws huge crowds and participants from several towns and spectators for miles around. The parade route today runs through the town and terminates at the base lodge of the ski slope for fireworks. (Courtesy of Windham Historical Society.)

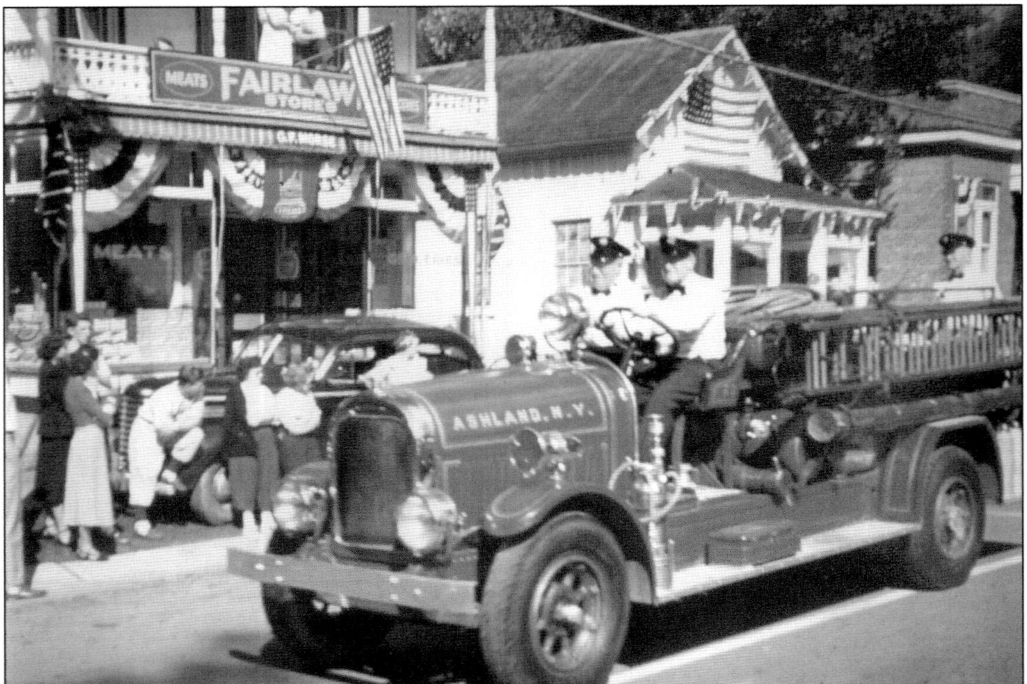

During this July 4, 1952, parade in Windham, the Ashland fire truck passes in front of Morse's Grocery. Over many decades, Windham had become the town with the largest parade and fireworks, which drew thousands. There was competition in various categories between the floats from businesses and boardinghouses. (Courtesy of Richard and Ruth Morse.)

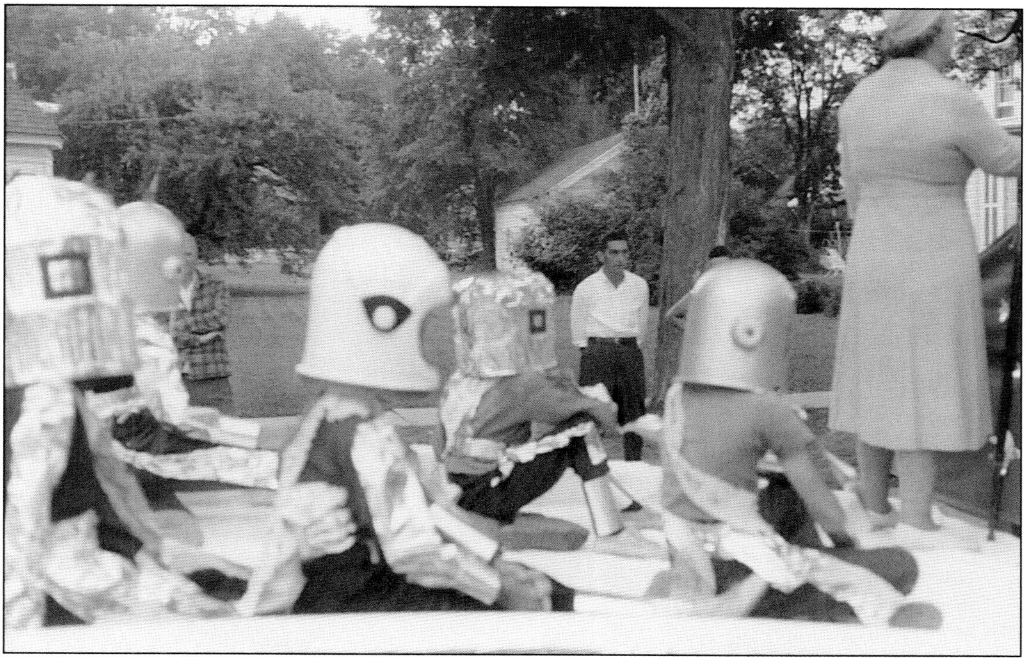

In the picture above, the 1962 Fourth of July parade float has a space travel theme, a popular subject matter of the time. Creative imaginations at area businesses would conjure up the most ingenious themes and methods to make the floats. The kids that did not have a helmet made one out of tin foil, which also covers the entire float. The photograph below shows the floats as they pass in front of Miller Brothers store. Cole's Pleasant View boardinghouse (second float) was located about two miles west of Windham near Old Road. The large hotel building is no longer there. Following behind is the Quinn's Service Station float. The Quinns had operated an automotive repair business on the west end of Windham.

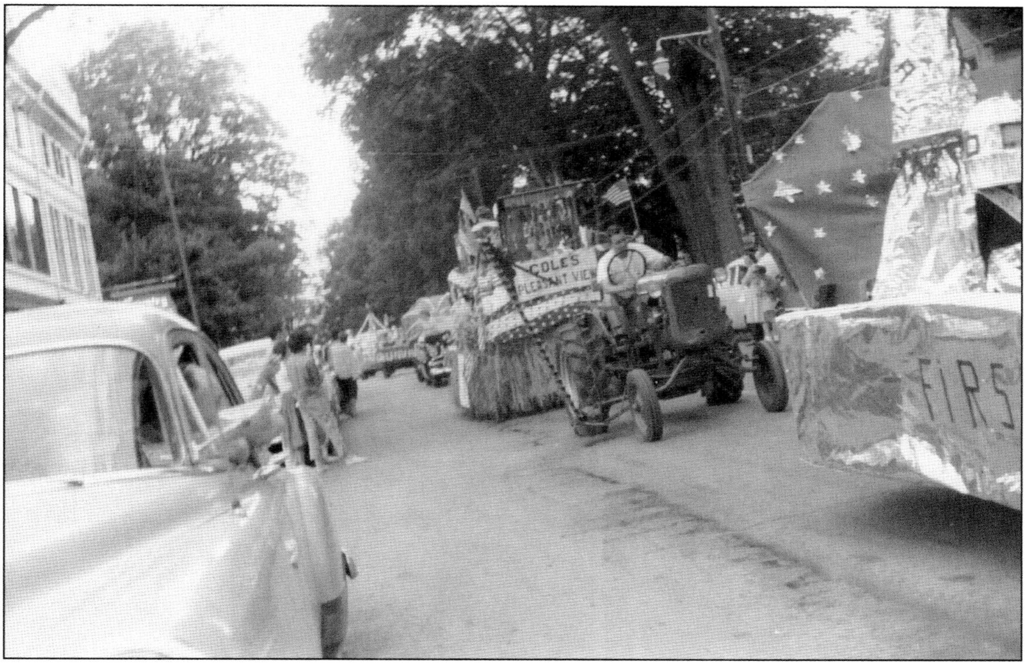

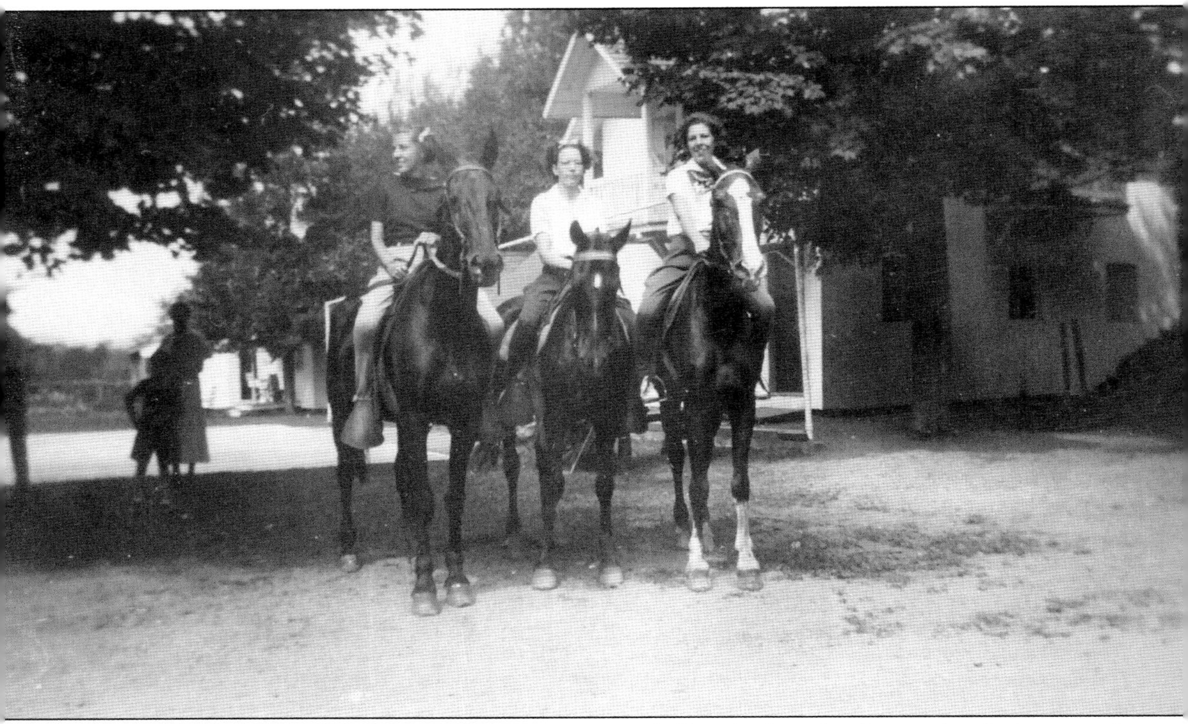

Horseback riding, one of the many activities provided by the boardinghouses for their guests, is yet another example of how the farms and boardinghouses complemented each other. In this mid-1930s photograph, from left to right, are Jan Schultz, Phoebe Munson, and Marge Usher at Crest Park. (Courtesy of Christopher Garraghan.)

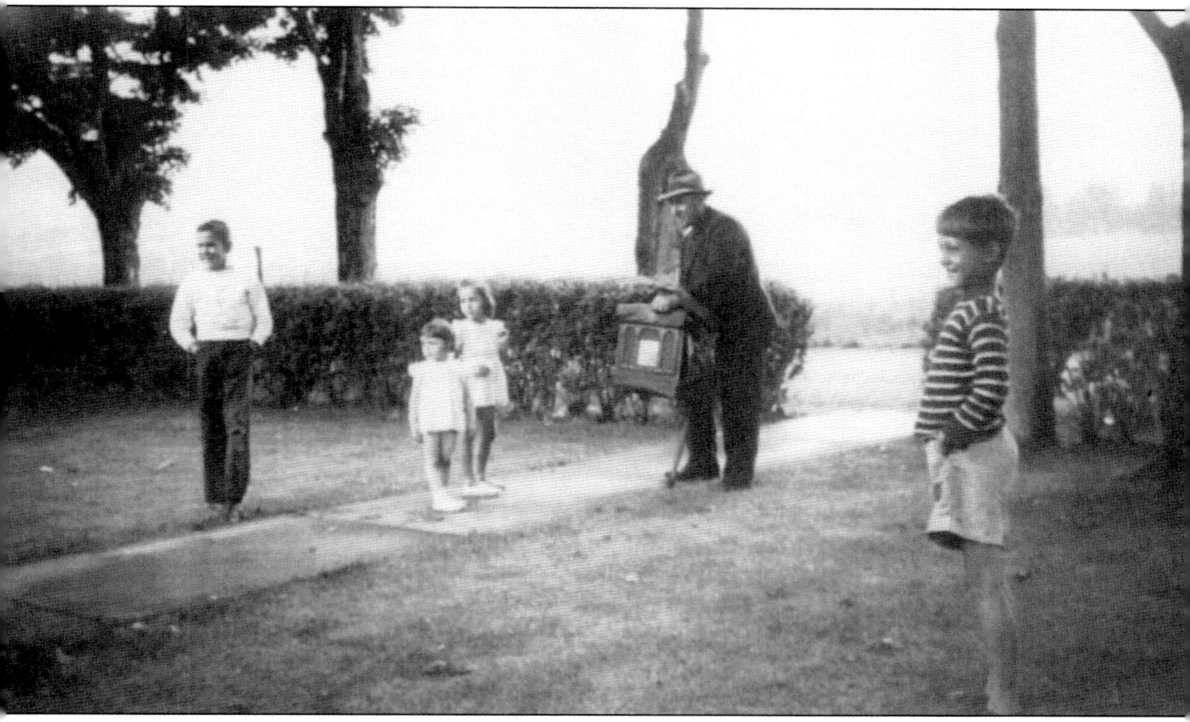

Entertainment for the boardinghouse guests was a high priority. Here, a gypsy organ grinder complete with a dancing monkey (out of frame) brings smiles to the kids at the Westmere in 1941. One-man bands, traveling circuses, and performers of all kinds traveled through Windham, stopping at boardinghouses, putting on shows, and passing the hat for their pay. Guests thoroughly enjoyed these impromptu acts. (Courtesy of Harold and Evelyn Munson.)

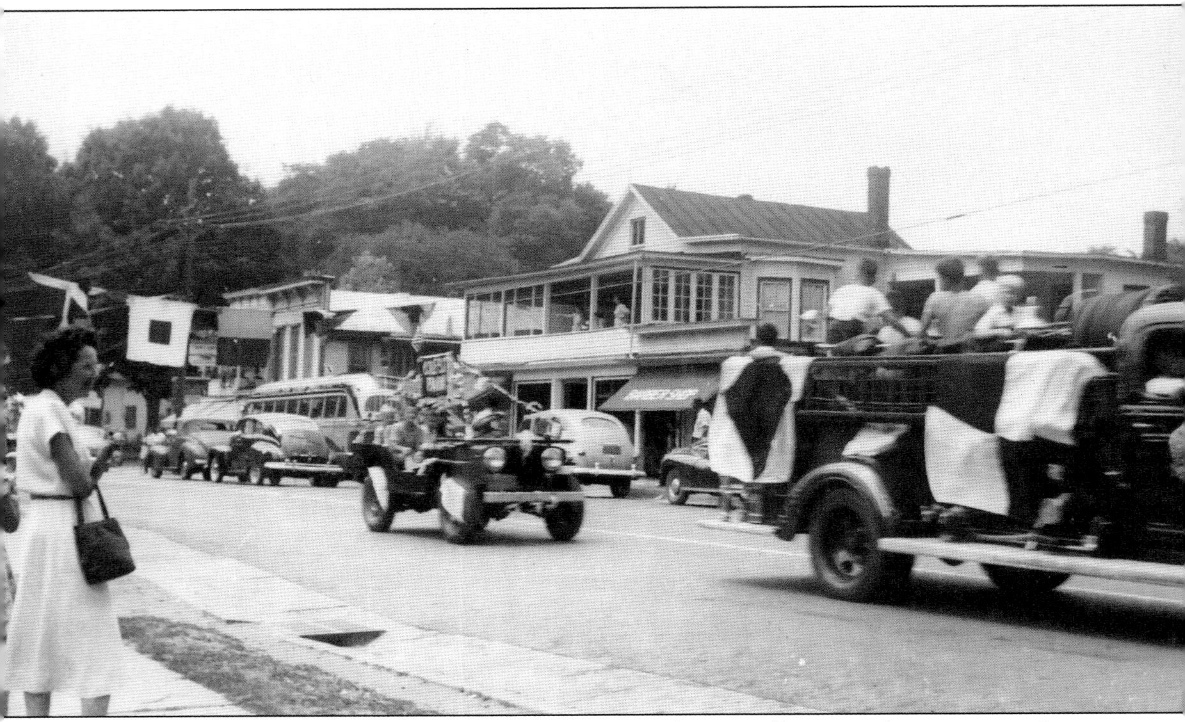

A typical Windham Fourth of July parade in the early 1950s illustrates the turnout such events created among residents and summer guests alike. The sign on top of the jeep says it represents the Crest Park boardinghouse. Floats were a fun project for workers and guests to make for the parade, which had numerous entries from area businesses.

Eight

After the Summer

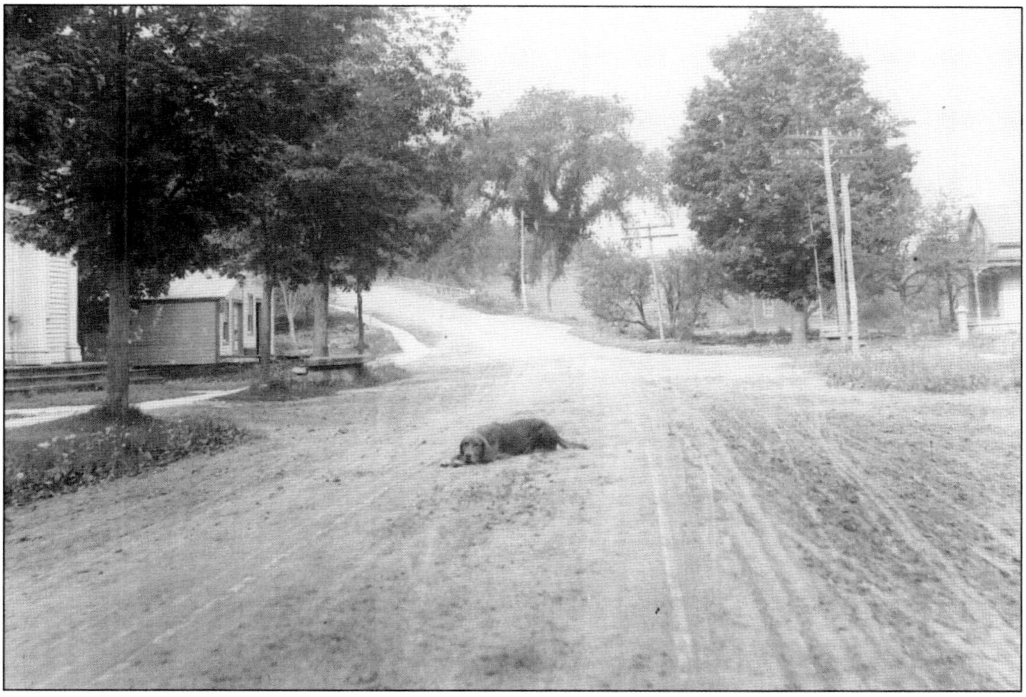

When the immense workload of summer was over, even the dogs had to rest, as this 1906 picture on the east end of town attests to. In 1890, it was reported that the Greene County population swelled from about 30,000 residents to well over 70,000 summer boarders. There were over 900 boardinghouses operating in Greene County at the time, and Windham had a large share of that number.

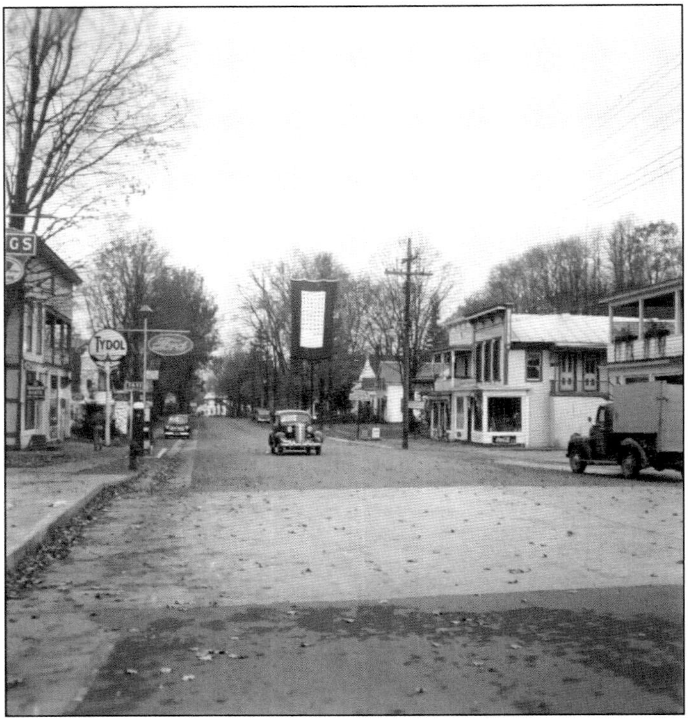

When the Labor Day weekend in September came to a close, every boardinghouse was empty as the summer visitors returned to their homes in the cities. Windham returned once again to being a calm, pastoral town, as this 1940s photograph of Main Street shows. By October, the leaves had fallen as the town braced for the coming winter. Residents could rest as another busy season passed.

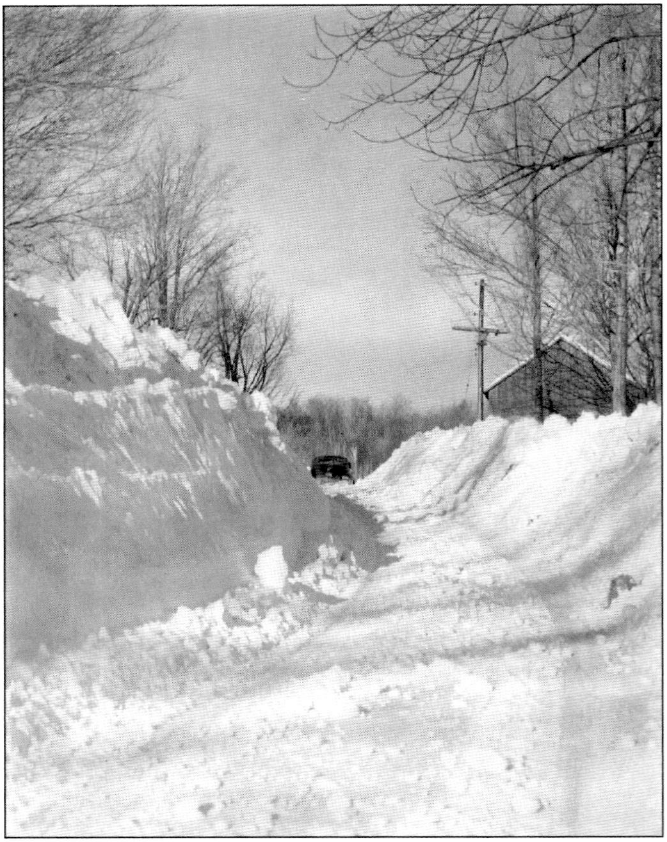

Windham's isolation from the outside world in winter was nearly total, as this 1940s picture on Begley Road illustrates. The mountain road ascending to Windham in winter was a very difficult climb, and a traveler had to have a very good reason to go there. (Courtesy of Richard and Ruth Morse.)

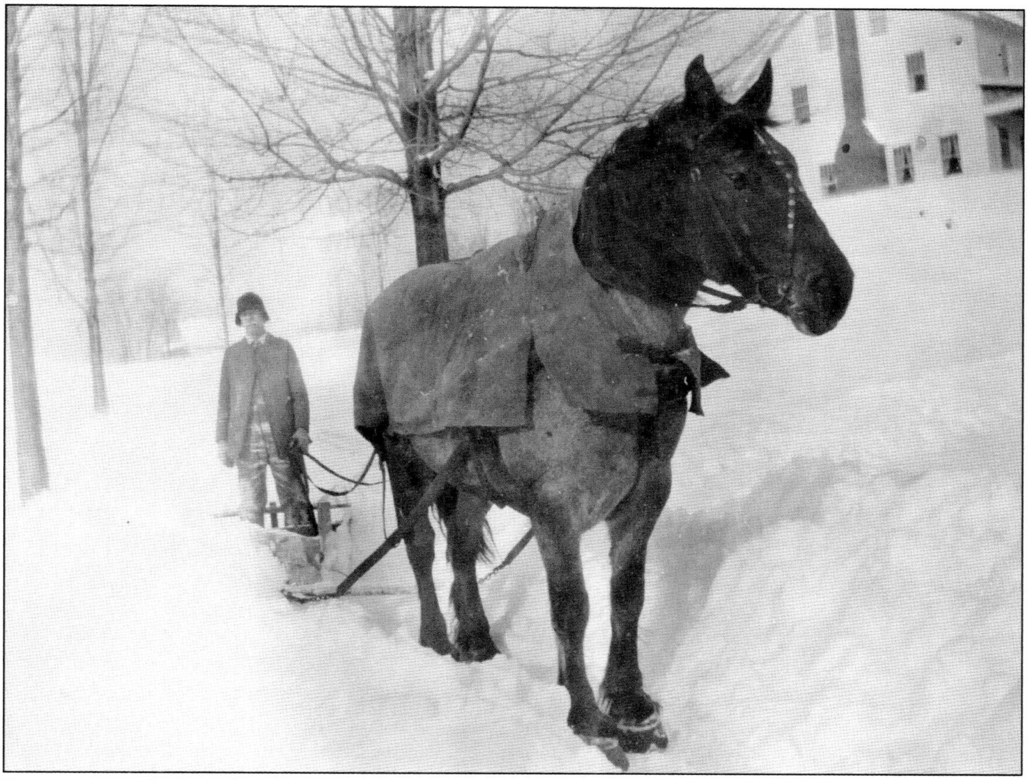

Snow removal of any kind in Windham was no easy matter prior to 1960. Above, Elmer Munson shows how it was done in 1926 with his horse Old Grey. Even when vacant through the winter months, the buildings at each boardinghouse required attention. Snow weight, as seen in the photograph below, could collapse roofs. Interior leaks had to be checked constantly, as damage could be expensive.

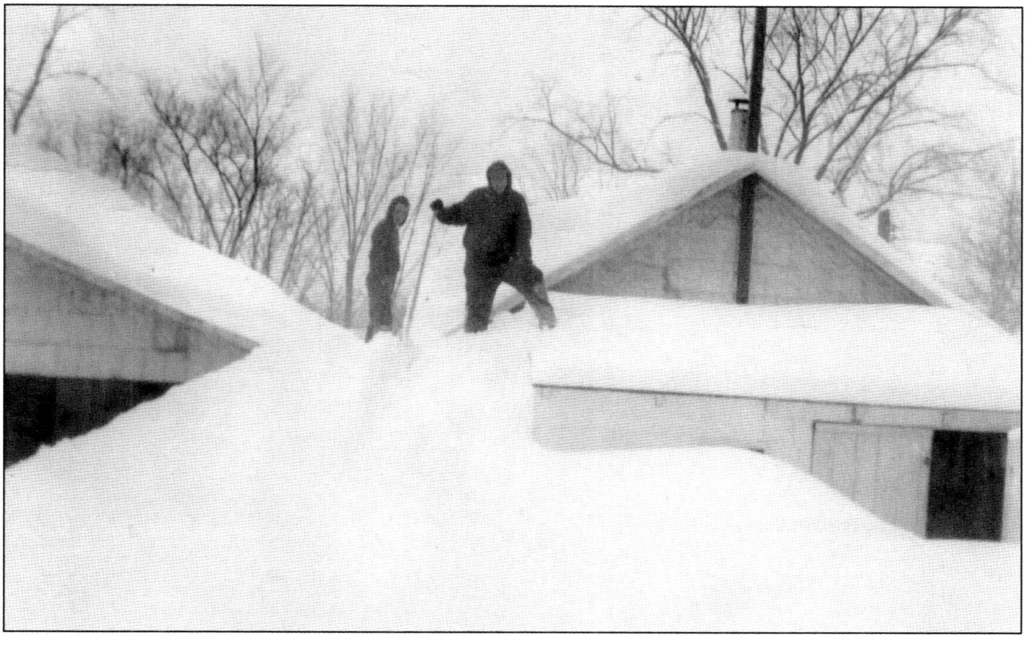

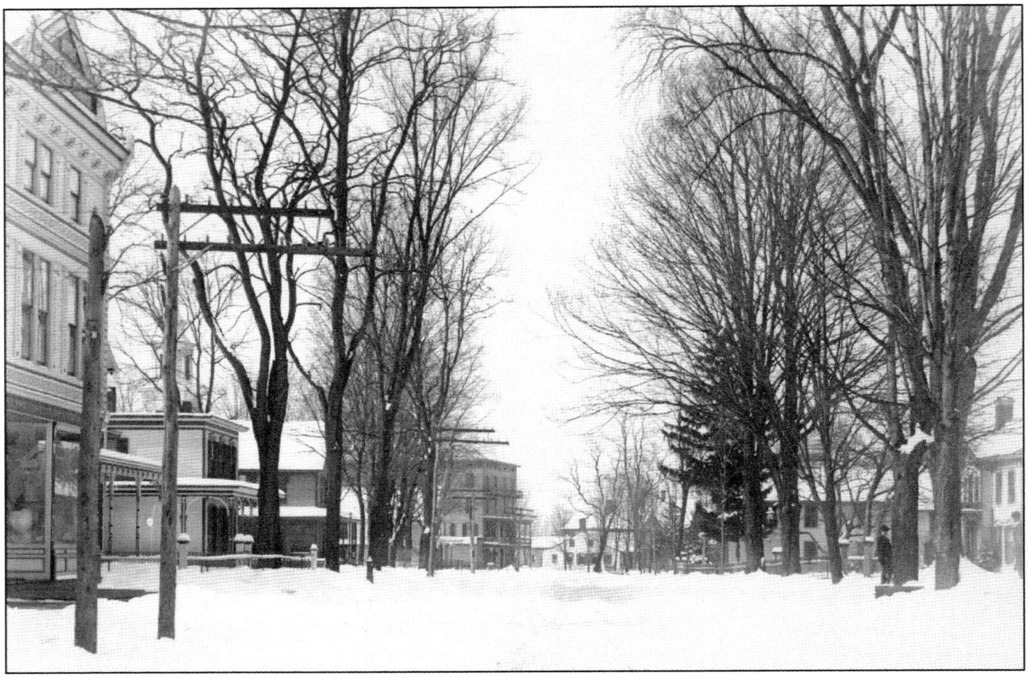

This c. 1907 photograph is looking west in front of Miller Brothers store on Main Street in Windham during the winter. The Windham Hotel, seen in the distant center, burned down in the late 1960s and was replaced by the Key Bank building. Winter travel in these mountains was very difficult—at times, impossible. Below, the 1912 postcard shows the view west on Main Street. The hardware store is on the right. The deep snow emphasizes just how difficult travel was then. The new fire company building, constructed in 1911, is next to the hardware store. Windham Hose Company has since moved to larger facilities on the west end of town. This original firehouse is currently vacant and in need of restoration.

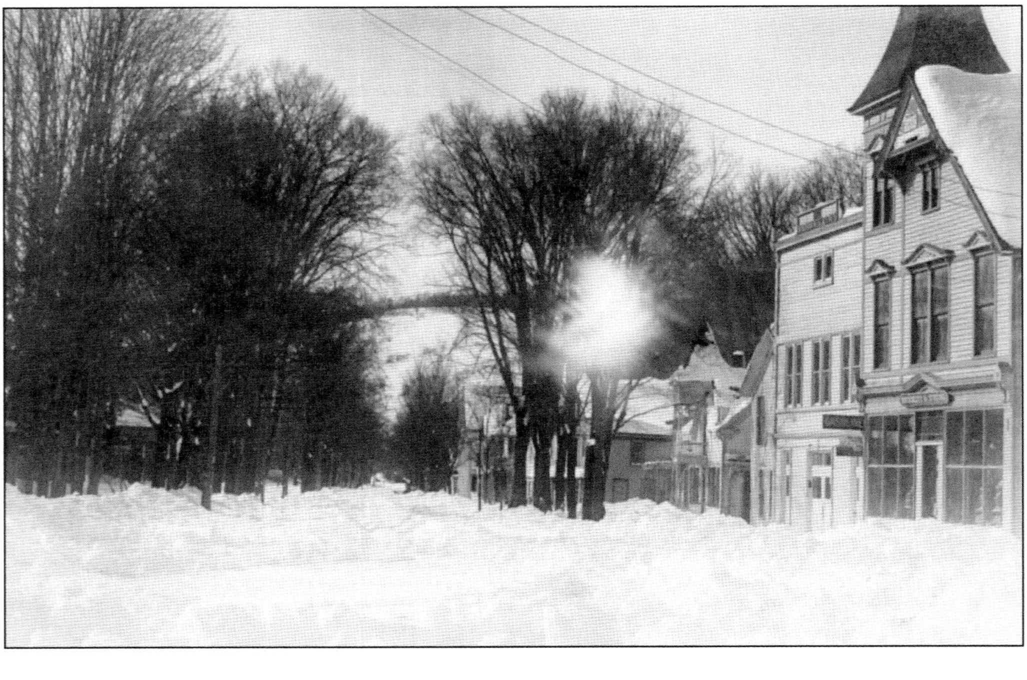

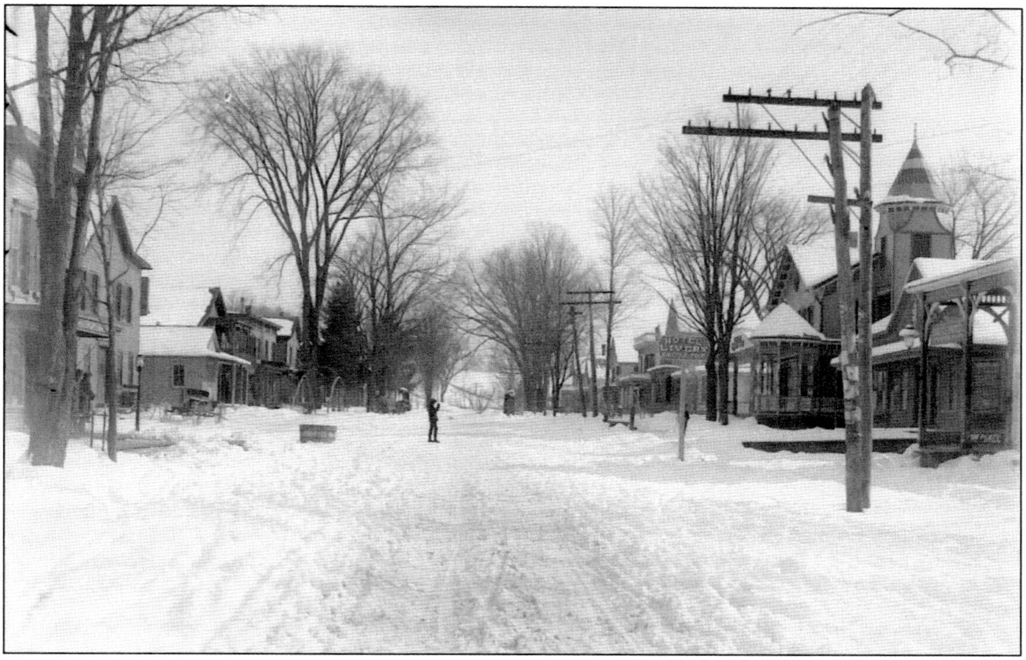

This 1905 view faces east on Main Street in Windham toward Cemetery Hill. A watering trough is at the corner of Mill Street. The building on the far left is Patterson's store, and beyond that is Brandow Photography, in the small building next to Mad Brook. The house on the right with the porch turret past the "Hotel/Livery" sign was the old Windham Pharmacy for almost 100 years.

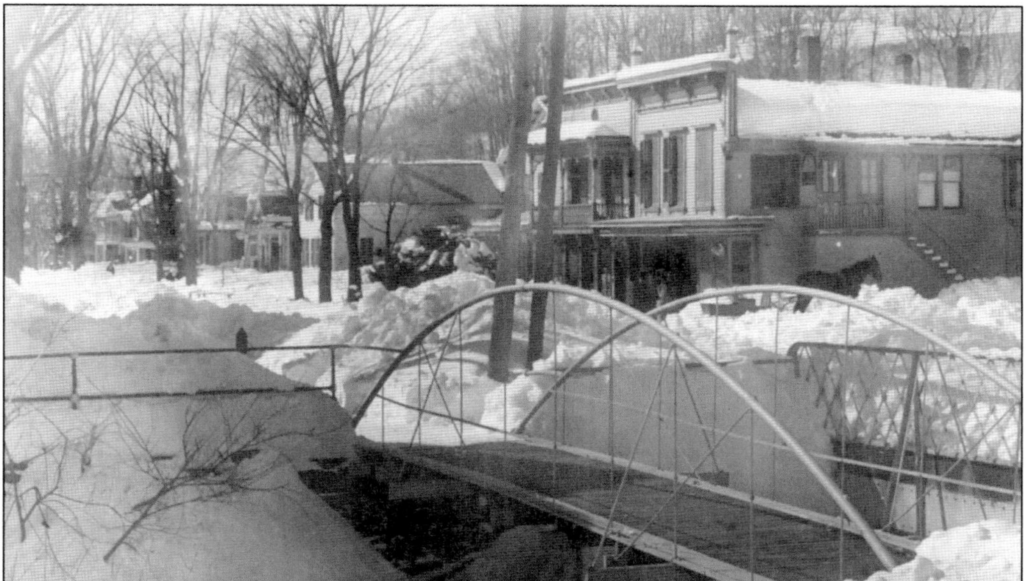

Seen in this c. 1905 image, a walkway spans Mad Brook on Main Street in Windham. Patterson's store in the background is at the corner of Mill and Main Streets. The second house to the left of Patterson's store was owned by Emma Patterson. She authored several books on the Revolutionary War. The next building is the Prentice Mack Jewelry store, constructed in 1899. (Courtesy of Richard and Ruth Morse.)

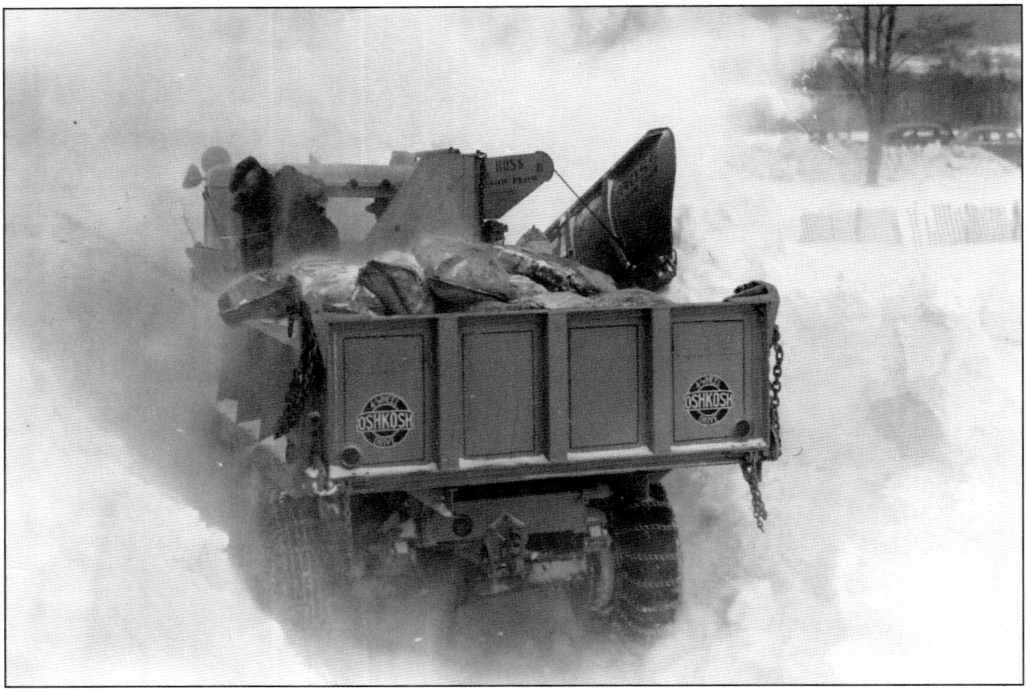

By the 1940s, snow-removal equipment had improved to the point that Windham's near total winter isolation could now be eased. This town snowplow is put to the test, plowing huge drifts piled up on the mountain roads. Windham's 2,000-foot elevation delivered more yearly snowfall than surrounding communities below the mountain. (Courtesy of Christopher Garraghan.)

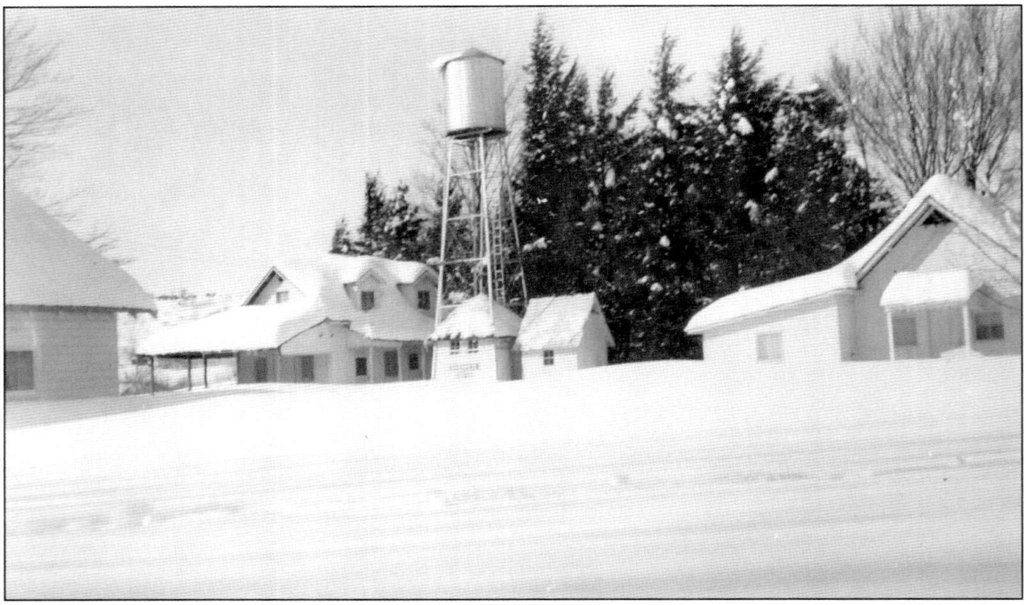

A water tower like the one in this 1955 picture was common at most of the larger boardinghouses. With the expansion to serve more guests came more demand for water. In those days, before deep well drilling, water was pumped from streams or small reservoirs to these types of tanks. Gravity feed from the tank to the faucets and showers did the rest. Notice the shower building directly under the tank.

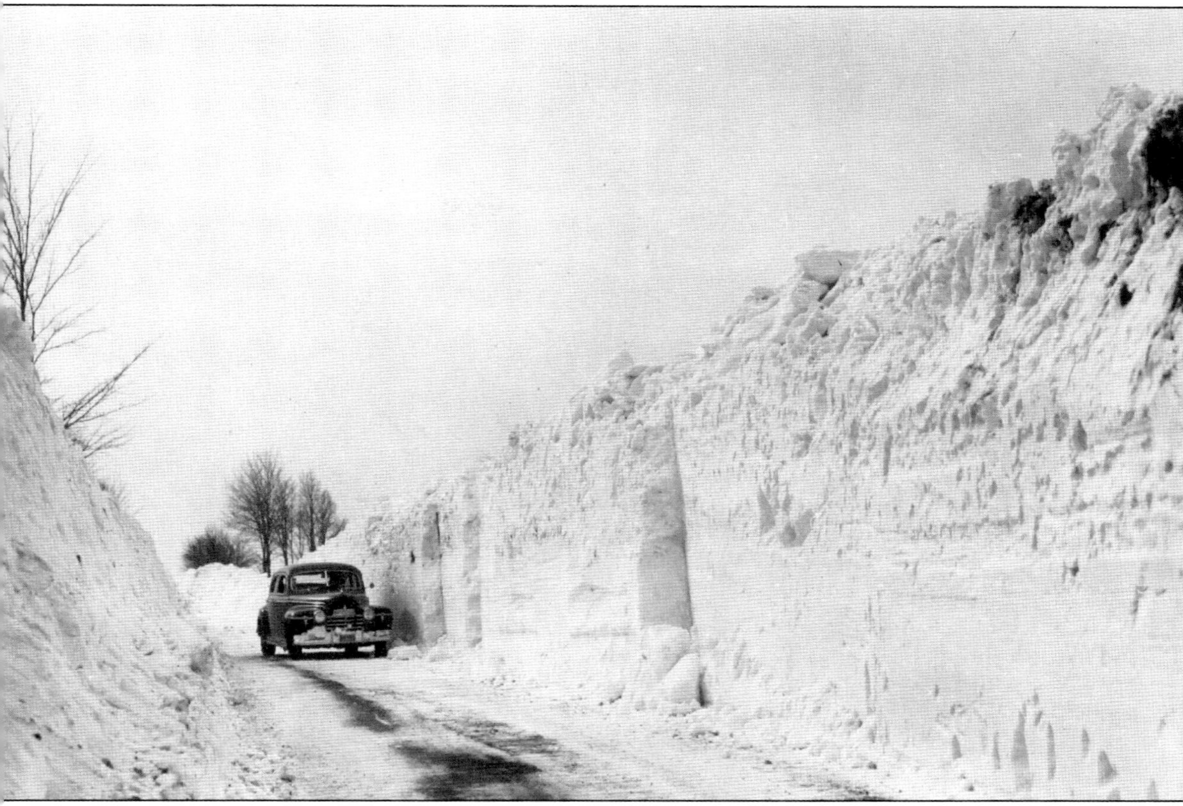

Windham's mountain roads, as seen in this c. 1940s photograph, clearly show how and why the town was so isolated from the world in winter before the use of plows and, especially, snowblowers. The availability of new equipment in the mid-20th century would finally open roads for travel to and from Windham in winter. The town is located in a mountain valley at almost 2,000 feet above sea level. This higher elevation often accounts for a larger snowfall accumulation in Windham compared to what the surrounding towns at lower altitudes might get. A recent example was in February 2010, when Windham had a storm that dropped over six feet of snow on the town in five days, while 25 miles away in Catskill, only two feet of snow fell. This was a big factor in selecting Windham for a ski slope location.

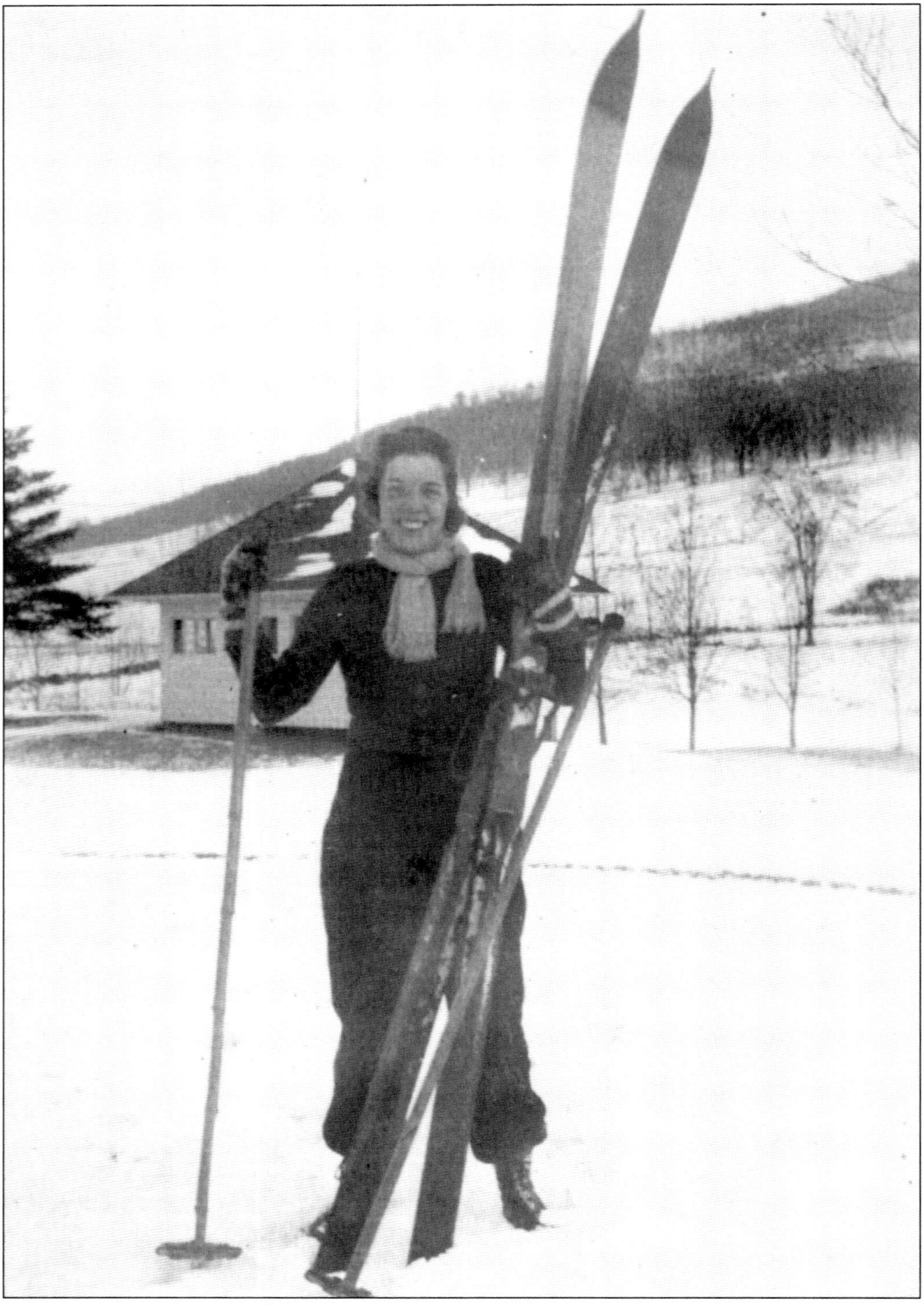

Harriett Munson poses with her skis in 1934. It would be a long time before a ski slope would come to Windham, but many local residents enjoyed skiing nevertheless. Of course, it was a long hike back up the mountainside to repeat the run. Cave Mountain is behind her, where 26 years later, the fledgling Cave Mountain Ski Area would start operations.

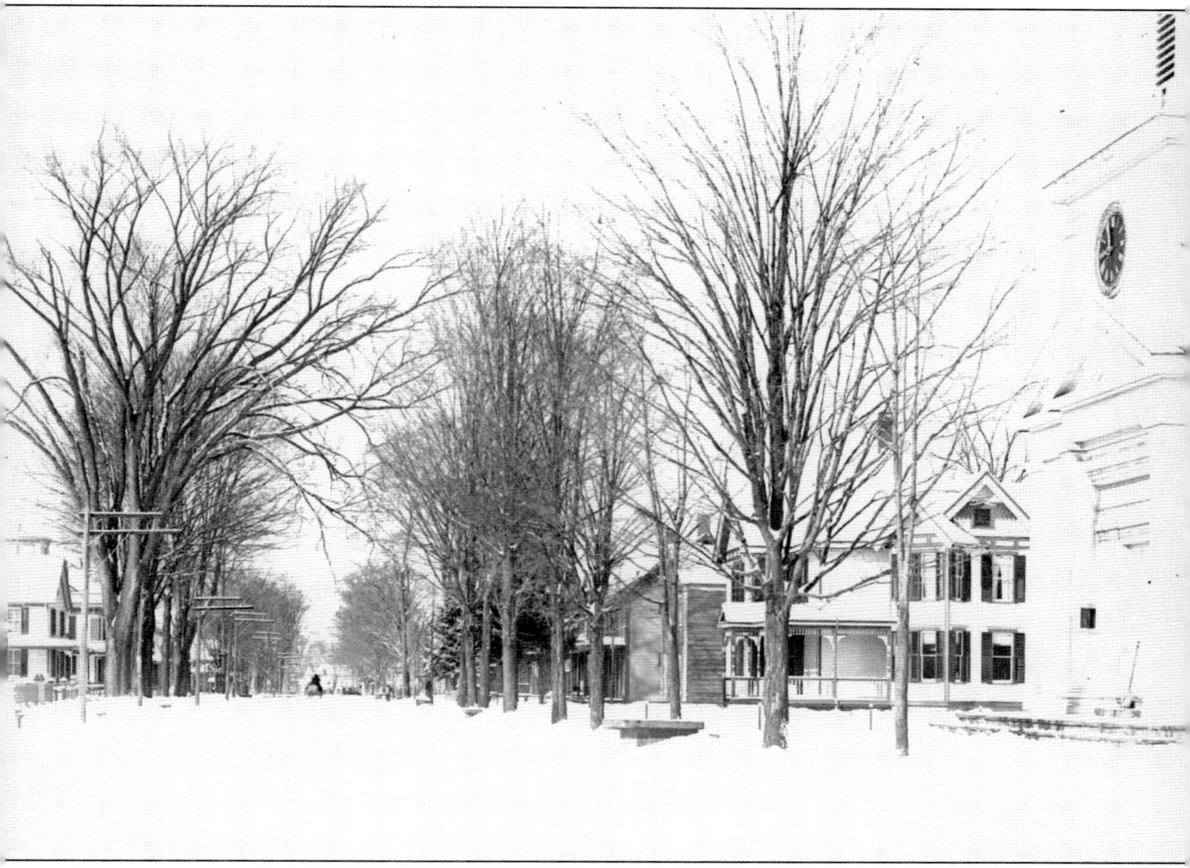

The quiet, picturesque 1905 winter scene of Main Street in Windham is a complete opposite of the hustle and bustle the summer vacationers brought to the town. After the beginning of September, Windham quite literally turned into a completely different village. When winter snow arrived, everything, including people and businesses, seemed to go into hibernation. Today, the winter ski business has invigorated Windham.

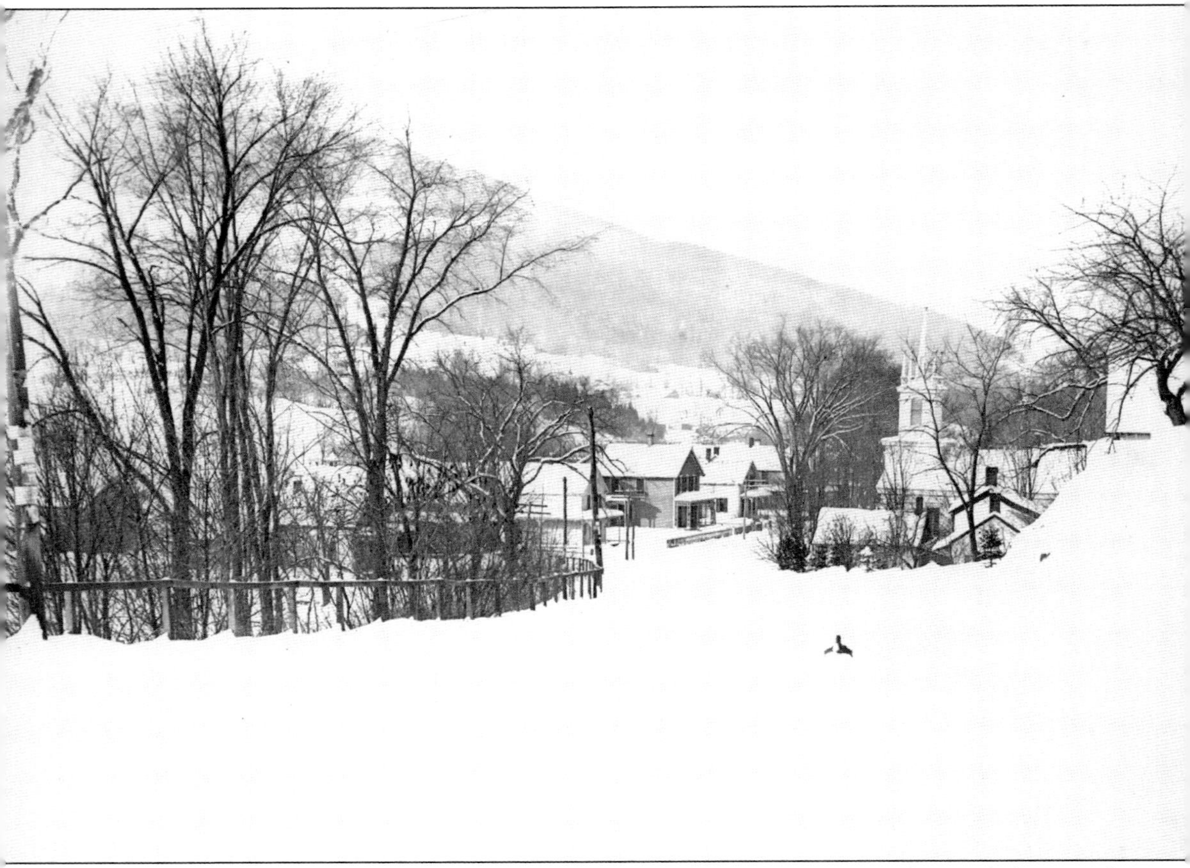

Cemetery Hill descends into Windham on the east end of town, as seen in this 1905 photograph. Prior to 1960, before heavy motor vehicle traffic and sanded highways, this hill was perfect for nighttime winter sledding for children of all ages. After dinner, it was not uncommon to see scores of villagers whisking down on their sleds in the moonlight. Crowds would gather at the Mitchell Hollow Road and Route 23 intersection for the run down. With vehicle in hand, a running start, and a belly flop onto the sled, a rider could go all the way through the dimly lit village to Church Street. For those who preferred ice-skating, the frozen Creamery Pond seen in the bottom left of this picture allowed them to glide to their heart's content. A roaring bonfire and benches at the pond provided comfort.

The Windham Historical Society

The Windham Historical Society was created and organized in 2006 by dedicated individuals who felt deeply that Windham's history must be preserved. Those founding members were Virginia Adams, Michael Avella, Margaret Davis, Janet Gooss, Regina Kazman, Lynne McGowan, Patricia Morrow, and Margaret Sokoll. It is chartered by the New York State Education Department and is a 501(c)(3) not-for-profit organization.

The Windham Historical Society has an annual June meeting with a historical presentation. In addition, it sponsors an archival day, postcard show, and bake sale in July.

The society accepts items such as historical artifacts, photographs, and documents relevant to Windham for collection and preservation. It hopes to acquire a permanent home to use as a headquarters, public display space for its collection of historical artifacts, and site for community events.

Nothing is more important to the Windham Historical Society than its members and serving the public's interest by preserving Windham's history. Interested individuals are encouraged to contact the society directly by mail: PO Box 1111, Windham, New York 12496. E-mails can be sent to Windham Historical Society president Roy Davis at roytd@hughes.net.

All author proceeds from the sale of this book will go to the Windham Historical Society.